The Lean and Green Meal Prep Cookbook

600 Lean and Green Recipes to Cook, Prep, Grab, and Go | With 6 Foolproof Step-by-step Meal Prepping Guide and Fueling Hack for 5&1, 4&2&1 and 3&3 Plans

Luetta J. Green

Table of Contents

Chapter 1 The Basics of Lean & Green Diet

My Lean & Green Journey

My weight loss journey began after my thirtieth birthday when I decided that I no longer felt comfortable with my weight. I had become so used to hiding my body in long and unflattering clothing, and declining invitations to parties where I needed to wear certain outfits. Over many years, my life had become full of excuses about why I couldn't sign up for a gym membership or why I couldn't commit to a healthy eating plan. Eventually, I became so sick and tired of my own excuses and I was motivated to set a weight loss goal and accomplish it within a year. I started researching credible diets that would help me lose weight and keep the weight off permanently. I realized that the internet is not short of diets, however, there were very few which actually delivered on its promises. You can name a diet and I guarantee you that I have tried it. Even though I would lose a pound or two with each diet, I would always regain the weight in a matter of weeks.

Feeling hopeless and discouraged, I reached out to a friend of mine who always had the best advice. Together, we were determined to find a diet that would be easy to follow and become a healthy lifestyle. Not long in our search, we stumbled across the Lean & Green diet. This diet, previously known as the Medifast diet, had a really unique offer. The company would assess my health needs and assign me to a program or eating plan. This eating plan would aid in reducing the number of calories I consumed a day, which would result in rapid weight loss. What further differentiated this diet from the rest is that most of the foods consumed were meal replacements that were prepared by the company and approved by dieticians. These meal replacements or fuelings could be delivered to my doorstep after placing an order, meaning that I didn't have to go on a grocery run every week. When I learned more about the Lean & Green diet, I was sold!

Today, after successfully losing sixty pounds on the program, I am a certified Lean & Green health coach, helping other dieters like myself lose weight and restore vitality in their bodies. I decided to write this cookbook to share some of the Lean and Green recipes I have whipped up in my kitchen which have positively promoted weight loss. Lean and Green meals are the portion of food that the diet allows people to prepare on their own at home. Depending on the particular eating plan, dieters can have between one to three Lean and Green meals per day.

What is Lean & Green?

Lean & Green is a wonderful and healthy diet program that has prepared meals and snacks that you can eat while trying to lose weight. It was created to help overweight and obese people lose weight by having healthy diet foods to prepare at home. Follow the Lean & Green Diet program and eat right, and you can lose your weight in a healthier and efficient way.

Lean & Green diet is based on a unique weight loss system that provides you with a low-calorie meal system while inspiring healthy and easy habits. This diet aims to help people reduce their calorie intake and manage their weight problems.

Lean & Green diet is designed especially for you if you don't have a lot of time and energy for cooking. It offers you a wide variety of daily meals, which are specifically balanced in vitamin levels and stimulates good habits for your health and weight loss.

The Lean & Green diet is not made for some or the others – it is especially for those who want to lose weight. Lean & Green even offers you meal plans and a system of rewards when you reach your target weight or go beyond and go for your personal goals.

Lean & Green diet doesn't provide you with long shopping lists. It only gives you a shopping list containing the necessary ingredients to make a 7-day menu for you and anyone else from your family.

The Lean & Green diet also doesn't require you to buy special meals or have a lot of supplements. It gives you a solution with a healthy combination of proteins, healthy fats, and carbs for better energy levels.

It will only be for you if you want a plan which includes delicious, calorie counting meals for your meals and for you to finally get your desired weight!

Losing Weight on the Lean & Green Diet: Truth or Fiction?

The Lean & Green diet has been designed to help dieters, like myself, lose weight and fat by reducing the number of calories and carbohydrates through a monitored program. The 5-and-1 plan, for instance, limits the number of calories consumed per day to 800 to 1,000, divided into six portion-controlled meals. There has been much research to suggest that meal replacement diets such as this one have a higher success rate at losing weight than traditional calorie-restrictive diets. A sixteen-week study conducted on 198 people who had excess weight or were obese, found that those who went on the Lean & Green 5-and-1 eating plan had lost a significant amount of weight, had lower fat levels, and reduced waist circumference when compared to the control group. More specifically, those who went on the 5-and-1 plan lost a total of 5.7% of their body weight on average, with 28.1% of the dieters losing over 10% of body weight.

Planning Meals: The Typical Foods to Eat on the Lean & Green Diet

I am never hungry on the Lean & Green diet. Even when I am out with friends or family, I can still enjoy healthy delicious meals without missing out on a fine dining experience. The Lean & Green diet emphasizes the importance of making healthier food choices rather than eliminating certain foods from my diet. Depending on the specific Lean & Green diet plan I choose, for example, I would eat between two to five of the company's prepackaged meal replacement foods (fuelings) per day. I am also given the opportunity to prepare one to three low-calorie meals of my own which consist primarily of lean protein and non-starchy vegetables. As mentioned before, there are no foods that are technically forbidden for me to eat. However, foods like alcohol or sweets are strongly discouraged. Below are some of the foods that are safe and healthy to consume on an Lean & Green diet:

Lean & Green Fuelings

Most of my meals on the Lean & Green diet are prepackaged meals bought directly from the company. These meals and snacks are known as fuelings. The company has a wide variety of meals, beverages, and snacks to choose from which are all carefully prepared to support weight loss. Some of the tasty meal replacement options available include bars, soups, shakes, pretzels, brownies, and so much more. What's also amazing about these meal replacements is that they have nearly the same nutrition profile. This means that the value, quality, and calories are nearly identical, thus the foods can be eaten interchangeably.

Lean Meats

As part of the "Lean and Green" meals I prepare, the diet allows me to include a five to seven-ounce (141 to 198 gram) portion of cooked lean protein. Lean & Green distinguishes proteins into three categories: leanest, leaner, and lean. The leanest protein options include fish (cod, flounder, tuna, or haddock), shellfish (crab, scallops, lobster, or shrimp), game meat (elk, buffalo, or deer), ground turkey, and meatless options (fourteen egg whites, two cups of liquid egg substitute, five ounces of seitan, or one and a half cups of 1% cottage cheese). The leaner protein options include fish (swordfish, trout, or halibut), chicken (breast without the skin), turkey or ground turkey, and meatless options (two whole eggs and four egg whites, two whole eggs and a cup of liquid egg substitute, one and a half cups of 1% cottage cheese or twelve ounces of low-fat 2% plain greek yogurt). The lean protein options include fish (salmon, tuna steak, farmed catfish, or mackerel), lean beef (either steak, ground, or roast), lamb, pork tenderloin or chops, chicken, turkey, and meatless options (fifteen ounces of Mori-nu extra firm or firm tofu, three whole eggs up to two times per week, one cup of shredded low-fat cheese, one cup low-fat ricotta cheese, or five ounces of tempeh).

Greens and Non-Starchy Vegetables

Optavia's 5-in-1 program allows for two non-starchy vegetables to be eaten with lean protein in a particular meal. The program also recommends that dieters consume three servings of vegetables for any particular meal. A serving is equal to half a cup of vegetables. Therefore, three servings would amount to one and a half cups of vegetables in any particular meal. Similarly, with the lean proteins, the vegetables are separated into three categories: lower carb, moderate carb, and high carb. The low carb vegetable category allows for a cup of collards, endive, lettuce, or spinach, and half a cup of cucumbers, celery, white mushrooms, jalapenos, or watercress. The moderate carb vegetable category allows for half a cup of asparagus, cauliflower, eggplant, cabbage, kale, or zucchini. The high carb vegetable category allows for half a cup of broccoli, red cabbage, cooked collards or mustard greens, cooked leeks, tomatoes, turnips, or cooked swiss chards.

Healthy Fats

In addition to lean protein and greens, healthy fats can be included in the diet. It is recommended to maintain two servings of healthy fats. Some of the healthy options available include olive oil, walnut oil, flaxseed oil, and avocado oil.

Low-Fat Dairy, Fruits, and Whole Grains

After I had achieved my desired weight loss goal through consuming meal replacements, lean proteins, and non-starchy vegetables, I could then move onto a maintenance plan which exposed me to more foods while maintaining all of my hard-earned work. At this point, I could consume low-fat dairy, fresh fruits, and whole grains. These new food groups were available on Optavia's "3-and-3" and "4-and-2-and-1" weight maintenance programs.

The 5-and-1 Plan

With the Lean & Green diet, I am constantly eating throughout the day. In fact, the diet advises eating six or seven times per day (about every two to three hours) depending on the specific plan you choose. There are three customized low-calorie plans to choose from depending on your personal weight loss goal. For instance, the 5-and-1 plan is suitable for those who desire to lose a considerable amount of weight in the shortest amount of time.

The Optavia 5-and-1 plan requires dieters to eat six small meals a day. This healthy eating habit promotes weight loss and ensures that dieters have sufficient energy throughout the day. Five out of the six meals consist of Optavia fuelings. There are over sixty delicious fuelings to choose from that are ready-made, convenient, and packed with nutrients. The friendly and helpful Optavia health coaches are available to guide dieters on the best selection of fuelings to choose for a varied diet plan. The sixth meal of the day is a homemade meal made using the "Lean and Green" meal guidelines. Preparing my own healthy meals gave me the opportunity to recognize what optimal nutrition looks like, and soon eating healthy became second nature to me.

The success of the optimal weight 5&1 plan depends greatly on whether you execute the following:

- Eat your first fueling within the first hour you get up, I would strongly recommend setting up an alarm clock, this is just how important the first meal is.
- Eat every 2.5 hours or 3 hours do not skip a meal, even if you are not hungry, if you miss a meal, you are gonna sabotage your results.
- Eat all 5 fuelings everyday even if you are not hungry
- Eat a plan-compliant lean and green meal every day, you can even use a food scale
- One condiment a day, only plan-approved snacks
- Drink half your weight in ounces of water every day
- Get at least 7 hours of sleep

For example, a day of meals in the 5 & 1 program might look like this:

Breakfast:	I supply
Mid-morning snack:	I fueling
Lunch:	I fueling
Afternoon snack:	I fueling
Dinner:	homemade "lean and green" meal
Evening snack:	I fueling

→ You are free to choose to eat the "lean and green" meal whenever you want during the day (one day you can select lunch, another one dinner...).

The Most Commonly Asked Questions about the Lean & Green Diet (and Answers)

Below are some of the frequently asked questions related to the Lean & Green diet. For more support and assistance, simply visit https://answers.optavia.com/help.

What are the "Habits of Health"?

The Habits of Health are the six building blocks to achieving optimal health. These six building blocks provide Lean & Green clients with an integrative framework for developing or maintaining healthy lifestyle habits every day. All of these habits place good health at the center of the client's life, so maintaining health is more of a lifestyle decision instead of something that is done when battling illness. Below is a list of the six habits or building blocks:

- Habits of healthy weight management
- Habits of healthy eating and hydration
- Habits of healthy motion
- Habits of healthy sleep
- Habits of a healthy mind
- Habits of a healthy surrounding

How Do I Handle My Cravings on the Lean & Green Diet?

It is normal to crave unhealthy foods when starting a new diet. These cravings are something to expect and aren't a sign of weakness or failure. It's important to realize where the cravings are coming from. Most of the time, these cravings may be triggered by thoughts, moods, stress, worry, or by environmental factors like social gatherings. Instead of suppressing the craving or pretending it doesn't exist, invite it in and try to understand it by asking the following questions:

- Why is this craving coming now?
- How am I feeling?
- Am I hungry?
- Am I stressed?
- Am I exhausted?

Once the craving is understood, there are several strategies for eliminating it. For instance, one can avoid the trigger, breathe in and out deeply, create a healthy distraction, take a walk, talk to someone, or create a healthy environment.

Can I Eat Out While on the Lean & Green Diet?

Yes, dieters can dine out while on the Lean & Green diet. However, it will take some careful planning. For instance, one would have to rearrange their fueling routine (if it is necessary) so that the Lean and Green meal can be enjoyed on a dinner out with friends, family get together, or business meeting. It is also important to consider serving and portion sizes when dining out. For example, the Lean and Green meal should consist of five to seven ounces of cooked lean protein, three servings of non-starchy vegetables, and zero to two servings of healthy fats (depending on your lean choices). Meat should be prepared without marinades, sauces, or added fats. Starchy vegetables like potatoes can be replaced with low-carb options like steamed broccoli or green beans. Alternatively, dieters can take along their fueling when dining out, and ask the waiter/waitress to bring cold or hot water to mix with the fueling.

What Type of Exercises are Suitable for the Lean & Green Diet?

There are typically three types of exercises recommended for dieters on the Lean & Green diet: aerobic exercises, strength training, and lifestyle exercises. Aerobic exercises include activities such as walking, cycling, running, and any other cardio activity that burns calories and increases heart rate. Dieters can aim for thirty minutes of aerobic exercise at least three times per week (this could be split up into ten minutes of exercise per day). Strength training involves lifting heavy weights or loads. Gradually increasing the amount of weight one can carry helps to build muscles throughout the body. Dieters should aim to do strength training at least two to three times per week. Lifestyle exercises include performing daily activities that increase your heart rate. This could include activities like shopping, gardening, cleaning, taking public transport to work, and so on. Dieters should aim for at least thirty to forty-five minutes of lifestyle exercise every day of the week.

Chapter 2: The Basics of Meal Prep

What is Meal Prepping

Simply put, meal prep is the act of preparing and storing in advance several individual servings of one or more weekly meals and snacks. Although meal planning is involved, meal prep takes the selection and scheduling of meals a step further by actually having them fully cooked and boxed. Meal prepping can be done one or two days each week, depending on your individual needs and schedule. The same meal will be divided and boxed for several meals throughout the week and be ready to heat-and-eat, like a casserole, or eat cold, like a salad. But the benefits of meal prepping go a lot further than just convenience.

Why Meal Prep?

Meal prepping is the number one reason I am able to feed myself and my family healthy, delicious meals each day. The benefits of meal prepping include:

Saving money: If you know what you are going to cook, you can purchase accordingly. You can purchase meat and other ingredients in bulk, divide them into meal portions, and place them in resealable plastic bags in the refrigerator or freezer. This stretches your food dollar.

Saving time: Although you will spend some time in the kitchen on a set day of your choosing, during the week you won't be slaving for hours over a hot stove. Plus, you won't have much cleanup to do during those busy weeknights. That extra 30 to 60 minutes can be spent as quality time with loved ones instead!

Controlling portions: In order to make a meal last, you need to divide the food and account for portions. Each of my recipes provides exact measurements for portions to help make your life easier. By controlling portions, you not only save money, but also keep meal and snack calories in check.

Getting more done with less effort: Some nights it just feels like you are cooking nonstop while your to-do list gets longer and longer. It takes less effort to prepare a double batch of chili or burgers in advance than it does to cook a new meal every night; even on busy weeknights you'll be able to sit down, breathe, and enjoy a healthy meal.

Eating healthier: A stop at a fast-food joint or hitting up the vending machine will be a thing of the past. These unhealthy choices are where many high-calorie, high-fat, and high-sugar foods are eaten. When you're armed with prepared meals and snacks, these unhealthy eating habits start to disappear.

Improving multitasking skills: Meal prepping will hone your multitasking skills and even improve them. You'll learn to set a timer for the oven while preparing the dressing for your lunch salad. Multitasking allows you to save time and become more efficient at meal prepping.

Meal Prep Principles

Developing smart meal prepping habits is part of the learning process. Here are some meal prep dos and don'ts worth keeping in mind as you get started:

✔ DO flag healthy recipes you love. After trying healthy recipes, keep the ones you love in a folder or mark them in the cookbook.

✔ DO go at your own pace. You can successfully meal prep with three recipes or six recipes. You don't need to prepare 10 or more recipes for the week. Start slowly and build your way up.

✔ DO work with your schedule. Some weeks you'll be able to prepare more recipes than other weeks. Do whatever works for you and your schedule.

✔ DO freeze extras. Some weeks you will have a few extra meals. Freezer-friendly meals can be frozen and kept for up to a few months, as noted in the recipes.

✔ DO make cleanup easy. You'll have many vegetable scraps, eggshells, and empty containers to toss, so keep your recycling, compost bin, and trash nearby for easy cleanup.

✔ DON'T leave everything until the last minute. Plan ahead for best results. Meal prepping is about scheduling your time in advance, so you can get to the market and buy the ingredients you need, then spend the necessary time at home preparing them.

✔ DON'T divide meals later. The last step of meal prepping is to divide recipes into individual portions and pack them into containers. Don't skip this step or divide meals right before digging into one. Dividing meals up front helps maintain good portion control, prevents last-minute scrambling to divide meals, and ensures your meals will last through the week.

✔ DON'T overprep. The last thing you want to do is prep meals that will go uneaten, unless of course you can freeze them. To get into the meal prepping jive, start slow and get to know your meal prepping needs. You can meal prep one or two days a week—do whatever works with your schedule.

The Art of Storage

I hope that meal prep will become a regular routine in your home like it is in ours. In order to make that happen, it is essential that you invest in and choose the right storage containers. When I was ready to invest in a set of containers, I bought a few different options—glass, metal, and plastic (BPA-free, of course). This way I could do a trial run to figure out what I liked best before I made a big purchase. Trying a few to see what you like and what works best in your kitchen will save you time and money in the long run.

Good-quality containers are essential for keeping your food fresh as long as possible. Here are some things to look for when buying containers for meal prepping:

BPA-free. I'm sure you have read or seen BPA-free on containers or other plastic items before, and here's why it's important. BPA stands for bisphenol A, which is a chemical found in plastics like food containers, water bottles, food cans, and consumer goods. Research has shown that BPA can seep into food or beverages from plastic containers made of BPA. Possible side effects of BPA exposure include increased blood pressure, mental health issues, and negative effects on fetuses, infants, and children.

Stackable. I know we all have a cupboard or a drawer packed full of containers and lids. If you begin to make meal prep a part of your regular routine, that means a lot of containers will start to accumulate. Having containers that are stackable will keep your cupboards functional and looking organized, making life easier.

Freezer-safe. There will be times when you prep and have more than you need for the week. That's when having containers that are freezer-safe is key. I will also purposely double recipes so I can throw them in the freezer for future use.

Microwave-safe. It is totally up to you how you reheat your meals. Most likely microwaving is going to be the most convenient method. So, choosing containers that are microwave-friendly is something you will want to pay attention to.

Dishwasher-safe. This one is obvious, at least it is for me.

Glass Containers

In our house we use glass containers for many reasons. Glass is environmentally friendly. It performs safely at different temperatures, allowing me to reheat meals in the prep containers right in the microwave or oven. Although glass is a little more of an investment than plastic, with glass containers you get safety and durability. They also don't retain any of the smells of food after cleaning, which is a nice bonus. Square, rectangular, and circular glass containers are available; choose a mixture of sizes for the most versatility.

Plastic Containers

Plastic containers are very popular for meal prep—they're lightweight, stack easily, and many are now microwavable as well as freezable. But as I mentioned, my go-to is glass. Plastic containers may leach harmful substances into the food stored in them. Plastic is not biodegradable, which means it isn't possible for our earth to naturally absorb the material back into the soil; instead, plastic actually contaminates it. Unlike glass and metal, plastic absorbs odors and tastes like whatever you stored in it previously. If you have ever stored fish in a plastic container, I'm guessing it still smells like fish to this day. While it's a fact that plastic is cheaper than other options, it's also true that it will not last as long. If you do choose to go with plastic containers, always look for an indicator that they are BPA-free.

Mason Jars

Mason (canning) jars are also great for storing food. Made of glass, Mason jars are inexpensive and perfect for storing salads and salad dressings. A combination of wide-mouth quart and pint jars, as well as some smaller four-ounce jars for dressings, will go a long way when doing meal preps. I incorporate them a few times throughout the preps for quick storage.

Stainless Steel

Stainless steel containers will last a lot longer than plastic. They look nicer, maintain hot and cold temperatures well, and are super durable. They are the most expensive option, and one drawback to keep in mind is that metal can't be reheated in the microwave.

Whichever type of storage container you decide to purchase, I recommend getting at least 15 containers as well as five pint-size or quart-size Mason jars so you have enough storage for your meals through one week of prep.

Food Storage Guidelines

When buying meats and dairy from your local grocery store, look for products with the "sell by" date farthest in the future. It may take some digging, but the food products will store longer for your meal prep.

Make sure to let your prepped meals completely cool before you cover them and put them in the refrigerator or freezer. If you don't wait and put the lid on while the meal is still hot, it will create steam within your storage container. This will result in the meal continuing to cook, which can lead to overcooked vegetables or dried-out proteins.

When storing food in your refrigerator and freezer, it's really important to always label and date the containers. Of course you'll want to rotate and use the earliest dates first to minimize food spoilage. When storing food in the refrigerator, place raw foods at the bottom, wrapped to catch any juices. Ready-to-eat foods like cooked dishes and fresh food like fruits, vegetables, and yogurt should be stored above the raw food. This will help minimize the risk of cross-contamination and potential foodborne illness. It's also important to use foods when they're at their peak of freshness and nutrition. Below is a chart illustrating freezer and refrigerator storage times of popular foods.

	FRIDGE	FREEZER
Salads: egg salad, tuna salad, chicken salad, pasta salad	3 TO 5 DAYS	DOES NOT FREEZE WELL
Hamburger, meatloaf, and other dishes made with ground meat (raw)	1 TO 2 DAYS	3 TO 4 MONTHS
Steaks: beef, lamb pork, (raw)	3 TO 5 DAYS	3 TO 4 MONTHS
Chops: beef, lamb pork, (raw)	3 TO 5 DAYS	4 TO 6 MONTHS
Roasts: beef, lamb pork, (raw)	3 TO 5 DAYS	4 TO 12 MONTHS
Whole chicken turkey or (raw)	1 TO 2 DAYS	1 YEAR
Pieces: chicken turkey or (raw)	1 TO 2 DAYS	9 MONTHS
Soups and stews with vegetables and meat	3 TO 4 DAYS	2 TO 3 MONTHS
Pizza	3 TO 4 DAYS	1 TO 2 MONTHS
Beef, lamb, pork, or chicken (cooked)	3 TO 4 DAYS	2 TO 6 MONTHS

How to Thaw Safely

You can thaw raw proteins like meat, poultry, and fish in several ways. First, you can place it in the refrigerator the night before. For a whole turkey or chicken you will need 2 to 3 days in the refrigerator for proper thawing. Smaller items, like frozen shrimp, can be run under cool water for 1 to 2 hours. Make sure there are no dishes in the sink when thawing food in this manner. You can also thaw frozen raw proteins in the microwave. However, because you get an uneven distribution of heat, some of the meats or fish may start to cook. If you do use the microwave to thaw, it is recommended to cook the food right away.

For cooked meals, you can use the same methods mentioned above. Thawing in the refrigerator is best since the food is at a safe temperature the entire time. After the food is thawed completely, it can be stored in the refrigerator for 3 to 4 days. The internal temperature of any reheated food should reach 165°F and should be measured with a thermometer placed in the thickest part of the dish.

Safe Reheating Guidelines

You can safely reheat your prepped meals by following a few simple guidelines in the microwave, in the oven, or on the stovetop.

Safely Reheating Meals in The Microwave

While a microwave won't always produce the same results as an oven, using a microwave for reheating prepped meals is often much faster and more convenient. Here are a few general tips for getting the best results when reheating your prepped meals in a microwave oven.

Always Remove The Lids

Always remove the lid from prep containers prior to microwaving to ensure the expanding heat does not create an explosion inside the microwave. You can cover the uncovered container with a damp paper towel to ensure moisture is retained during the reheating process.

Be Sure to Thaw Frozen Meals Before Reheating

Many of the meals in this book include instructions for freezing. If you're reheating a frozen meal, be sure to remove the meal from the freezer at least one day prior to reheating and serving to ensure that the meal is reheated properly and evenly. If you forget to remove the meal from the freezer, most microwave ovens have a defrost mode that can be used to partially thaw the meal prior to cooking.

Three Minutes on High Usually Does The Trick

As a general rule, microwaving refrigerated prepped meals for about 3 minutes on high should be sufficient for most of the recipes in this book. If possible, larger ingredients such as proteins should be removed from containers and reheated in the microwave first to ensure other foods don't become overcooked in the process. Also, make sure the surface of the food is as even as possible to ensure even reheating.

Only Reheat Glass Containers

You should never reheat food in containers made of anything other than glass. Microwaving metal can cause a dangerous arcing effect in a microwave oven, and microwaving plastic can leach dangerous chemicals into your meals.

Safely Reheating Meals in an Oven or on The Stovetop

Reheating prepped meals in the oven is simple. And while it might take a little longer than it would in a microwave, an oven reheats food more evenly than a microwave and can result in more desirable textures for some foods. Here are a few best practices for reheating meals in the oven or on the stovetop.

Reheat to the Same Temperature the Meal Was Prepared to

When reheating your meals, the meals should be reheated to the same temperatures they were originally cooked to, and for most recipes in this book, reheating your meals on the middle oven rack for 20 minutes in a preheated oven set to 350°F (180°C) should be sufficient. Use a thermometer to check the meals every 5 minutes, after 10 minutes have passed.

Only Use Metal or Glass Containers That are Marked "Oven-Safe"

Be sure to only reheat meals in glass or metal prep containers that are marked "oven-safe," and always remove the lid from the container before placing it in the oven. Some oven-safe containers may have lids that are not actually oven-safe, and these lids can melt or become superheated inside an oven, which can be dangerous.

Use a Baking Sheet to Minimize the Mess

Whenever reheating a meal in the oven, place it on a baking tray lined with parchment paper. This will prevent any liquids that bubble over from the container from dripping onto the surface of your oven, which can create a mess.

When Time is Short, Opt for the Broiler

If you want to speed up the reheating process in the oven, you can place meals under a broiler set to 350°F (180°C). However, this method can result in some foods burning more quickly, and it may not heat the meals as evenly from top to bottom, so watch the meals carefully. Also, it's best to use a metal container under the broiler since some oven-safe glass containers may still crack at higher temperatures.

Stick to the Stovetop for Certain Recipes

While a conventional oven or microwave oven will work for reheating the majority of the recipes in this book, some recipes that were originally prepared in a frying pan or in a pot, such as soups, are best reheated in a large frying pan or pot placed over medium heat on the stovetop.

Use a Thermometer to Check the Temperature

Whichever method you follow to reheat your meals, it's best to check the internal temperature of the food to ensure it's been reheated to the proper cooking temperature. A simple oven or kitchen thermometer is all you'll need to do this.

4 Steps for Meal Prep

For whatever day you get started, you're going to want to streamline the process as much as possible. To do that, just follow the simple steps below to help you get started.

Step 1: Make a Shopping List

You'll want to make a shopping list the day before for best results. In the beginning of your 21-day plan, you'll need to make it for a few short days, but at the end, your shopping list will be for a week at a time. Expect to dedicate most of the day to meal prep but remember that it will make life easier.

Step 2: Go Shopping

You'll want to go in and get out when it comes to the grocery store so that you aren't tempted by unhealthy snacks. If you have mostly vegetables, try going to the local farmers market where there's less temptation too.

Step 3: Start with a Clean Area

It's going to be easier to start cooking if you clean your area beforehand, and make sure that you have your containers clean too. It's important to make sure you have everything on hand, and it'll help to make it all go by a little quicker.

Step 4: Start Cooking!

Now the only thing left is to start cooking, but make sure that you let your food completely cool before packing it up. If you don't let your food cool, then you can ruin the texture and it may become soggy upon reheating.

Chapter 3 Step-By-Step Meal Plans

5 & 1 Plan

Day 1

1st Meal	2nd Meal	3rd Meal	4th Meal	5th Meal	6th Meal
Iced Vanilla Shake	Pumpkin Coffee Frappe	Hot Chocolate with Cinnamon	Vanilla Frappe	Pumpkin Almond Gingerbread Latte	Chicken, Mushroom and Tomato Stew

Change your relation with food.

We were trained from childbirth that food is comfort, from the pacifier to candies to the pizzas, and there are tons of triggers for you to munch on. like i had a bad day at work, i deserve an ice cream sundae; got a promotion at work, lets go out and celebrate with food. This is exactly the mindset we need to change about ourselves, we need to rebrand food as things that fuel us, not a hugging bear.

Day 2

1st Meal	2nd Meal	3rd Meal	4th Meal	5th Meal	6th Meal
Pumpkin Almond Gingerbread Latte	Iced Vanilla Shake	Pumpkin Coffee Frappe	Hot Chocolate with Cinnamon	Vanilla Frappe	Chicken, Mushroom and Tomato Stew

Take some aspins, ibuprofen, or have chicken broth, pickles.

You will feel Sluggishness, fatigue, headache in the beginning, it is because the toxins and and electrons are leaving your body, so your body needs the salt to reset your body back to balance.

Day 3

1st Meal	2nd Meal	3rd Meal	4th Meal	5th Meal	6th Meal
Vanilla Frappe	Pumpkin Almond Gingerbread Latte	Iced Vanilla Shake	Pumpkin Coffee Frappe	Hot Chocolate with Cinnamon	Chicken, Mushroom and Tomato Stew

Listen to Optavia weight loss podcasts.

Retrain your brain by exposing yourself to the new information, just type in the keyword"optavia" in the podcast search box and two channels you should subscribe to are "the habit of health"podcast and the client support podcast, these two are value packed podcasts, you will definitely love it and learn ton of applicable knowledge there. Listen to these two podcast every day and get inspired(this is not a sponsored tip, though. Lol)

Day 4

1st Meal	2nd Meal	3rd Meal	4th Meal	5th Meal	6th Meal
Hot Chocolate with Cinnamon	Vanilla Frappe	Pumpkin Almond Gingerbread Latte	Iced Vanilla Shake	Pumpkin Coffee Frappe	Chicken, Mushroom and Tomato Stew
Get Enough Z's. Sleep is highly underrated but may be just as important as eating healthy and exercising. Studies show that poor sleep is one of the strongest risk factors for obesity, as it's linked to an 89% increased risk of obesity in children and 55% in adults					

Day 5

1st Meal	2nd Meal	3rd Meal	4th Meal	5th Meal	6th Meal
Pumpkin Coffee Frappe	Hot Chocolate with Cinnamon	Vanilla Frappe	Pumpkin Almond Gingerbread Latte	Iced Vanilla Shake	Chicken, Mushroom and Tomato Stew
Drink Water, Especially Before Meals.. It is often claimed that drinking water can help with weight loss — and that's true. Drinking water can boost metabolism by 24–30% over a period of 1–1.5 hours, helping you burn off a few more calories, One study showed that drinking a half-liter (17 ounces) of water about half an hour before meals helped dieters eat fewer calories and lose 44% more weight, compared to those who didn't drink the water.					

Day 6

1st Meal	2nd Meal	3rd Meal	4th Meal	5th Meal	6th Meal
Iced Vanilla Shake	Pumpkin Coffee Frappe	Hot Chocolate with Cinnamon	Vanilla Frappe	Pumpkin Almond Gingerbread Latte	Chicken, Mushroom and Tomato Stew
Drink Coffee (Preferably Black). Coffee has been unfairly demonized. Quality coffee is loaded with antioxidants and can have numerous health benefits. Studies show that the caffeine in coffee can boost metabolism by 3–11% and increase fat burning by up to 10–29%. Just make sure not to add a bunch of sugar or other high-calorie ingredients to your coffee. That will completely negate any benefits.					

Day 7

1st Meal	2nd Meal	3rd Meal	4th Meal	5th Meal	6th Meal
Pumpkin Almond Gingerbread Latte	Iced Vanilla Shake	Pumpkin Coffee Frappe	Hot Chocolate with Cinnamon	Vanilla Frappe	Chicken, Mushroom and Tomato Stew
Drink Green Tea. Like coffee, green tea also has many benefits, one of them being weight loss. Though green tea contains small amounts of caffeine, it is loaded with powerful antioxidants called catechins, which are believed to work synergistically with caffeine to enhance fat burning. Although the evidence is mixed, many studies show that green tea (either as a beverage or a green tea extract supplement) can help you lose weight.					

6 Prep Plan to Start Your Journey

Prep Plan #1

This is a fantastic starter plan with five Optavia fuelings and one "lean and green" meal per day that will keep you covered up to 7 days of eating.

Recipe 1 : Iced Vanilla Shake | Calories: 62 | Fat: 1g | Protein: 1g | Carbs: 12g | Net Carbs: 11g | Fiber: 1g

---

Prep time: 5 minutes | Cook time: 0 minutes | Serves 11 sachet Optavia Essential Velvety Hot Chocolate

---

½ packet Optavia Vanilla Shake Fueling
½ packet Optavia Gingerbread Fueling
½ cup unsweetened almond milk
½ cup water
8 ice cubes

Steps:
1. In a small blender, place all ingredients and pulse until smooth.
2. Transfer the shake into a serving glass and serve immediately.

Recipe 2 : Pumpkin Coffee Frappe | Calories: 195 | Fat: 9g | Protein: 6g | Carbs: 21g | Net Carbs: 18g | Fiber: 3g

---

Prep time: 5 minutes | Cook time: 0 minutes | Serves 1

---

1 sachet Optavia Essential Spiced Gingerbread
4 ounces (113 g) strong brewed coffee
4 ounces (113 g) unsweetened almond milk
⅛ teaspoon pumpkin pie spice
½ cup ice
1 tablespoon whipped topping

Steps:
1. In a blender, add the Spiced Gingerbread sachet, coffee, almond milk, pumpkin pie spice and ice and pulse until smooth.
2. Transfer the mixture into a glass and top with whipped topping.
3. Serve immediately.

Recipe 3 : Hot Chocolate with Cinnamon | Calories: 142 | Fat: 8g | Protein: 6g | Carbs: 10g | Net Carbs: 9g | Fiber: 1g

---

Prep time: 10 minutes | Cook time: 2 minutes | Serves 1

---

1 sachet Optavia Essential Velvety Hot Chocolate
½ teaspoon ground cinnamon
Pinch of cayenne pepper
6 ounces (170 g) unsweetened almond milk
1 tablespoon whipped cream

Steps:
1. In a serving mug, place all the ingredients except for whipped cream and beat until well blended.
2. Microwave on high for about 2 minutes.
3. Top with whipped cream and serve.

Recipe 4 : Vanilla Frappe | Calories: 266 | Fat: 13g | Protein: 9g | Carbs: 26g | Net Carbs: 23g | Fiber: 3g

---

Prep time: 5 minutes | Cook time: 0 minutes | Serves 1

---

1 sachet Optavia Essential Vanilla Shake
8 ounces unsweetened almond milk
½ cup ice
1 tablespoon whipped topping

Steps:
1. In a blender, add the Vanilla Shake sachet, almond milk and ice and pulse until smooth.
2. Transfer the mixture into a glass and top with whipped topping.
3. Serve immediately.

Recipe 5 : Pumpkin Almond Gingerbread Latte | Calories: 73 | Fat: 4g | Protein: 6g |
Carbs: 2g | Net Carbs: 1g | Fiber: 1g

Prep time: 5 minutes | Cook time: 1 minutes | Serves 1

2 tablespoons pumpkin purée
½ cup unsweetened almond milk
1 sachet Optavia Essential Spiced Gingerbread
½ cup strong brewed coffee

Steps:
1. Combine the pumpkin purée and milk in a microwave-safe mug. Microwave for 1 minute and stir.
2. Mix in the coffee and Spiced Gingerbread. Serve immediately.

Recipe 6 : Chicken, Mushroom and Tomato Stew | Calories: 282 | Fat: 24g | Protein: 10g |
Carbs: 7g | Net Carbs: 3g | Fiber: 4g

Prep time: 15 minutes | Cook time: 15 minutes | Serves 4

2 tablespoons olive oil
4 (5-ounce / 142-g) skinless chicken thighs
¾ pound (340 g) fresh cremini mushrooms, stemmed and quartered
1 small onion, chopped
1 tablespoon tomato paste
3 garlic cloves, minced
¼ cup green olives, pitted and halved
1 cup fresh cherry tomatoes
½ cup chicken broth
Salt and ground black pepper, as required
2 tablespoons fresh parsley, chopped

Steps:
1. Add the oil in Instant Pot and select "Sauté". Then add the chicken thighs and cook for about 2-3 minutes per side.
2. Transfer chicken thighs onto a plate.
3. In the Instant pot, add mushrooms and onion and cook for about 4-5 minutes.
4. Add tomato paste and garlic and cook for about 1 minute.
5. Press "Cancel" and stir in the chicken, olives, tomatoes and broth.
6. Secure the lid and turn to "Seal" position.
7. Cook on "Manual" with "High Pressure" for about 10 minutes.
8. Press "Cancel" and carefully do a "Quick" release.
9. Remove the lid and stir in salt, black pepper and parsley.
10. Serve hot.

Shopping Lists

Dairy

- Almond Milk

Meats and Seafoods

- Chicken

Fruits, Vegetables, Spices & Herbs

- Optavia Essential Velvety Hot Chocolate
- Optavia Vanilla Shake Fueling
- Optavia Gingerbread Fueling
- Optavia Essential Spiced Gingerbread
- Brewed Coffee
- Pumpkin Pie Spice
- Whipped Topping

- Cinnamon
- Cayenne Pepper
- Whipped Cream
- Optavia Essential Vanilla Shake
- Pumpkin Purée
- Cremini Mushrooms
- Onion
- Tomato Paste
- Garlic Cloves
- Green Olives

- Cherry
- Tomatoes
- Salt
- Black
- Pepper
- Parsley

Meal Prep Plan

Start your breakfast with **Iced Vanilla Shake.** First, In a small blender, place all ingredients and pulse until smooth. Transfer the shake into a serving glass and serve immediately.

Next is **Pumpkin Coffee Frappe** for your light snacks. In a blender, add the Spiced Gingerbread sachet, coffee, almond milk, pumpkin pie spice and ice and pulse until smooth. Transfer the mixture into a glass and top with whipped topping. Serve immediately.

For your lunch, prepare your ingredients for **Hot Chocolate with Cinnamon.** In a serving mug, place all the ingredients except for whipped cream and beat until well blended. Microwave on high for about 2 minutes. Top with whipped cream and serve.

Then, you can start a **Vanilla Frappe** for make your snacks. In a blender, add the Vanilla Shake sachet, almond milk and ice and pulse until smooth. Transfer the mixture into a glass and top with whipped topping. Serve immediately.

For your dinner, you can now prepare **Pumpkin Almond Gingerbread Latte.** Combine the pumpkin purée and milk in a microwave-safe mug. Microwave for 1 minute and stir. Mix in the coffee and Spiced Gingerbread. Serve immediately.

Finally, for your after snacks on your dinner. You can now prepare a **Chicken, Mushroom and Tomato Stew.** Add the oil in Instant Pot and select "Sauté". Then add the chicken thighs and cook for about 2-3 minutes per side. Transfer chicken thighs onto a plate. In the Instant pot, add mushrooms and onion and cook for about 4-5 minutes. Add tomato paste and garlic and cook for about 1 minute. Press "Cancel" and stir in the chicken, olives, tomatoes and broth. Secure the lid and turn to "Seal" position. Cook on "Manual" with "High Pressure" for about 10 minutes. Press "Cancel" and carefully do a "Quick" release. Remove the lid and stir in salt, black pepper and parsley. Serve hot.

5 & 1 Plan

Day 1

1st Meal	2nd Meal	3rd Meal	4th Meal	5th Meal	6th Meal
Cappuccino Shake	Vanilla-Almond Frappe	Classic Eggnog	Iced Ginger Ale Coconut Colada	Iced Pumpkin Frappe	Cod and Bell Peppers with Capers
Cut Back on Added Sugar.					
Added sugar is one of the worst ingredients in the modern diet. Most people consume way too much. Studies show that sugar (and high-fructose corn syrup) consumption is strongly associated with an increased risk of obesity, as well as conditions including type 2 diabetes and heart disease. If you want to lose weight, cut back on added sugar. Just make sure to read labels, because even so-called health foods can be loaded with sugar.					

Day 2

1st Meal	2nd Meal	3rd Meal	4th Meal	5th Meal	6th Meal
Iced Pumpkin Frappe	Cappuccino Shake	Vanilla-Almond Frappe	Classic Eggnog	Iced Ginger Ale Coconut Colada	Cod and Bell Peppers with Capers

Day 3

1st Meal	2nd Meal	3rd Meal	4th Meal	5th Meal	6th Meal
Iced Ginger Ale Coconut Colada	Iced Pumpkin Frappe	Cappuccino Shake	Vanilla-Almond Frappe	Classic Eggnog	Cod and Bell Peppers with Capers

Keep Healthy Food Around in Case You Get Hungry.

Keeping healthy food nearby can help prevent you from eating something unhealthy if you become excessively hungry. Snacks that are easily portable and simple to prepare include whole fruits, nuts, baby carrots, yogurt and hard-boiled eggs.

Day 4

1st Meal	2nd Meal	3rd Meal	4th Meal	5th Meal	6th Meal
Classic Eggnog	Iced Ginger Ale Coconut Colada	Iced Pumpkin Frappe	Cappuccino Shake	Vanilla-Almond Frappe	Cod and Bell Peppers with Capers

Do Aerobic Exercise.

Doing aerobic exercise (cardio) is an excellent way to burn calories and improve your physical and mental health. It appears to be particularly effective for losing belly fat, the unhealthy fat that tends to build up around your organs and cause metabolic disease

Day 5

1st Meal	2nd Meal	3rd Meal	4th Meal	5th Meal	6th Meal
Vanilla-Almond Frappe	Classic Eggnog	Iced Ginger Ale Coconut Colada	Iced Pumpkin Frappe	Cappuccino Shake	Cod and Bell Peppers with Capers

Lift Weights.

One of the worst side effects of dieting is that it tends to cause muscle loss and metabolic slowdown, often referred to as starvation mode. The best way to prevent this is to do some sort of resistance exercise such as lifting weights. Studies show that weight lifting can help keep your metabolism high and prevent you from losing precious muscle mass. Of course, it's important not just to lose fat — you also want to build muscle. Resistance exercise is critical for a toned body.

Day 6

1st Meal	2nd Meal	3rd Meal	4th Meal	5th Meal	6th Meal
Cappuccino Shake	Vanilla-Almond Frappe	Classic Eggnog	Iced Ginger Ale Coconut Colada	Iced Pumpkin Frappe	Cod and Bell Peppers with Capers

Eat More Fiber.

Fiber is often recommended for weight loss. Although the evidence is mixed, some studies show that fiber (especially viscous fiber) can increase satiety and help you control your weight over the long term

Day 7

1st Meal	2nd Meal	3rd Meal	4th Meal	5th Meal	6th Meal
Iced Pumpkin Frappe	Cappuccino Shake	Vanilla-Almond Frappe	Classic Eggnog	Iced Ginger Ale Coconut Colada	Cod and Bell Peppers with Capers
Eat More Vegetables.					
Vegetables have several properties that make them effective for weight loss. They contain few calories but a lot of fiber. Their high water content gives them low energy density, making them very filling.					

6 Prep Plan to Start Your Journey

Prep Plan #2

This is a fantastic starter plan with five Optavia fuelings and one "lean and green" meal per day that will keep you covered up to 7 days of eating.

Recipe 1 : Cappuccino Shake | Calories: 150 | Fat: 8g | Protein: 3g | Carbs: 17g | Net Carbs: 13g | Fiber: 4g

Prep time: 5 minutes | Cook time: 0 minutes | Serves 1

1 packet Medifast cappuccino mix
1 tablespoon sugar-free chocolate syrup
½ cup water
½ cup ice, crushed

Steps:
1. In a small blender, place all ingredients and pulse until smooth and creamy.
2. Transfer the shake into a serving glass and serve immediately.

Recipe 2 :Vanilla-Almond Frappe | Calories: 146 | Fat: 8g | Protein: 4g | Carbs: 32g | Net Carbs: 30g | Fiber: 2g

Prep time: 5 minutes | Cook time: 0 minutes | Serves 1

1 sachet Optavia Essential Vanilla Shake
8 ounces (227 g) unsweetened almond milk
½ cup ice
1 tablespoon whipped topping

Steps:
1. In a blender, add the Vanilla Shake sachet, almond milk and ice and pulse until smooth.
2. Transfer the mixture into a glass and top with whipped topping.
3. Serve immediately.

Recipe 3 : Classic Eggnog | Calories: 246 | Fat: 14g | Protein: 16g | Carbs: 12g | Net Carbs: 12g | Fiber: 0g

Prep time: 10 minutes | Cook time: 0 minutes | Serves 1

1 sachet Optavia Essential Vanilla Shake
8 ounces (227 g) unsweetened almond milk
1 organic egg (yolk and white separated)
¼ teaspoon rum extract
Pinch of ground nutmeg

Steps:
1. In a blender, add the Vanilla Shake sachet, almond milk and egg yolk and pulse until smooth.
2. In the bowl of a stand mixer, place egg white and beat on medium speed until stiff peaks form.
3. Place the whipped egg whites into a serving glass and top with shake mixture.
4. Stir the mixture and sprinkle with nutmeg.
5. Serve immediately.

Recipe 4 : Iced Ginger Ale Coconut Colada | Calories: 611 | Fat: 50g | Protein: 6g | Carbs: 40g | Net Carbs: 33g | Fiber: 7g

Prep time: 10 minutes | Cook time: 0 minutes | Serves 1

1 sachet Optavia Essential Creamy Vanilla Shake
6 ounces (170 g) unsweetened, original coconut milk
¼ teaspoon rum extract
6 ounces (170 g) diet ginger ale
½ cup ice
2 tablespoons shredded, unsweetened coconut, plus 2 teaspoons for topping

Steps:
1. Combine all the ingredients in a blender. Pulse until creamy.
2. Divide the mixture among two pina colada glasses. Spread remaining 2 teaspoons of shredded coconut on top.
3. Serve immediately.

Recipe 5 : Iced Pumpkin Frappe | Calories: 222 | Fat: 11g | Protein: 6g | Carbs: 22g | Net Carbs: 20g | Fiber: 2g

Prep time: 5 minutes | Cook time: 0 minutes | Serves 1

1 sachet Optavia Essential Spiced Gingerbread
4 ounces (113 g) strong brewed coffee, chilled
4 ounces (113 g) unsweetened almond milk
⅛ teaspoon pumpkin pie spice
½ cup ice
2 tablespoons pressurized whipped topping

Steps:
1. Combine all the ingredients, except for the whipped topping, in a blender. Pulse until smooth.
2. Pour the mixture in a serving bowl. Top with whipped topping and serve.

Recipe 6 : Cod and Bell Peppers with Capers | Calories: 181 | Fat: 10g | Protein: 21g | Carbs: 3g | Net Carbs: 2g | Fiber: 1g

Prep time: 15 minutes | Cook time: 4 minutes | Serves 4

¼ cup water
4 (4-ounce / 113-g) frozen cod fillets
12 cherry tomatoes
12 to 14 black olives
2 tablespoons capers
⅓ cup bell peppers, seeded and sliced
2 tablespoons olive oil
Salt, as required
Pinch of red pepper flakes

Steps:
1. In the pot of Instant Pot, pour the water.
2. Place the fish fillets in water and top with tomatoes, followed by the olives, capers and red peppers.
3. Drizzle with olive oil and sprinkle with salt and red pepper flakes.
4. Secure the lid and turn to "Seal" position.
5. Cook on "Manual" with "High Pressure" for about 4 minutes.
6. Press "Cancel" and do a "Natural" release for about 8 minutes, then do a "Quick" release.
7. Remove the lid and transfer the fish mixture onto serving plates.
8. Serve hot.

Shopping Lists

Dairy

- Almond Milk
- Coconut Milk
- Eggs

Fruits, Vegetables, Spices & Herbs

- Optavia Essential Velvety Hot Chocolate
- Medifast Cappuccino Mix
- Sugar-Free Chocolate Syrup
- Optavia Essential Vanilla Shake

- Whipped Topping
- Optavia Essential Vanilla Shake
- Rum Extract
- Nutmeg
- Optavia Essential Creamy Vanilla Shake
- Ginger Ale
- Coconut
- Optavia Essential Spiced Gingerbread
- Brewed Coffee
- Pumpkin Pie Spice
- Whipped Topping
- Frozen Cod Fillets

- Cherry Tomatoes
- Black Olives
- Capers
- Bell
- Peppers
- Olive
- Oil
- Salt
- Red
- Pepper
- Flakes

Meal Prep Plan

Start your breakfast with **Cappuccino Shake.** First, In a small blender, place all ingredients and pulse until smooth and creamy. Transfer the shake into a serving glass and serve immediately.

Next is **Vanilla-Almond Frappe** for your light snacks. In a blender, add the Vanilla Shake sachet, almond milk and ice and pulse until smooth. Transfer the mixture into a glass and top with whipped topping. Serve immediately.

For your lunch, prepare your ingredients for **Classic Eggnog**. In a blender, add the Vanilla Shake sachet, almond milk and egg yolk and pulse until smooth. In the bowl of a stand mixer, place egg white and beat on medium speed until stiff peaks form. Place the whipped egg whites into a serving glass and top with shake mixture. Stir the mixture and sprinkle with nutmeg. Serve immediately.

Then, you can start a **Iced Ginger Ale Coconut Colada** for make your snacks. Combine all the ingredients in a blender. Pulse until creamy. Divide the mixture among two pina colada glasses. Spread remaining 2 teaspoons of shredded coconut on top. Serve immediately.

For your dinner, you can now prepare **Iced Pumpkin Frappe**. Combine all the ingredients, except for the whipped topping, in a blender. Pulse until smooth. Pour the mixture in a serving bowl. Top with whipped topping and serve.

Finally, for your after snacks on your dinner. You can now prepare a **Cod and Bell Peppers with Capers.** In the pot of Instant Pot, pour the water. Place the fish fillets in water and top with tomatoes, followed by the olives, capers and red peppers. Drizzle with olive oil and sprinkle with salt and red pepper flakes. Secure the lid and turn to "Seal" position. Cook on "Manual" with "High Pressure" for about 4 minutes. Press "Cancel" and do a "Natural" release for about 8 minutes, then do a "Quick" release. Remove the lid and transfer the fish mixture onto serving plates. Serve hot.

4 & 2 & 1 Plan

Day 1

1st Meal	2nd Meal	3rd Meal	4th Meal	5th Meal	6th Meal	7th Meal
Pumpkin Coffee Frappe	Macadamia Smoothie Bowl with Chia Seeds	Iced Ginger Ale Coconut Colada	Vanilla Zombie Frappe	Spicy Chicken Meatballs with Arugula	Shrimp and Green Bean Chili	Plan-Approved Snack (eat whenever you crave for it)

Eat More Protein.

Protein is the single most important nutrient for losing weight. Eating a high-protein diet has been shown to boost metabolism by 80–100 calories per day while shaving 441 calories per day off your diet. One study also showed that eating 25% of your daily calories as protein reduced obsessive thoughts about food by 60% while cutting desire for late-night snacking in half. Simply adding protein to your diet is one of the easiest and most effective ways to lose weight.

Day 2

1st Meal	2nd Meal	3rd Meal	4th Meal	5th Meal	6th Meal	7th Meal
Shrimp and Green Bean Chili	Pumpkin Coffee Frappe	Macadamia Smoothie Bowl with Chia Seeds	Iced Ginger Ale Coconut Colada	Vanilla Zombie Frappe	Spicy Chicken Meatballs with Arugula	Plan-Approved Snack (eat whenever you crave for it)

Don't Do Sugary Drinks, Including Soda and Fruit Juice.

Sugar is bad, but sugar in liquid form is even worse. Studies show that calories from liquid sugar may be the single most fattening aspect of the modern diet; For example, one study showed that sugar-sweetened beverages are linked to a 60% increased risk of obesity in children for each daily serving. Keep in mind that this applies to fruit juice as well, which contains a similar amount of sugar as a soft drink like Coke.

Day 3

1st Meal	2nd Meal	3rd Meal	4th Meal	5th Meal	6th Meal	7th Meal
Spicy Chicken Meatballs with Arugula	Shrimp and Green Bean Chili	Pumpkin Coffee Frappe	Macadamia Smoothie Bowl with Chia Seeds	Iced Ginger Ale Coconut Colada	Vanilla Zombie Frappe	Plan-Approved Snack (eat whenever you crave for it)

Eat Whole, Single-Ingredient Foods (Real Food).

If you want to be a leaner, healthier person, then one of the best things you can do for yourself is to eat whole, single-ingredient foods. These foods are naturally filling, and it's very difficult to gain weight if the majority of your diet is based on them.

Day 4

1st Meal	2nd Meal	3rd Meal	4th Meal	5th Meal	6th Meal	7th Meal
Vanilla Zombie Frappe	Spicy Chicken Meatballs with Arugula	Shrimp and Green Bean Chili	Pumpkin Coffee Frappe	Macadamia Smoothie Bowl with Chia Seeds	Iced Ginger Ale Coconut Colada	Plan-Approved Snack (eat whenever you crave for it)

Chew More Slowly.

Your brain may take a while to register that you've had enough to eat. Some studies show that chewing more slowly can help you eat fewer calories and increase the production of hormones linked to weight loss. Also consider chewing your food more thoroughly. Studies show that increased chewing may reduce calorie intake at a meal

These practices are a component of mindful eating, which aims to help you slow down your food intake and pay attention to each bite.

Day 5

1st Meal	2nd Meal	3rd Meal	4th Meal	5th Meal	6th Meal	7th Meal
Iced Ginger Ale Coconut Colada	Vanilla Zombie Frappe	Spicy Chicken Meatballs with Arugula	Shrimp and Green Bean Chili	Pumpkin Coffee Frappe	Macadamia Smoothie Bowl with Chia Seeds	Plan-Approved Snack (eat whenever you crave for it)

Eat regular meals.

Eating at regular times during the day helps burn calories at a faster rate. It also reduces the temptation to snack on foods high in fat and sugar.

Day 6

1st Meal	2nd Meal	3rd Meal	4th Meal	5th Meal	6th Meal	7th Meal
Macadamia Smoothie Bowl with Chia Seeds	Iced Ginger Ale Coconut Colada	Vanilla Zombie Frappe	Spicy Chicken Meatballs with Arugula	Shrimp and Green Bean Chili	Pumpkin Coffee Frappe	Plan-Approved Snack (eat whenever you crave for it)

Read food labels.

Knowing how to read food labels can help you choose healthier options. Use the calorie information to work out how a particular food fits into your daily calorie allowance on the weight loss plan.

Day 7

1st Meal	2nd Meal	3rd Meal	4th Meal	5th Meal	6th Meal	7th Meal
Pumpkin Coffee Frappe	Macadamia Smoothie Bowl with Chia Seeds	Iced Ginger Ale Coconut Colada	Vanilla Zombie Frappe	Spicy Chicken Meatballs with Arugula	Shrimp and Green Bean Chili	Plan-Approved Snack (eat whenever you crave for it)

Do not stock junk food.

To avoid temptation, do not stock junk food – such as chocolate, biscuits, crisps and sweet fizzy drinks – at home. Instead, opt for healthy snacks, such as fruit, unsalted rice cakes, oat cakes, unsalted or unsweetened popcorn, and fruit juice.

6 Prep Plan to Start Your Journey

Prep Plan #3

This is a fantastic starter plan with four Optavia fuelings, two "lean and green" meals, and one snack per day that will keep you covered up to 7 days of eating.

Recipe 1 : Pumpkin Coffee Frappe | Calories: 195 | Fat: 9g | Protein: 6g | Carbs: 21g | Net Carbs: 18g | Fiber: 3g

Prep time: 5 minutes | Cook time: 0 minutes | Serves 1

1 sachet Optavia Essential Spiced Gingerbread
4 ounces (113 g) strong brewed coffee
4 ounces (113 g) unsweetened almond milk
⅛ teaspoon pumpkin pie spice
½ cup ice
1 tablespoon whipped topping

Steps:
1. In a blender, add the Spiced Gingerbread sachet, coffee, almond milk, pumpkin pie spice and ice and pulse until smooth.
2. Transfer the mixture into a glass and top with whipped topping.
3. Serve immediately.

Recipe 2 : Macadamia Smoothie Bowl with Chia Seeds | Calories: 545 | Fat: 49g | Protein: 6g | Carbs: 26g | Net Carbs: 19g | Fiber: 7g

Prep time: 10 minutes | Cook time: 0 minutes | Serves 1

1 sachet Optavia Essential Tropical Fruit Smoothie
½ cup unsweetened coconut milk
½ cup ice
1 tablespoon shredded, unsweetened coconut
½ ounce (14 g) macadamias, chopped
½ teaspoon lime zest
½ tablespoon chia seeds

Steps:
1. Add the Tropical Fruit Smoothie, coconut milk, and ice to a blender. Pulse until smooth.
2. Pour the smoothie into a bowl. Spread the remaining ingredients on top and serve.

Recipe 3 : Iced Ginger Ale Coconut Colada | Calories: 611 | Fat: 50g | Protein: 6g | Carbs: 40g | Net Carbs: 33g | Fiber: 7g

Prep time: 10 minutes | Cook time: 0 minutes | Serves 1

1 sachet Optavia Essential Creamy Vanilla Shake
6 ounces (170 g) unsweetened, original coconut milk
¼ teaspoon rum extract
6 ounces (170 g) diet ginger ale
½ cup ice
2 tablespoons shredded, unsweetened coconut, plus 2
    teaspoons for topping

Steps:
1. Combine all the ingredients in a blender. Pulse until creamy.
2. Divide the mixture among two pina colada glasses. Spread remaining 2 teaspoons of shredded coconut on top.
3. Serve immediately.

Recipe 4 : Vanilla Zombie Frappe | Calories: 201 | Fat: 9g | Protein: 5g | Carbs: 23g | Net Carbs: 21g | Fiber: 2g

Prep time: 15 minutes | Cook time: 0 minutes | Serves 1

1 sachet Optavia Essential Creamy Vanilla Shake
1 cup unsweetened almond milk
1 tablespoon caramel syrup
½ cup ice
McCormick Color From Nature Food Colors- blue, yellow, and red
2 tablespoons plain, low-fat Greek yogurt
1 tablespoon unsweetened vanilla milk
2 tablespoons pressurized whipped topping

Steps:
1. Put the Creamy Vanilla Shake, almond milk, caramel syrup, and ice in a blender. Pulse until smooth.
2. Add equal portions of blue and yellow food coloring until the shade of green is achieved.
3. In a bowl, mix the Greek yogurt and equal portions of blue and red food coloring until the shade of purple is achieved.
4. In a separate bowl, mix the vanilla milk with equal portions of blue and red food coloring until the shade of purple is achieved.
5. Drizzle purple Greek yogurt mixture down the sides of a cup. Fill cup with green shake mixture. Top with whipped topping and sprinkle with purple milk mixture.
6. Serve immediately.

Recipe 5 : Spicy Chicken Meatballs with Arugula | Calories: 545 | Fat: 43g | Protein: 30g | Carbs: 5g | Net Carbs: 3g | Fiber: 2g

Prep time: 15 minutes | Cook time: 25 minutes | Serves 4

For Meatballs:
1½ pounds (680 g) ground chicken
¾ cup almond meal
2 scallions, sliced thinly
2 garlic cloves, minced
Salt and ground black pepper, as required
5 tablespoons olive oil, divided
6 tablespoons hot sauce

For Serving:
4 cups fresh baby arugula

Steps:
1. In a large bowl, add chicken, almond meal, scallion, garlic, salt and black pepper and mix until well combined.
2. With slightly, greased hands, make 1-2 inches wide balls from mixture.
3. Add 1 tablespoons of the oil in the Instant Pot and select "Sauté". Then add the meatballs and cook until browned from all sides.
4. In a bowl, add the remaining oil and hot sauce and mix until well combined.
5. Press "Cancel" and place the sauce on top evenly.
6. Secure the lid and turn to "Seal" position.
7. Select "Poultry" and just use the default time of 15-20 minutes.
8. Press "Cancel" and carefully do a "Quick" release.
9. Divide the arugula onto serving plates.
10. Remove the lid and transfer the meatballs onto serving plates with meatballs.
11. Serve immediately.

Recipe 6 : Shrimp and Green Bean Chili | Calories: 197 | Fat: 6g | Protein: 28g | Carbs: 9g | Net Carbs: 5g | Fiber: 4g

Prep time: 15 minutes | Cook time: 2 minutes | Serves 4

2 tablespoons fresh lemon juice
1 teaspoon red chili powder
1 teaspoon garam masala powder
1 teaspoon ground cumin
Salt and ground black pepper, as required
1 pound (454 g) medium frozen shrimp, peeled and deveined
¾ pound (340 g) green beans, trimmed
1 tablespoon olive oil

Steps:
1. In a small bowl, mix together lemon juice and spices.
2. In the bottom of Instant Pot, arrange a steamer trivet and pour 1 cup of water.
3. Arrange green beans on top of trivet in a single layer and top with shrimp.
4. Drizzle with oil and sprinkle with spice mixture.
5. Secure the lid and turn to "Seal" position.
6. Select "Steam" and just use the default time of 2 minutes.
7. Press "Cancel" and do a "Natural" release.
8. Remove the lid and serve hot.

Recipe 7 : Plan-Approved Snack (eat whenever you crave for it)

Shopping Lists

Dairy

- Almond Milk
- Coconut Milk
- Greek Yogurt

Meats And Seafoods

- Chicken
- Shrimp

Fruits, Vegetables, Spices & Herbs

- Optavia Essential Spiced Gingerbread
- Optavia Essential Creamy Vanilla Shake
- Brewed Coffee
- Pumpkin Pie Spice
- Whipped Topping
- Optavia Essential Tropical Fruit Smoothie
- Macadamias
- Lime Zest

- Chia Seeds
- Rum Extract
- Ginger Ale
- Caramel Syrup
- Mccormick Color From Nature Food Colors- Blue, Yellow, And Red
- Whipped Topping
- Almond
- Scallions
- Green Beans

- Garlic Cloves
- Salt
- Ground Black Pepper
- Olive Oil
- Hot Sauce
- Arugula
- Lemon Juice
- Red Chili Powder
- Garam Masala Powder
- Ground Cumin

Meal Prep Plan

Start your breakfast with **Pumpkin Coffee Frappe.** First, In a blender, add the Spiced Gingerbread sachet, coffee, almond milk, pumpkin pie spice and ice and pulse until smooth. Transfer the mixture into a glass and top with whipped topping. Serve immediately.

Next is **Macadamia Smoothie Bowl with Chia Seeds** for your drinks. Add the Tropical Fruit Smoothie, coconut milk, and ice to a blender. Pulse until smooth. Pour the smoothie into a bowl. Spread the remaining ingredients on top and serve.

For your lunch, prepare your ingredients for **Iced Ginger Ale Coconut Colada**. Combine all the ingredients in a blender. Pulse until creamy. Divide the mixture among two pina colada glasses. Spread remaining 2 teaspoons of shredded coconut on top. Serve immediately.

Then, you can start a **Vanilla Zombie Frappe** for make your snacks. Put the Creamy Vanilla Shake, almond milk, caramel syrup, and ice in a blender. Pulse until smooth. Add equal portions of blue and yellow food coloring until the shade of green is achieved. In a bowl, mix the Greek yogurt and equal portions of blue and red food coloring until the shade of purple is achieved. In a separate bowl, mix the vanilla milk with equal portions of blue and red food coloring until the shade of purple is achieved. Drizzle purple Greek yogurt mixture down the sides of a cup. Fill cup with green shake mixture. Top with whipped topping and sprinkle with purple milk mixture. Serve immediately.

For your dinner, you can now prepare **Spicy Chicken Meatballs with Arugula**. In a large bowl, add chicken, almond meal, scallion, garlic, salt and black pepper and mix until well combined. With slightly, greased hands, make 1-2 inches wide balls from mixture. Add 1 tablespoons of the oil in the Instant Pot and select "Sauté". Then add the meatballs and cook until browned from all sides. In a bowl, add the remaining oil and hot sauce and mix until well combined. Press "Cancel" and place the sauce on top evenly. Secure the lid and turn to "Seal" position. Select "Poultry" and just use the default time of 15-20 minutes. Press "Cancel" and carefully do a "Quick" release. Divide the arugula onto serving plates. Remove the lid and transfer the meatballs onto serving plates with meatballs. Serve immediately.

Finally, for your after snacks on your dinner. You can now prepare a **Shrimp and Green Bean Chili.** In a small bowl, mix together lemon juice and spices. In the bottom of Instant Pot, arrange a steamer trivet and pour 1 cup of water. Arrange green beans on top of trivet in a single layer and top with shrimp. Drizzle with oil and sprinkle with spice mixture. Secure the lid and turn to "Seal" position. Select "Steam" and just use the default time of 2 minutes. Press "Cancel" and do a "Natural" release. Remove the lid and serve hot.

4 & 2 & 1 Plan

Day 1

1st Meal	2nd Meal	3rd Meal	4th Meal	5th Meal	6th Meal	7th Meal
Chocolate Peppermint Mocha	Cheese Smashed Potatoes with Spinach	Boo-Nila Shake	Chocolate Shake	Salmon Fillets with Zucchini	Beef and Spinach Bibimbap	Plan-Approved Snack (eat whenever you crave for it)

Cut down on alcohol.
A standard glass of wine can contain as many calories as a piece of chocolate. Over time, drinking too much can easily contribute to weight gain.

Day 2

1st Meal	2nd Meal	3rd Meal	4th Meal	5th Meal	6th Meal	7th Meal
Beef and Spinach Bibimbap	Chocolate Peppermint Mocha	Cheese Smashed Potatoes with Spinach	Boo-Nila Shake	Chocolate Shake	Salmon Fillets with Zucchini	Plan-Approved Snack (eat whenever you crave for it)

Stimulus and cue control.
Many social and environmental cues might encourage unnecessary eating. For example, some people are more likely to overeat while watching television. Others have trouble passing a bowl of candy to someone else without taking a piece. By being aware of what may trigger the desire to snack on empty calories, people can think of ways to adjust their routine to limit these triggers.

Day 3

1st Meal	2nd Meal	3rd Meal	4th Meal	5th Meal	6th Meal	7th Meal
Salmon Fillets with Zucchini	Beef and Spinach Bibimbap	Chocolate Peppermint Mocha	Cheese Smashed Potatoes with Spinach	Boo-Nila Shake	Chocolate Shake	Plan-Approved Snack (eat whenever you crave for it)

Seek social support.

Embracing the support of loved ones is an integral part of a successful weight loss journey. Some people may wish to invite friends or family members to join them, while others might prefer to use social media to share their progress.

Other avenues of support may include:

a positive social network

group or individual counseling

exercise clubs or partners

employee-assistance programs at work

Day 4

1st Meal	2nd Meal	3rd Meal	4th Meal	5th Meal	6th Meal	7th Meal
Chocolate Shake	Salmon Fillets with Zucchini	Beef and Spinach Bibimbap	Chocolate Peppermint Mocha	Cheese Smashed Potatoes with Spinach	Boo-Nila Shake	Plan-Approved Snack (eat whenever you crave for it)

Stay positive.

Weight loss is a gradual process, and a person may feel discouraged if the pounds do not drop off at quite the rate that they had anticipated. Some days will be harder than others when sticking to a weight loss or maintenance program. A successful weight-loss program requires the individual to persevere and not give up when self-change seems too difficult. Some people might need to reset their goals, potentially by adjusting the total number of calories they are aiming to eat or changing their exercise patterns.

The important thing is to keep a positive outlook and be persistent in working toward overcoming the barriers to successful weight loss.

Day 5

1st Meal	2nd Meal	3rd Meal	4th Meal	5th Meal	6th Meal	7th Meal
Boo-Nila Shake	Chocolate Shake	Salmon Fillets with Zucchini	Beef and Spinach Bibimbap	Chocolate Peppermint Mocha	Cheese Smashed Potatoes with Spinach	Plan-Approved Snack (eat whenever you crave for it)

Keep a Daily Gratitude Journal.

"Our eating habits are usually connected to our emotions — whether we realize it or not. When we're stressed, we tend to reach for sweets. I tell clients that by keeping a daily journal of things you're grateful for, you're better able to cope with the stress by acknowledging it rather than reaching for dessert."

Day 6

1st Meal	2nd Meal	3rd Meal	4th Meal	5th Meal	6th Meal	7th Meal
Cheese Smashed Potatoes with Spinach	Boo-Nila Shake	Chocolate Shake	Salmon Fillets with Zucchini	Beef and Spinach Bibimbap	Chocolate Peppermint Mocha	Plan-Approved Snack (eat whenever you crave for it)

Day 7

1ˢᵗ Meal	2ⁿᵈ Meal	3ʳᵈ Meal	4ᵗʰ Meal	5ᵗʰ Meal	6ᵗʰ Meal	7ᵗʰ Meal
Chocolate Peppermint Mocha	Cheese Smashed Potatoes with Spinach	Boo-Nila Shake	Chocolate Shake	Salmon Fillets with Zucchini	Beef and Spinach Bibimbap	Plan-Approved Snack (eat whenever you crave for it)

6 Prep Plan to Start Your Journey

Prep Plan #4

This is a fantastic starter plan with four Optavia fuelings, two "lean and green" meals, and one snack per day that will keep you covered up to 7 days of eating.

Recipe 1 : Chocolate Peppermint Mocha | Calories: 53 | Fat: 2g | Protein: 1g | Carbs: 8g | Net Carbs: 8g | Fiber: 0g

Prep time: 5 minutes | Cook time: 0 minutes | Serves 1

1 sachet Optavia Essential Velvety Hot Chocolate
6 ounces (170 g) brewed coffee
¼ teaspoon peppermint extract
¼ cup unsweetened almond milk, warmed
2 tablespoons pressurized whipped topping
Pinch cinnamon

Steps:
1. Combine the Velvety Hot Chocolate, coffee, peppermint extract, and milk in a mug and stir to mix well.
2. Spread with whipped topping and sprinkle with cinnamon. Serve immediately.

Recipe 2 : Cheese Smashed Potatoes with Spinach |
Calories: 199 | Fat: 6g | Protein: 10g | Carbs: 26g | Net Carbs: 23g | Fiber: 3g

Prep time: 5 minutes | Cook time: 0 minutes | Serves 1

1 sachet Optavia Essential Roasted Garlic
   Creamy Smashed Potatoes
1 cup baby spinach
1 teaspoon water
½ cup reduced-fat shredded Mozzarella
   cheese
1 tablespoon grated Parmesan cheese

Steps:
1. Cook the Roasted Garlic Creamy Smashed Potatoes according to package directions.
2. Steam the spinach with water in a microwave-safe bowl in the microwave for 1 minute or until wilted.
3. Combine the Roasted Garlic Creamy Smashed Potatoes, spinach, and cheeses in a large serving bowl.
4. Serve warm.

Recipe 3 : Boo-Nila Shake | Calories: 151 | Fat: 8g | Protein: 4g | Carbs: 13g | Net Carbs: 7g | Fiber: 8g

Prep time: 5 minutes | Cook time: 0 minutes | Serves 1

1 sachet Optavia Essential Creamy Vanilla
  Shake
8 ounces (227 g) unsweetened almond milk
½ cup ice
2 tablespoons pressurized whipped
  topping

Steps:
1. Combine the Creamy Vanilla Shake, almond milk, and ice in a food processor. Pulse until smooth.
2. Pour the mixture in a mason jar and spread with whipped topping over.
3. Serve immediately.

Recipe 4 : Chocolate Shake | calories: 150 | fat: 8g | protein: 2g | carbs: 17g | net carbs: 14g | fiber: 3g

Prep time: 5 minutes | Cook time: 0 minutes | Serves 1

1 packet Medifast cappuccino mix
1 tablespoon sugar-free chocolate syrup
½ cup water
½ cup ice, crushed

Steps:
1. In a small blender, place all ingredients and pulse until smooth and creamy.
2. Transfer the shake into a serving glass and serve immediately.

Recipe 5 : Salmon Fillets with Zucchini | calories: 204 | fat: 11g | protein: 23g | carbs: 6g | net carbs: 4g | fiber: 2g

Prep time: 15 minutes | Cook time: 6 minutes | Serves 4

1 pound (454 g) skin-on salmon fillets
Salt and ground black pepper, as
  required
1 fresh parsley sprig
1 fresh dill sprig
3 teaspoons coconut oil, melted and
  divided
½ lemon, sliced thinly
1 carrot, peeled and julienned
1 zucchini, peeled and julienned
1 red bell pepper, seeded and julienned

Steps:
1. Season the salmon fillets with salt and black pepper evenly.
2. In the bottom of Instant Pot, arrange a steamer trivet and place herb sprigs and 1 cup of water.
3. Place the salmon fillets on top of trivet, skin side down.
4. Drizzle salmon fillets with 2 teaspoons of coconut oil and top with lemon slices.
5. Secure the lid and turn to "Seal" position.
6. Select "Steam" and just use the default time of 3 minutes.
7. Press "Cancel" and do a "Natural" release.
8. Meanwhile, for sauce: in a bowl, add remaining ingredients and mix until well combined.
9. Remove the lid and transfer the salmon fillets onto a platter.
10. Remove the steamer trivet, herbs and cooking water from pot. With paper towels, pat dry the pot.

Recipe 6 : Beef and Spinach Bibimbap | Calories: 495 | Fat: 32g | Protein: 41g | Carbs: 8g | Net Carbs: 5g | Fiber: 3g

Prep time: 10 minutes | Cook time: 12 minutes | Serves 4

1 teaspoon olive oil
5 cups baby spinach
1 teaspoon toasted sesame oil
¼ teaspoon salt
1 pound (454 g) 95 to 97% lean ground beef
1 tablespoon reduced-sodium soy sauce
2 tablespoons chili garlic sauce
2 cups riced cauliflower
1 cup thinly sliced cucumber
4 hard-boiled eggs
½ cup chopped green onions
1 tablespoon sesame seeds

Steps:
1. Heat the olive oil in a skillet over medium high heat until it shimmers. Add the baby spinach and sauté for 2 to 3 minutes until just wilted. Drizzle with the sesame oil and season with salt.
2. Remove the spinach from the skillet and set aside.
3. Place the ground beef in the same skillet and cook until fully browned. Stir in the chili garlic sauce and soy sauce and cook for 1 minute. Remove the skillet from the heat and set aside.
4. Place the riced cauliflower with 1 tablespoon water in a large microwave-safe dish. Microwave on High for 3 to 4 minutes or until tender.
5. Divide ½ cup of riced cauliflower into each bowl. Top each bowl evenly with the spinach, beef, and sliced cucumber. Place an egg on top of each bowl. Serve garnished with the green onions and green onions.

Recipe 7 : Plan-Approved Snack (eat whenever you crave for it)

Shopping Lists

Dairy

- Almond Milk
- Mozzarella Cheese
- Parmesan Cheese
- Eggs

Meats and Seafoods

- Salmon
- Beef
- Shrimp

Fruits, Vegetables, Spices & Herbs

- Optavia Essential Velvety Hot Chocolate
- Brewed Coffee
- Peppermint Extract
- Whipped Toppings
- Cinnamon
- Optavia Essential Roasted Garlic Creamy Smashed Potatoes
- Baby Spinach
- Optavia Essential Creamy Vanilla Shake
- Cappuccino
- Sugar Free Syrup
- Black Pepper
- Parsley
- Dill
- Coconut Oil
- Lemon
- Carrot
- Zucchini
- Red Bell Pepper
- Olive Oil
- Sesame Oil
- Salt
- Soy Sauce
- Cauliflower
- Cucumber
- Green Onions
- Sesame Seeds

Meal Prep Plan

Start your breakfast with **Chocolate Peppermint Mocha.** First, Combine the Velvety Hot Chocolate, coffee, peppermint extract, and milk in a mug and stir to mix well. Spread with whipped topping and sprinkle with cinnamon. Serve immediately.

Next is **Cheese Smashed Potatoes with Spinach** for your light snacks. Cook the Roasted Garlic Creamy Smashed Potatoes according to package directions. Steam the spinach with water in a microwave-safe bowl in the microwave for 1 minute or until wilted. Combine the Roasted Garlic Creamy Smashed Potatoes, spinach, and cheeses in a large serving bowl. Serve warm.

For your lunch, prepare your ingredients for **Boo-Nila Shake**. In a small blender, place all ingredients and pulse until smooth and creamy. Transfer the shake into a serving glass and serve immediately.

Then, you can start **a Chocolate Shake** for make your snacks. In a small blender, place all ingredients and pulse until smooth and creamy. Transfer the shake into a serving glass and serve immediately.

For your dinner, you can now prepare **Salmon Fillets with Zucchini**. Season the salmon fillets with salt and black pepper evenly. In the bottom of Instant Pot, arrange a steamer trivet and place herb sprigs and 1 cup of water. Place the salmon fillets on top of trivet, skin side down. Drizzle salmon fillets with 2 teaspoons of coconut oil and top with lemon slices. Secure the lid and turn to "Seal" position. Select "Steam" and just use the default time of 3 minutes. Press "Cancel" and do a "Natural" release. Meanwhile, for sauce: in a bowl, add remaining ingredients and mix until well combined. Remove the lid and transfer the salmon fillets onto a platter. Remove the steamer trivet, herbs and cooking water from pot. With paper towels, pat dry the pot.

Finally, for your after snacks on your dinner. You can now prepare a **Beef and Spinach Bibimbap.** Heat the olive oil in a skillet over medium high heat until it shimmers. Add the baby spinach and sauté for 2 to 3 minutes until just wilted. Drizzle with the sesame oil and season with salt. Remove the spinach from the skillet and set aside. Place the ground beef in the same skillet and cook until fully browned. Stir in the chili garlic sauce and soy sauce and cook for 1 minute. Remove the skillet from the heat and set aside. Place the riced cauliflower with 1 tablespoon water in a large microwave-safe dish. Microwave on High for 3 to 4 minutes or until tender. Divide ½ cup of riced cauliflower into each bowl. Top each bowl evenly with the spinach, beef, and sliced cucumber. Place an egg on top of each bowl. Serve garnished with the green onions and green onions.

3 & 3 Plan

Day 1

1st Meal	2nd Meal	3rd Meal	4th Meal	5th Meal	6th Meal
Pumpkin Almond Gingerbread Latte	Berry Mojito	Vanilla and Rum Eggnog	Simple Steak	Tuna Omelet	Chicken Chili
Be Choosy at Restaurants					
The foods we eat away from home tend to be higher in calories and lower in nutrients than the ones we make at home. A study published in April 2016 in the Journal of the Academy of Nutrition and Dietetics found that the average restaurant entrée contains more than 1,000 calories, and an entire day's worth of sodium and fat. To save calories, split your entrée or ask the server to substitute extra green veggies or a salad for potato or rice.					

Day 2

1st Meal	2nd Meal	3rd Meal	4th Meal	5th Meal	6th Meal
Chicken Chili	Pumpkin Almond Gingerbread Latte	Berry Mojito	Vanilla and Rum Eggnog	Simple Steak	Tuna Omelet
Start Where You Are and Do What You Can					
Don't feel like you need to overhaul your entire life starting immediately. Assess where you are currently and then figure out where you'd like to be in the future. A great starting point for mostly sedentary people is to get a step counter and see how much you walk on a normal day. Then set a step goal slightly higher than the norm and strive for that, working your way up slowly to a goal of 10,000 steps per day.					

Day 3

1st Meal	2nd Meal	3rd Meal	4th Meal	5th Meal	6th Meal
Tuna Omelet	Chicken Chili	Pumpkin Almond Gingerbread Latte	Berry Mojito	Vanilla and Rum Eggnog	Simple Steak
Tell the difference between a real plateau and an imaginary one					
During the first days of the diet, extra fluids leave our bodies which makes the number on the scale drop quickly. But in order to lose just 1 lb, you need to have a 3,500-calorie deficit. It doesn't matter how you achieve it, but the progress won't be fast. Many people think that losing weight slowly is a plateau, so they lose interest and drop the diet. Be patient and don't step on the scale more than once a week: this way, the progress will seem bigger.					

Day 4

1st Meal	2nd Meal	3rd Meal	4th Meal	5th Meal	6th Meal
Simple Steak	Tuna Omelet	Chicken Chili	Pumpkin Almond Gingerbread Latte	Berry Mojito	Vanilla and Rum Eggnog

Take some aspins, ibuprofen, or have chicken broth, pickles

You will feel Sluggishness, fatigue, headache in the beginning, it is because the toxins and and electrons are leaving your body, so your body needs the salt to reset your body back to balance.

Day 5

1st Meal	2nd Meal	3rd Meal	4th Meal	5th Meal	6th Meal
Vanilla and Rum Eggnog	Simple Steak	Tuna Omelet	Chicken Chili	Pumpkin Almond Gingerbread Latte	Berry Mojito

Drink Coffee (Preferably Black)

Coffee has been unfairly demonized. Quality coffee is loaded with antioxidants and can have numerous health benefits. Studies show that the caffeine in coffee can boost metabolism by 3–11% and increase fat burning by up to 10–29%. Just make sure not to add a bunch of sugar or other high-calorie ingredients to your coffee. That will completely negate any benefits.

Day 6

1st Meal	2nd Meal	3rd Meal	4th Meal	5th Meal	6th Meal
Berry Mojito	Vanilla and Rum Eggnog	Simple Steak	Tuna Omelet	Chicken Chili	Pumpkin Almond Gingerbread Latte

Cut Back on Added Sugar

Added sugar is one of the worst ingredients in the modern diet. Most people consume way too much. Studies show that sugar (and high-fructose corn syrup) consumption is strongly associated with an increased risk of obesity, as well as conditions including type 2 diabetes and heart disease. If you want to lose weight, cut back on added sugar. Just make sure to read labels, because even so-called health foods can be loaded with sugar.

Day 7

1st Meal	2nd Meal	3rd Meal	4th Meal	5th Meal	6th Meal
Pumpkin Almond Gingerbread Latte	Berry Mojito	Vanilla and Rum Eggnog	Simple Steak	Tuna Omelet	Chicken Chili

Eat Less Refined Carbs

Refined carbohydrates include sugar and grains that have been stripped of their fibrous, nutritious parts. These include white bread and pasta. Studies show that refined carbs can spike blood sugar rapidly, leading to hunger, cravings and increased food intake a few hours later. Eating refined carbs is strongly linked to obesity. If you're going to eat carbs, make sure to eat them with their natural fiber.

6 Prep Plan to Start Your Journey

Prep Plan #5

This is a fantastic starter plan with three Optavia fuelings and three "lean and green" meals per day that will keep you covered up to 7 days of eating.

Recipe 1 : Pumpkin Almond Gingerbread Latte | Calories: 73 | Fat: 4g | Protein: 6g | Carbs: 2g | Net Carbs: 1g | Fiber: 1g

Prep time: 5 minutes | Cook time: 1 minutes | Serves 1

2 tablespoons pumpkin purée
½ cup unsweetened almond milk
1 sachet Optavia Essential Spiced Gingerbread
½ cup strong brewed coffee

Steps:
1. Combine the pumpkin purée and milk in a microwave-safe mug. Microwave for 1 minute and stir.
2. Mix in the coffee and Spiced Gingerbread. Serve immediately.

Recipe 2 : Berry Mojito | Caloriesc: 99| fat: 0g | protein: 1g | carbs: 23g | net carbs: 22g | fiber: 1g

Prep time: 5 minutes | Cook time: 0 minutes | Serves 2

2 tablespoons fresh lime juice
6 fresh mint leaves
1 packet Mixed Berry Flavor Infuser
16 ounces (453 g) seltzer water
Ice cubes, as required

Steps:
1. In the bottom of 2 cocktail glasses, divide the lime juice and mint leaves.
2. With the bottom end of a spoon, gently muddle the mint leaves.
3. Now, divide the Berry Infuser and seltzer water into each glass and stir to combine.
4. Place ice cubes in each glass and serve.

Recipe 3 :Vanilla and Rum Eggnog | Calories: 688 | Fat: 68g | Protein: 25g | Carbs: 24g | Net Carbs: 7g | Fiber: 14g

Prep time: 5 minutes | Cook time: 0 minutes | Serves 1

1 sachet Optavia Essential Creamy Vanilla Shake
8 ounces (227 g) unsweetened almond milk
1 egg, white and yolk separated
¼ teaspoon rum extract
Pinch nutmeg

Steps:
1. Combine the Creamy Vanilla Shake, almond milk, and egg yolk in a blender and pulse until smooth.
2. Whip the egg white until stiff peaks form in a bowl. Pour the whipped egg white in a glass.
3. Pour the Vanilla Shake mixture over the egg white. Sprinkle with nutmeg and serve.

Recipe 4 : Simple Steak | Calories:284| Fat: 38g | Protein: 12g | Carbs: 3g | Net Carbs: 1g | Fiber: 2g

Prep time: 5 minutes | Cook time: 5 minutes | Serves 4

1 tablespoon olive oil
4 (6-ounce/ 170 g) flank steaks
Salt and ground black pepper, as required
6 cups fresh salad greens

Steps:
1. In a wok, heat the oil over medium-high heat and cook steaks with salt and black pepper for about 3 to 5 minutes per side.
2. Transfer the steaks onto serving plates and serve alongside the greens.

Recipe 5 : Tuna Omelet | Calories: 284| Fat: 38g | Protein: 12g | Carbs: 3g | Net Carbs: 1g | Fiber: 2g

Prep time: 15 minutes | Cook time: 5 minutes | Serves 2

4 eggs
¼ cup unsweetened almond milk
1 tablespoon scallions, chopped
1 garlic clove, minced
½ of jalapeño pepper, minced
Salt and ground black pepper, as required
1 (5-ounce/ 142 g) can water-packed tuna, drained and flaked
1 tablespoon olive oil
3 tablespoons green bell pepper, seeded and chopped
3 tablespoons tomato, chopped
¼ cup low-fat cheddar cheese, shredded

Steps:
1. In a bowl, add the eggs, almond milk, scallions, garlic, jalapeño pepper, salt, and black pepper, and beat well.
2. Add the tuna and stir to combine.
3. In a large nonstick frying pan, heat oil over medium heat.
4. Place the egg mixture in an even layer and cook for about 1 to 2 minutes, without stirring.
5. Carefully lift the edges to run the uncooked portion flow underneath.
6. Spread the veggies over the egg mixture and sprinkle with the cheese.
7. Cover the frying pan and cook for about 30 to 60 seconds.
8. Remove the lid and fold the omelet in half.
Remove from the heat and cut the omelet into 2 portions.

Recipe 6 : Chicken Chili| Calories: 306 | Fat: 15.6g | Protein: 33.4g | Carbs: 7.1g | Net Carbs: 5.2g | Fiber: 1.9g

Prep time: 10 minutes | Cook time: 10 minutes | Serves 2

3 (5-ounce/ 142 g) chicken breasts
1 carrot, peeled and chopped
1 celery stalk, chopped
1 medium yellow onion, chopped
2 garlic cloves, chopped
1 teaspoon dried oregano
1 teaspoon ground cumin
Salt and ground black pepper, as required
½ cup unsweetened coconut milk
1 cup chicken broth

Steps:
1. In the pot of Instant Pot, add all ingredients and stir to combine.
2. Secure the lid and turn to "Seal" position.
3. Select "Poultry" and just use the default time of 20 minutes.
4. Press "Cancel" and do a "Natural" release.
5. Remove the lid and with a slotted spoon, transfer the chicken breasts into a bowl.
6. With 2 forks, shred chicken breasts and then return into the pot.
7. Serve immediately.

Shopping Lists

Dairy

- Almond Milk
- Coconut Milk
- Eggs
- Cheddar Cheese

Meats and Seafoods

- Chicken
- Steak
- Tuna

Fruits, Vegetables, Spices & Herbs

- Carrot
- Celery Stalk
- Orange
- Yellow Onion
- Garlic Cloves
- Dried Oregano
- Cumin
- Salt
- Black Pepper
- Lime
- Fresh Mint Leaves
- Mixed Berry Flavor Infuser
- Optavia Essential Creamy Vanilla Shake
- Rum Extract
- Nutmeg
- Olive Oil
- Fresh Salad Greens
- Scallions
- Garlic Clove
- Jalapeño Pepper
- Tomato

Meal Prep Plan

Start your breakfast with **Pumpkin Almond Gingerbread Latte.** First, Combine the pumpkin purée and milk in a microwave-safe mug. Microwave for 1 minute and stir. Mix in the coffee and Spiced Gingerbread. Serve immediately.

Next is **Berry Mojito** for your drinks. In the bottom of 2 cocktail glasses, divide the lime juice and mint leaves. With the bottom end of a spoon, gently muddle the mint leaves. Now, divide the Berry Infuser and seltzer water into each glass and stir to combine. Place ice cubes in each glass and serve.

For your lunch, prepare your ingredients for **Vanilla and Rum Eggnog.** Combine the Creamy Vanilla Shake, almond milk, and egg yolk in a blender and pulse until smooth. Whip the egg white until stiff peaks form in a bowl. Pour the whipped egg white in a glass. Pour the Vanilla Shake mixture over the egg white. Sprinkle with nutmeg and serve.

Then, you can start **a Simple Steak** for make your dinner. In a wok, heat the oil over medium-high heat and cook steaks with salt and black pepper for about 3 to 5 minutes per side. Transfer the steaks onto serving plates and serve alongside the greens.

For your dinner, you can now prepare **Tuna Omelet.** In a bowl, add the eggs, almond milk, scallions, garlic, jalapeño pepper, salt, and black pepper, and beat well. Add the tuna and stir to combine. In a large nonstick frying pan, heat oil over medium heat. Place the egg mixture in an even layer and cook for about 1 to 2 minutes, without stirring. Carefully lift the edges to run the uncooked portion flow underneath. Spread the veggies over the egg mixture and sprinkle with the cheese. Cover the frying pan and cook for about 30 to 60 seconds. Remove the lid and fold the omelet in half. Remove from the heat and cut the omelet into 2 portions.

Finally, for your after snacks on your dinner. You can now prepare a **Chicken Chili.** In the pot of Instant Pot, add all ingredients and stir to combine. Secure the lid and turn to "Seal" position. Select "Poultry" and just use the default time of 20 minutes. Press "Cancel" and do a "Natural" release. Remove the lid and with a slotted spoon, transfer the chicken breasts into a bowl. With 2 forks, shred chicken breasts and then return into the pot. Serve immediately.

3 & 3 Plan

Day 1

1ˢᵗ Meal	2ⁿᵈ Meal	3ʳᵈ Meal	4ᵗʰ Meal	5ᵗʰ Meal	6ᵗʰ Meal
Classic Eggnog	Iced Pumpkin Frappe	Cappuccino Shake	Chicken and Cauliflower Risotto	Beef with Broccoli	Shrimp with Green Beans
Keep Healthy Food Around in Case You Get Hungry Keeping healthy food nearby can help prevent you from eating something unhealthy if you become excessively hungry. Snacks that are easily portable and simple to prepare include whole fruits, nuts, baby carrots, yogurt and hard-boiled eggs.					

Day 2

1st Meal	2nd Meal	3rd Meal	4th Meal	5th Meal	6th Meal
Shrimp with Green Beans	Classic Eggnog	Iced Pumpkin Frappe	Cappuccino Shake	Chicken and Cauliflower Risotto	Beef with Broccoli

Do Aerobic Exercise
Doing aerobic exercise (cardio) is an excellent way to burn calories and improve your physical and mental health. It appears to be particularly effective for losing belly fat, the unhealthy fat that tends to build up around your organs and cause metabolic disease

Day 3

1st Meal	2nd Meal	3rd Meal	4th Meal	5th Meal	6th Meal
Beef with Broccoli	Shrimp with Green Beans	Classic Eggnog	Iced Pumpkin Frappe	Cappuccino Shake	Chicken and Cauliflower Risotto

Lift Weights
One of the worst side effects of dieting is that it tends to cause muscle loss and metabolic slowdown, often referred to as starvation mode. The best way to prevent this is to do some sort of resistance exercise such as lifting weights. Studies show that weight lifting can help keep your metabolism high and prevent you from losing precious muscle mass. Of course, it's important not just to lose fat — you also want to build muscle. Resistance exercise is critical for a toned body.

Day 4

1st Meal	2nd Meal	3rd Meal	4th Meal	5th Meal	6th Meal
Chicken and Cauliflower Risotto	Beef with Broccoli	Shrimp with Green Beans	Classic Eggnog	Iced Pumpkin Frappe	Cappuccino Shake

Eat More Fiber
Fiber is often recommended for weight loss. Although the evidence is mixed, some studies show that fiber (especially viscous fiber) can increase satiety and help you control your weight over the long term

Day 5

1st Meal	2nd Meal	3rd Meal	4th Meal	5th Meal	6th Meal
Cappuccino Shake	Chicken and Cauliflower Risotto	Beef with Broccoli	Shrimp with Green Beans	Classic Eggnog	Iced Pumpkin Frappe

Eat More Vegetables
Vegetables have several properties that make them effective for weight loss. They contain few calories but a lot of fiber. Their high water content gives them low energy density, making them very filling.

Day 6

1st Meal	2nd Meal	3rd Meal	4th Meal	5th Meal	6th Meal
Iced Pumpkin Frappe	Cappuccino Shake	Chicken and Cauliflower Risotto	Beef with Broccoli	Shrimp with Green Beans	Classic Eggnog

Eat More Protein

Protein is the single most important nutrient for losing weight. Eating a high-protein diet has been shown to boost metabolism by 80–100 calories per day while shaving 441 calories per day off your diet. One study also showed that eating 25% of your daily calories as protein reduced obsessive thoughts about food by 60% while cutting desire for late-night snacking in half. Simply adding protein to your diet is one of the easiest and most effective ways to lose weight.

Day 7

1st Meal	2nd Meal	3rd Meal	4th Meal	5th Meal	6th Meal
Classic Eggnog	Iced Pumpkin Frappe	Cappuccino Shake	Chicken and Cauliflower Risotto	Beef with Broccoli	Shrimp with Green Beans

Eat regular meals

Eating at regular times during the day helps burn calories at a faster rate. It also reduces the temptation to snack on foods high in fat and sugar.

6 Prep Plan to Start Your Journey

Prep Plan #6

This is a fantastic starter plan with three Optavia fuelings and three "lean and green" meals per day that will keep you covered up to 7 days of eating.

Recipe 1 : Classic Eggnog | Calories: 246 | Fat: 14g | Protein: 16g | Carbs: 12g | Net Carbs: 12g | Fiber: 0g

Prep time: 10 minutes | Cook time: 0 minutes | Serves 1

1 sachet Optavia Essential Vanilla Shake
8 ounces (227 g) unsweetened almond milk
1 organic egg (yolk and white separated)
¼ teaspoon rum extract
Pinch of ground nutmeg

Steps:
1. In a blender, add the Vanilla Shake sachet, almond milk and egg yolk and pulse until smooth.
2. In the bowl of a stand mixer, place egg white and beat on medium speed until stiff peaks form.
3. Place the whipped egg whites into a serving glass and top with shake mixture.
4. Stir the mixture and sprinkle with nutmeg.
5. Serve immediately.

Recipe 2 : Iced Pumpkin Frappe | Calories: 222 | Fat: 11g | Protein: 6g | Carbs: 22g | Net Carbs: 20g | Fiber: 2g

Prep time: 5 minutes | Cook time: 0 minutes | Serves 1

1 sachet Optavia Essential Spiced Gingerbread
4 ounces (113 g) strong brewed coffee, chilled
4 ounces (113 g) unsweetened almond milk
⅛ teaspoon pumpkin pie spice
½ cup ice
2 tablespoons pressurized whipped topping

Steps:
1. Combine all the ingredients, except for the whipped topping, in a blender. Pulse until smooth.
2. Pour the mixture in a serving bowl. Top with whipped topping and serve.

Recipe 3 : Cappuccino Shake | Calories: 150 | Fat: 8g | Protein: 3g | Carbs: 17g | Net Carbs: 13g | Fiber: 4g

Prep time: 5 minutes | Cook time: 0 minutes | Serves 1

1 packet Medifast cappuccino mix
1 tablespoon sugar-free chocolate syrup
½ cup water
½ cup ice, crushed

Steps:
1. In a small blender, place all ingredients and pulse until smooth and creamy.
2. Transfer the shake into a serving glass and serve immediately.

Recipe 4 : Chicken and Cauliflower Risotto | Calories: 532 | Fat: 19g | Protein: 29g | Carbs: 60g | Net Carbs: 52g | Fiber: 8g

Prep time: 0 minutes | Cook time: 30 minutes | Serves 4

2 pounds (907 g) boneless, skinless chicken breasts
¼ teaspoon salt
¼ teaspoon ground black pepper
2 tablespoons butter, melted
1¼ pounds (567 g) riced cauliflower
¼ pound (113 g) asparagus, chopped
½ cup chicken stock
4 tablespoons nutritional yeast

Steps:
1. Preheat the oven to 350°F (180°C).
2. Place the chicken in a casserole dish and season with salt and pepper.
3. Pour melted butter over, and roast in the preheated oven for 30 minutes or until an internal temperature reaches at least 165°F (74°C). Remove from oven and allow to cool.
4. Meanwhile, combine the cauliflower rice, asparagus, and chicken stock in a pot and simmer over medium heat for 6 minutes or until soft.
5. Remove the cauliflower and asparagus from the stovetop and stir in the nutritional yeast.
6. Serve with roasted chicken breast.

Recipe 5 : Beef with Broccoli | Calories: 498 | Fat: 35.6g | Protein: 33.6g | Carbs: 11g | Net Carbs: 8g | Fiber: 3g

Prep time: 15 minutes | Cook time: 32 minutes | Serves 4

1 tablespoon olive oil
1 pound (454 g) beef chuck roast, trimmed and cut into thin strips
Salt and ground black pepper, as required
1 yellow onion, chopped
2 garlic cloves, minced
Pinch of red pepper flakes, crushed
½ cup beef broth

2 tablespoons low-sodium soy sauce
1 tablespoon Erythritol
1 tablespoon arrowroot starch
1½ tablespoons cold water
¾ pound (340 g) broccoli florets
2 tablespoons water
2 tablespoons fresh cilantro, chopped

Steps:

1. Add the oil in Instant Pot and select "Sauté". Then add the beef, salt and black pepper and cook for about 5 minutes.
2. Transfer the beef into a bowl.
3. Now, add the onion and cook for about 4 to 5 minutes.
4. Add the garlic and red pepper flakes and cook for about 1 minute.
5. Press "Cancel" and stir in beef broth, soy sauce and Erythritol and stir well.
6. Secure the lid and turn to "Seal" position.
7. Cook on "Manual" with "High Pressure" for about 12 minutes.
8. Press "Cancel" and carefully do a "Quick" release.
9. Meanwhile, in a small bowl, dissolve arrowroot starch in cold water.
10. Remove the lid and select "Sauté".
11. Add arrowroot mixture in Instant Pot, stirring continuously and cook for about 4 to 5 minutes or until desired thickness.
12. Meanwhile, in a large microwave-safe bowl, add broccoli and 2 tablespoons of water and microwave on High for about 3 to 4 minutes.
13. Add the broccoli in Instant Pot and stir well.
14. Press "Cancel" and serve with the garnishing of cilantro.

Recipe 6 : Shrimp with Green Beans | Calories: 197 | Fat: 5.8g | Protein: 27.6g | Carbs: 8.5g | Net Carbs: 5.2g | Fiber: 3.3g

Prep time: 10 minutes | Cook time: 2 minutes | Serves 4

2 tablespoons fresh lemon juice
1 teaspoon red chili powder
1 teaspoon garam masala powder
1 teaspoon ground cumin
Salt and ground black pepper, as required
1 pound (454 g) medium frozen shrimp, peeled and deveined
¾ pound green beans, trimmed
1 tablespoon olive oil

Steps:

1. In a small bowl, mix together lemon juice and spices.
2. In the bottom of Instant Pot, arrange a steamer trivet and pour 1 cup of water.
3. Arrange green beans on top of trivet in a single layer and top with shrimp.
4. Drizzle with oil and sprinkle with spice mixture.
5. Secure the lid and turn to "Seal" position.
6. Select "Steam" and just use the default time of 2 minutes.
7. Press "Cancel" and do a "Natural" release.
8. Remove the lid and serve hot.

Shopping Lists

Dairy

- Almond Milk
- Coconut Milk
- Organic Eggs

Meats and Seafoods

- Chicken
- Beef
- Shrimp

Fruits, Vegetables, Spices & Herbs

- Rum Extract
- Optavia Essential Spiced Gingerbread
- Nutmeg
- Brewed Coffee
- Pumpkin Pie Spice
- Ice
- Whipped Toppings
- Medifast Cappuccino Mix
- Sugar-free Chocolate Syrup
- Salt
- Black Pepper
- Butter
- Cauliflower
- Asparagus
- Chicken Stock
- Yeast
- Olive Oil
- Yellow Onion
- Garlic Cloves
- Red Pepper Flakes
- Soy Sauce
- Erythritol
- Starch
- Broccoli
- Cilantro
- Lemon
- Red Chili powder
- Garam Masala
- Cumin
- Green Beans

Meal Prep Plan

Start your breakfast with **Classic Eggnog.** First, In a blender, add the Vanilla Shake sachet, almond milk and egg yolk and pulse until smooth. In the bowl of a stand mixer, place egg white and beat on medium speed until stiff peaks form. Place the whipped egg whites into a serving glass and top with shake mixture. Stir the mixture and sprinkle with nutmeg. Serve immediately.

Next is **Iced Pumpkin Frappe** for your drinks. Combine all the ingredients, except for the whipped topping, in a blender. Pulse until smooth. Pour the mixture in a serving bowl. Top with whipped topping and serve.

For your lunch, prepare your ingredients for **Cappuccino Shake**. In a small blender, place all ingredients and pulse until smooth and creamy. Transfer the shake into a serving glass and serve immediately.

Then, you can start **a Chicken and Cauliflower Risotto** for make your snacks. Preheat the oven to 350°F (180°C). Place the chicken in a casserole dish and season with salt and pepper. Pour melted butter over, and roast in the preheated oven for 30 minutes or until an internal temperature reaches at least 165°F (74°C). Remove from oven and allow to cool. Meanwhile, combine the cauliflower rice, asparagus, and chicken stock in a pot and simmer over medium heat for 6 minutes or until soft. Remove the cauliflower and asparagus from the stovetop and stir in the nutritional yeast. Serve with roasted chicken breast.

For your dinner, you can now prepare **Beef with Broccoli**. Add the oil in Instant Pot and select "Sauté". Then add the beef, salt and black pepper and cook for about 5 minutes. Transfer the beef into a bowl. Now, add the onion and cook for about 4 to 5 minutes. Add the garlic and red pepper flakes and cook for about 1 minute. Press "Cancel" and stir in beef broth, soy sauce and Erythritol and stir well. Secure the lid and turn to "Seal" position. Cook on "Manual" with "High Pressure" for about 12 minutes. Press "Cancel" and carefully do a "Quick" release. Meanwhile, in a small bowl, dissolve arrowroot starch in cold water. Remove the lid and select "Sauté". Add arrowroot mixture in Instant Pot, stirring continuously and cook for about 4 to 5 minutes or until desired thickness. Meanwhile, in a large microwave-safe bowl, add broccoli and 2 tablespoons of water and microwave on High for about 3 to 4 minutes. Add the broccoli in Instant Pot and stir well. Press "Cancel" and serve with the garnishing of cilantro.

Finally, for your after snacks on your dinner. You can now prepare a **Shrimp with Green Beans.** In a small bowl, mix together lemon juice and spices. In the bottom of Instant Pot, arrange a steamer trivet and pour 1 cup of water. Arrange green beans on top of trivet in a single layer and top with shrimp. Drizzle with oil and sprinkle with spice mixture. Secure the lid and turn to "Seal" position. Select "Steam" and just use the default time of 2 minutes. Press "Cancel" and do a "Natural" release. Remove the lid and serve hot.

Chapter 4 Lean and Green Meals

Chicken and Tomato Stew with Celery

1 Leaner | 3 Greens | 1 Healthy Fat | 3 Condiments
Prep time: 15 minutes | Cook time: 30 minutes | Serves 4

2 tablespoons extra-virgin olive oil
4 (6-ounce / 170-g) bone-in, skin-on chicken thighs
1 (4-ounce / 113-g) package sliced fresh mushrooms
3 celery stalks, chopped
½ of onion, chopped
2 garlic cloves, minced
1 (14-ounce / 397-g) can stewed tomatoes
2 tablespoons tomato paste
2 teaspoons Herbes de Provence
¾ cup water
Pinch of red pepper flakes
Ground black pepper, as required

1. Add the oil in Instant Pot and select "Sauté". Then add the chicken thighs and cook for about 5-6 minutes per side.
2. With a slotted spoon, transfer chicken thighs onto a plate.
3. In the pot, add the mushrooms, celery and onion and cook for about 5 minutes.
4. Add the garlic and cook for about 2 minutes.
5. Press "Cancel" and stir in the chicken, tomatoes, tomato paste, Herbes de Provence and water.
6. Secure the lid and turn to "Seal" position.
7. Cook on "Manual" with "High Pressure" for about 11 minutes.
8. Press "Cancel" and carefully do a "Quick" release.
9. Remove the lid and stir in red pepper flakes and black pepper.
10. Serve hot.

Per Serving
calories: 430 | fat: 25g | protein: 52g | carbs: 9g | net carbs: 7g | fiber: 2g

Balsamic Lemon Chicken with Bell Peppers

1 Leaner | 2 Greens | 1 Healthy Fat | 3 Condiments
Prep time: 15 minutes | Cook time: 18 minutes | Serves 4

4 (4-ounce / 113-g) skinless, boneless chicken thighs
Salt, as required
2 tablespoons olive oil
½ of large red onion, sliced
2 garlic cloves, chopped
½ cup chicken broth
2 cups green bell peppers, seeded and sliced
2 fresh rosemary sprigs
2 tablespoons balsamic vinegar
2 tablespoons fresh lemon juice

1. Season the chicken thighs with salt evenly and set aside.
2. Add the oil in Instant Pot and select "Sauté". Then add 4 chicken thighs and cook for about 1-2 minutes per side.
3. With a slotted spoon, transfer the chicken thighs onto a plate.
4. Repeat with the remaining chicken thighs.
5. In the pot, add the onion and garlic and cook for about 1-2 minutes.
6. Add the broth and cook for about 1 minute, scraping up the browned bits from the bottom.
7. Press "Cancel" and stir in the remaining ingredients.
8. Place the cooked chicken thighs on top and gently, cover with some of onions and peppers.
9. Secure the lid and turn to "Seal" position.
10. Cook on "Manual" with "High Pressure" for about 10 minutes.
11. Press "Cancel" and carefully do a "Quick" release.
12. Remove the lid and with a slotted spoon, transfer the chicken thighs onto a plate.
13. Select "Sauté" and cook for about 5 minutes.
14. Press "Cancel" and pour the sauce over chicken thighs.
15. Serve immediately.

Per Serving
calories: 239 | fat: 12g | protein: 27g | carbs: 7g | net carbs: 1g | fiber: 6g

Spicy Chicken Meatballs with Arugula

1 Leaner | 3 Greens | 1 Healthy Fat | 3 Condiments
Prep time: 15 minutes | Cook time: 25 minutes | Serves 4

For Meatballs:

1½ pounds (680 g) ground chicken
¾ cup almond meal
2 scallions, sliced thinly
2 garlic cloves, minced
Salt and ground black pepper, as required
5 tablespoons olive oil, divided
6 tablespoons hot sauce

For Serving:

4 cups fresh baby arugula

1. In a large bowl, add chicken, almond meal, scallion, garlic, salt and black pepper and mix until well combined.
2. With slightly, greased hands, make 1-2 inches wide balls from mixture.
3. Add 1 tablespoons of the oil in the Instant Pot and select "Sauté". Then add the meatballs and cook until browned from all sides.
4. In a bowl, add the remaining oil and hot sauce and mix until well combined.
5. Press "Cancel" and place the sauce on top evenly.
6. Secure the lid and turn to "Seal" position.
7. Select "Poultry" and just use the default time of 15-20 minutes.
8. Press "Cancel" and carefully do a "Quick" release.
9. Divide the arugula onto serving plates.
10. Remove the lid and transfer the meatballs onto serving plates with meatballs.
11. Serve immediately.

Per Serving
calories: 545 | fat: 43g | protein: 30g | carbs: 5g | net carbs: 3g | fiber: 2g

Mustard Chicken with Bell Peppers

1 Leaner | 3 Greens | 1 Healthy Fat | 3 Condiments
Prep time: 15 minutes | Cook time: 25 minutes | Serves 4

2 tablespoons extra-virgin olive oil
1 pound (454 g) chicken breast, cut into bite-sized pieces
1 lemon, peeled and sliced very thinly
¼ cup green olives, pitted
2 bell peppers, seeded and cut into long, wide, strips
1 onion, quartered
2 garlic cloves, chopped
2 tablespoons tomato paste
1 tablespoon Dijon Mustard
1 teaspoon ground cumin
1 teaspoon ground turmeric
½ teaspoons ground ginger
½ teaspoons ground cinnamon
Salt and ground black pepper, as required

1. Add the oil in Instant Pot and select "Sauté". Then add the chicken pieces and cook for about 3-5 minutes or browned from all sides.
2. Press "Cancel" and stir in the remaining ingredients.
3. Secure the lid and turn to "Seal" position.
4. Cook on "Manual" with "High Pressure" for about 20 minutes.
5. Press "Cancel" and carefully do a "Quick" release.
6. Remove the lid and serve hot.

Per Serving
calories: 243 | fat: 11g | protein: 26g | carbs: 9g | net carbs: 7g | fiber: 2g

Cheddar Chicken Breasts with Broccoli

1 Leaner | 2 Greens | 1 Healthy Fat | 3 Condiments
Prep time: 15 minutes | Cook time: 25 minutes | Serves 4

2 tablespoons olive oil
4 (4-ounce / 113-g) skinless, boneless chicken breasts
Salt and ground black pepper, as required
1 medium onion, chopped
1 garlic clove, minced

2 cups chicken broth
1½ tablespoons arrowroot starch
4 tablespoons water, divided
1 cup low-fat Cheddar cheese, shredded
4 cups small broccoli florets

1. Add the oil in Instant Pot and select "Sauté". Then add the chicken breasts and cook for about 4-5 minutes.
2. With a slotted spoon, transfer the chicken breasts into a plate.
3. Add the onion and cook for about 2-3 minutes.
4. Add the garlic and cook for about 1 minute.
5. Press "Cancel" and stir in the cooked chicken and broth.
6. Secure the lid and turn to "Seal" position.
7. Cook on "Manual" with "High Pressure" for about 5 minutes.
8. Press "Cancel" and carefully do a "Quick" release.
9. Remove the lid and with tongs, transfer chicken breasts onto a cutting board.
10. With a sharp knife, cut chicken into desired sized pieces.
11. Meanwhile, in a small bowl, dissolve arrowroot starch in 1½ tablespoons of water.
12. Now, select "Sauté" of Instant Pot.
13. Add the arrowroot starch mixture, stirring continuously.
14. Add the Cheddar cheese and cook until melted completely, stirring continuously.
15. Meanwhile, in a large microwave-safe bowl, add broccoli and 2 tablespoons of water.
16. Microwave on High for about 3-4 minutes.
17. Add the chopped chicken and broccoli in Instant Pot and stir well.
18. Cook for about 4-5 minutes.
19. Press "Cancel" and serve hot.

Per Serving
calories: 380 | fat: 21g | protein: 38g | carbs: 10g | net carbs: 7g | fiber: 3g

Chicken and Cabbage with Jalapeño

1 Leaner | 2 Greens | 1 Healthy Fat | 2½ Condiments
Prep time: 15 minutes | Cook time: 8 minutes | Serves 4

1 tablespoon olive oil
1 small yellow onion, chopped
1 jalapeño pepper, seeded and chopped
2 cups cooked chicken, chopped
1½ pounds (680 g) cabbage, sliced into thin strips
½ cup chicken broth
½ tablespoon fresh lemon juice
Salt and freshly ground black pepper, as required

1. Add the oil in Instant Pot and select "Sauté". Then add the onion and cook for about 3 minutes.
2. Add chicken and cook for about 2 minutes.
3. Press "Cancel" and stir in the chicken, cabbage and broth.
4. Secure the lid and turn to "Seal" position.
5. Cook on "Manual" with "High Pressure" for about 3 minutes.
6. Press "Cancel" and carefully do a Quick release.
7. Remove the lid and stir in lemon juice, salt and black pepper.
8. Serve hot.

Per Serving
calories: 192 | fat: 6g | protein: 23g | carbs: 10g | net carbs: 5g | fiber: 5g

Mushroom and Chicken with Zucchini

1 Leaner | 3 Greens | 1 Healthy Fat | 2 Condiments
Prep time: 15 minutes | Cook time: 17 minutes | Serves 4

1 tablespoon olive oil
12 ounces (340 g) boneless, skinless chicken breasts, cubed
12 ounces (340 g) fresh mushrooms, sliced
½ cup onion, chopped
2 garlic cloves, minced
1 medium zucchini, cut into ½-inch slices
2 tablespoons fresh basil, chopped
Salt and freshly ground black pepper, to taste
1 cup tomatoes, chopped
1 cup chicken broth

1. Add the oil in Instant Pot and select "Sauté". Then add the chicken cubes and cook for about 4-5 minutes.
2. Add the mushrooms, onion and garlic and cook for about 5 minutes.
3. Add the zucchinis, basil, salt and black pepper and cook for about 1-2 minutes.
4. Press "Cancel" and stir in the tomatoes and broth.
5. Secure the lid and turn to "Seal" position.
6. Cook on "Manual" with "High Pressure" for about 5 minutes.
7. Press "Cancel" and do a "Natural" release.
8. Remove the lid and serve hot.

Per Serving
calories: 244 | fat: 11g | protein: 30g | carbs: 8g | net carbs: 6g | fiber: 2g

Chicken, Mushroom and Tomato Stew

1 Leaner | 3 Greens | 1 Healthy Fat | 3 Condiments
Prep time: 15 minutes | Cook time: 15 minutes | Serves 4

2 tablespoons olive oil
4 (5-ounce / 142-g) skinless chicken thighs
¾ pound (340 g) fresh cremini mushrooms, stemmed and
    quartered
1 small onion, chopped
1 tablespoon tomato paste
3 garlic cloves, minced
¼ cup green olives, pitted and halved
1 cup fresh cherry tomatoes
½ cup chicken broth
Salt and ground black pepper, as required
2 tablespoons fresh parsley, chopped

1. Add the oil in Instant Pot and select "Sauté". Then add the chicken thighs and cook for about 2-3 minutes per side.
2. Transfer chicken thighs onto a plate.
3. In the Instant pot, add mushrooms and onion and cook for about 4-5 minutes.
4. Add tomato paste and garlic and cook for about 1 minute.
5. Press "Cancel" and stir in the chicken, olives, tomatoes and broth.
6. Secure the lid and turn to "Seal" position.
7. Cook on "Manual" with "High Pressure" for about 10 minutes.
8. Press "Cancel" and carefully do a "Quick" release.
9. Remove the lid and stir in salt, black pepper and parsley.
10. Serve hot.

Per Serving
calories: 282 | fat: 24g | protein: 10g | carbs: 7g | net carbs: 3g | fiber: 4g

Chicken and Bell Pepper Curry with Basil

1 Leaner | 3 Greens | 1 Healthy Fat | 4 Condiments
Prep time: 15 minutes | Cook time: 12 minutes | Serves 4

1 ((14-ounce / 397-g) can unsweetened coconut milk
2 tablespoons Thai red curry paste
1 pound (454 g) boneless chicken breasts, cut into thin bite-
    size pieces
1 cup carrots, peeled and sliced
1½ cups green bell pepper, seeded and cubed
½ cup onion, sliced
¼ cup chicken broth
2 tablespoon fish sauce
1 tablespoon fresh lime juice
12 fresh basil leaves, chopped
Salt and ground black pepper, as required

1. Add the oil in Instant Pot and select "Sauté". Then add half of coconut milk and curry paste and cook for about 1-2 minutes.
2. Press "Cancel" and stir in remaining coconut milk, chicken, carrot, bell pepper, onion and broth.
3. Secure the lid and turn to "Seal" position.
4. Cook on "Manual" with "High Pressure" for about 5 minutes.
5. Press "Cancel" and carefully do a "Quick" release.
6. Remove the lid and select "Sauté".
7. Stir in the remaining ingredients and cook for about 4-5 minutes.
8. Stir in the salt and black pepper and press "Cancel".
9. Serve hot.

Per Serving
calories: 524 | fat: 13g | protein: 47g | carbs: 56g | net carbs: 34g | fiber: 22g

Chickens and Cauliflower Curry with Cilantro

1 Leaner | 3 Greens | 1 Healthy Fat | 4 Condiments
Prep time: 15 minutes | Cook time: 22 minutes | Serves 4

1½ pounds (680 g) skinless, boneless chicken thighs, cubed
Salt, as required
½ tablespoon olive oil
½ of onion, chopped
1 teaspoon ginger root, minced
3 garlic cloves, minced
1 teaspoon ground cumin
1 teaspoon ground coriander
½ teaspoon garam masala

½ teaspoon ground turmeric
½ teaspoon cayenne pepper
¼ teaspoon red pepper flakes, crushed
1 ((14-ounce / 397-g) can diced tomatoes, drained
2 cups cauliflower florets
½ cup frozen peas
½ cup full-fat coconut milk
¼ cup fresh cilantro leaves, chopped

1. Season the chicken with 1 teaspoon of salt. Keep aside.
2. Add the oil in Instant Pot and select "Sauté". Then add the onion, ginger, garlic and spices and cook for about 2-3 minutes.
3. Add tomatoes and with an immersion blender, blend until smooth.
4. Press "Cancel" and stir in the chicken.
5. Secure the lid and turn to "Seal" position.
6. Cook on "Manual" with "High Pressure" for about 15 minutes.
7. Press "Cancel" and carefully do a "Quick" release.
8. Remove the lid and stir in the cauliflower and peas.
9. Secure the lid and turn to "Seal" position.
10. Cook on "Manual" with "High Pressure" for about 2 minutes.
11. Press "Cancel" and carefully do a "Quick" release.
12. Remove the lid and stir in coconut milk.
13. Serve hot with the garnishing of cilantro.

Per Serving
calories: 345 | fat: 16g | protein: 41g | carbs: 10g | net carbs: 7g | fiber: 3g

Curried Chicken Thighs and Mushrooms

1 Leaner | 2 Greens | 1 Healthy Fat | 3 Condiments
Prep time: 15 minutes | Cook time: 15 minutes | Serves 4

2 tablespoons olive oil
1 pound (454 g) chicken thighs, sliced thinly
2 tablespoons curry paste
1 cup unsweetened coconut milk
2 tablespoons fresh lemon juice
1 teaspoon red chili powder
1 teaspoon ground coriander
3 cups fresh mushrooms, sliced
1 cup onion, sliced

1. Add the oil in Instant Pot and select "Sauté". Then add the curry paste and cook for about 1 minute.
2. Add the chicken pieces and cook for about 3-4 minutes.
3. Press "Cancel" and stir in coconut milk and spices.
4. Secure the lid and turn to "Seal" position.
5. Cook on "Manual" with "High Pressure" for about 5 minutes.
6. Press "Cancel" and carefully do a "Quick" release.
7. Remove the lid and select "Sauté".
8. Stir in mushroom and onion and cook for about 5 minutes
9. Press "Cancel" and serve hot.

Per Serving
calories: 366 | fat: 21g | protein: 35g | carbs: 8g | net carbs: 6g | fiber: 2g

Chicken Lettuce Wraps with Carrots

1 Leaner | 2 Greens | 1 Healthy Fat | 2 Condiments
Prep time: 15 minutes | Cook time: 29 minutes | Serves 4

3 (6-ounce / 170-g) boneless skinless chicken breasts
1 cup chicken broth
⅓ cup hot sauce
8 large lettuce leaves
2 cups carrots, peeled and shredded

1. In the pot of Instant Pot, place chicken breasts and broth.
2. Secure the lid and turn to "Seal" position.
3. Cook on "Manual" with "High Pressure" for about 26 minutes.
4. Press "Cancel" and carefully do a "Quick" release.
5. Remove the lid and transfer the chicken breasts onto a platter.
6. With 2 forks, shred the chicken breasts.
7. Remove the broth from pot, reserving about ½ cup inside.
8. Select "Sauté" and stir in shredded chicken and hot sauce.
9. Cook for about 2-3 minutes, stirring continuously.
10. Press "Cancel" and transfer the chicken mixture into a bowl.
11. Arrange the lettuce leaves onto serving plates.
12. Place chicken mixture over each leaf evenly and top with carrot.
13. Serve immediately.

Per Serving
calories: 278 | fat: 10g | protein: 39g | carbs: 6g | net carbs: 4g | fiber: 2g

Mozzarella Chicken and Zucchini Casserole

1 Leaner | 3 Greens | 1 Healthy Fat | 4 Condiments
Prep time: 15 minutes | Cook time: 30 minutes | Serves 4

½ cup unsweetened almond milk
½ cup almond flour
8 large eggs
Salt and ground black pepper, as required
1 cup cooked chicken, chopped
1 medium zucchini, chopped
1 medium green bell pepper, seeded and chopped
1 cup part-skim Mozzarella cheese, shredded

1. In a baking dish, add milk, flour, eggs, salt and black pepper and beat until well combined.
2. Add the chicken, vegetables and cheese and stir to combine.
3. In the bottom of Instant Pot, arrange a steamer trivet and pour 1 cup of water.
4. With a piece of foil, cover the baking dish and place on top of trivet.
5. Secure the lid and turn to "Seal" position.
6. Cook on "Manual" with "High Pressure" for about 30 minutes.
7. Press "Cancel" and do a "Natural" release for about 10 minutes. Then do a "Quick" release.
8. Remove the lid and serve immediately.

Per Serving
calories: 328 | fat: 20g | protein: 26g | carbs: 8g | net carbs: 5g | fiber: 3g

Ginger-Garlic Chicken Curry with Peas

1 Leaner | 2 Greens | 1 Healthy Fat | 4 Condiments
Prep time: 15 minutes | Cook time: 9 minutes | Serves 4

2 tablespoons olive oil
½ teaspoon cumin seeds
1 cinnamon stick
1 bay leaf
1 large onion, chopped
1 tablespoons ginger paste
1 tablespoons garlic paste
1 green chili pepper, chopped
2 medium tomatoes, chopped
2 teaspoons ground coriander
1 teaspoons garam masala
1 teaspoon red chili powder
Salt, as required
1 pound (454 g) ground chicken
¼ cup water
½ cup frozen green peas
1 tablespoon fresh lemon juice
2 tablespoons fresh cilantro, chopped

1. Add the oil in the Instant Pot and select "Sauté". Then add the cumin seeds, cinnamon stick and bay leaf and cook for about 30 seconds.
2. Add the onions, ginger, garlic and green chili and cook for about 3 minutes.
3. Add the tomatoes and spices and cook for about 2 minutes.
4. Press "Cancel" and stir in the ground chicken and water.
5. Secure the lid and turn to "Seal" position.
6. Cook on "Manual" with "High Pressure" for about 5 minutes.
7. Press "Cancel" and carefully do a "Natural" release for about 10 minutes. Then do a "Quick" release.
8. Remove the lid and select "Sauté".
9. Stir in the green peas and lemon juice and cook for about 2 minutes.
10. Press "Cancel" and serve hot with the garnishing of cilantro.

Per Serving
calories: 328 | fat: 16g | protein: 35g | carbs: 11g | net carbs: 8g | fiber: 3g

Cauliflower and Chicken Soup with Cheddar

1 Leaner | 3 Greens | 1 Healthy Fat | 3 Condiments
Prep time: 15 minutes | Cook time: 23 minutes | Serves 4

1 tablespoon olive oil
1 pound (454 g) ground chicken
1 small yellow onion, chopped
2 garlic cloves, minced

1 head cauliflower, chopped roughly
Salt and ground black pepper, as required
4 cups chicken broth
1 cups low-fat Cheddar cheese, shredded

1. Add the oil in Instant Pot and select "Sauté". Then add the ground chicken and cook for about 3-4 minutes.
2. Add the onion and cook for about 3 minutes.
3. Add garlic and red pepper flakes and cook for about 1 minute.
4. Press "Cancel" and stir in cauliflower, salt, black pepper and broth.
5. Secure the lid and turn to "Seal" position.
6. Cook on "Manual" with "High Pressure" for about 15 minutes.
7. Press "Cancel" and carefully do a "Quick" release.
8. Remove the lid and stir in the Cheddar until melted.
9. Serve immediately.

Per Serving
calories: 424 | fat: 23g | protein: 46g | carbs: 7g | net carbs: 5g | fiber: 2g

Chicken and Carrot Chili

1 Leaner | 3 Greens | 1 Healthy Fat | 3 Condiments
Prep time: 15 minutes | Cook time: 20 minutes | Serves 4

3 (5-ounce / 142-g) chicken breasts
1 carrot, peeled and chopped
1 celery stalk, chopped
1 medium yellow onion, chopped
2 garlic cloves, chopped
1 teaspoon dried oregano
1 teaspoon ground cumin
Salt and ground black pepper, as required
½ cup unsweetened coconut milk
1 cup chicken broth

1. In the pot of Instant Pot, add all ingredients and stir to combine.
2. Secure the lid and turn to "Seal" position.
3. Select "Poultry" and just use the default time of 20 minutes.
4. Press "Cancel" and do a "Natural" release.
5. Remove the lid and with a slotted spoon, transfer the chicken breasts into a bowl.
6. With 2 forks, shred chicken breasts and then return into the pot.
7. Serve immediately.

Per Serving
calories: 306 | fat: 16g | protein: 33g | carbs: 7g | net carbs: 5g | fiber: 2g

Garlic Turkey with Tomatoes

1 Leaner | 3 Greens | 1 Healthy Fat | 2½ Condiments
Prep time: 15 minutes | Cook time: 35 minutes | Serves 4

2 tablespoons olive oil
10 ounces (284 g) fresh mushrooms, trimmed and chopped finely
1 carrot, peeled and chopped finely
1 small onion, chopped finely
2 garlic cloves, chopped finely
1 pound (454 g) 93% lean ground turkey
½ cup chicken broth
1 ((14-ounce / 397-g) can crushed tomatoes
1 bay leaf
1 teaspoon dried thyme
Salt and ground black pepper, as required

1. Add the oil in Instant Pot and select "Sauté". Then add the
2. Add chopped vegetables and cook for about 4-5 minutes.
3. Add the ground turkey and cook for about 8-10 minutes, breaking up with a wooden spoon.
4. Add the broth and scrape the brown bits from the bottom.
5. Press "Cancel" and stir in the remaining ingredients.
6. Secure the lid and turn to "Seal" position.
7. Cook on "Manual" with "High Pressure" for about 20 minutes.
8. Press "Cancel" and carefully do a "Natural" release for about 10 minutes. Then do a "Quick" release.
9. Remove the lid and serve hot.

Per Serving
calories: 335 | fat: 20g | protein: 35g | carbs: 10g | net carbs: 7g | fiber: 3g

Paprika Turkey with Carrots

1 Leaner | 3 Greens | 1 Healthy Fat | 3 Condiments
Prep time: 15 minutes | Cook time: 38 minutes | Serves 4

2 tablespoons olive oil
2 medium carrots, peeled and chopped
1 small yellow onion, chopped finely
Salt, to taste
1¼ pounds (567 g) ground turkey
2 garlic cloves, chopped finely
2 tablespoons low-sodium soy sauce
1 teaspoon paprika
½ teaspoon ground cinnamon
1 ((14-ounce / 397-g) cans diced tomatoes with juice
⅓ cup chicken broth

1. Add the oil in Instant Pot and select "Sauté". Then add the carrot, celery and onion and cook for about 5 minutes.
2. Add the turkey and cook for about 2-3 minutes.
3. Add the garlic, soy sauces and spices and cook for about 5 minutes.
4. Press "Cancel" and stir in tomatoes with juice and broth.
5. Secure the lid and turn to "Seal" position.
6. Cook on "Manual" with "High Pressure" for about 20 minutes.
7. Press "Cancel" and carefully do a "Quick" release.
8. Remove the lid and select "Sauté".
9. Cook for about 5-10 minutes or until desired thickness of sauce.
10. Press "Cancel" and serve hot.

Per Serving
calories: 384 | fat: 23g | protein: 41g | carbs: 10g | net carbs: 7g | fiber: 3g

Turkey and Cabbage Soup with Carrots

1 Leaner | 3 Greens | 1 Healthy Fat | 3 Condiments
Prep time: 15 minutes | Cook time: 30 minutes | Serves 4

1 tablespoon olive oil
1 pound (454 g) lean ground turkey
1 small onion, chopped
1 cup carrot, peeled and shredded
½ head cabbage, chopped
3½ cups chicken broth
¼ cup low-sodium soy sauce
1 teaspoon ground ginger
Salt and ground black pepper, as required

1. Add the oil in Instant Pot and select "Sauté". Now, add the ground turkey and cook for about 5 minutes or until browned completely.
2. Press "Cancel" and stir in the remaining ingredients.
3. Secure the lid and turn to "Seal" position.
4. Cook on "Manual" with "High Pressure" for about 25 minutes.
5. Press "Cancel" and do a "Quick" release.
6. Remove the lid and serve immediately.

Per Serving
calories: 273 | fat: 13g | protein: 29g | carbs: 10g | net carbs: 7g | fiber: 3g

Turkey, Carrot and Pea Stew

1 Leaner | 3 Greens | 1 Healthy Fat | 4 Condiments
Prep time: 15 minutes | Cook time: 25 minutes | Serves 4

1 tablespoon olive oil
1 pound (454 g) ground turkey
1½ cups carrots, peeled and chopped
1 cup frozen peas
2 garlic cloves, minced
1 teaspoon dried oregano
1 teaspoon dried basil
½ teaspoon dried thyme
Salt, as required
3 cups chicken broth
2 tablespoons arrowroot starch
2 tablespoons water

1. Add the oil in Instant Pot and select "Sauté". Now, add the ground turkey and cook for about 8-10 minutes or until browned completely.
2. Press "Cancel" and stir in the remaining ingredients except arrowroot starch and water.
3. Secure the lid and turn to "Seal" position.
4. Cook on "Manual" with "High Pressure" for about 15 minutes.
5. Press "Cancel" and do a "Natural" release.
6. Meanwhile, in a small bowl, dissolve arrowroot starch in water.
7. Remove the lid and select "Sauté".
8. Add the arrowroot mixture and stir until smooth.
9. Cook for about 1-2 minutes.
10. Press "Cancel" and serve hot.

Per Serving
calories: 345 | fat: 17g | protein: 37g | carbs: 11g | net carbs: 7g | fiber: 4g

Turkey Chili with Cumin

1 Leaner | 3 Greens | 1 Healthy Fat | 3 Condiments
Prep time: 15 minutes | Cook time: 35 minutes | Serves 4

1 tablespoon olive oil
1 green bell pepper, seeded and chopped
1 yellow onion, chopped
2 garlic cloves, minced
1 pound (454 g) ground turkey
1 cup tomatoes, chopped finely
⅓ cup homemade pumpkin puree
2 tablespoons red chili powder
1 tablespoon ground cumin
½ tablespoon pumpkin pie spice
1 tablespoon dried oregano
Salt, as required
½ cup chicken broth

1. Add the oil in Instant Pot and select "Sauté". Then add the bell pepper, onion and garlic and cook for about 4-5 minutes.
2. Add the turkey and cook for about 8-10 minutes.
3. Press "Cancel" and stir in remaining ingredients.
4. Secure the lid and turn to "Seal" position.
5. Cook on "Manual" with "High Pressure" for about 20 minutes.
6. Press "Cancel" and do a "Natural" release.
7. Remove the id and serve hot.

Per Serving
calories: 310 | fat: 17g | protein: 34g | carbs: 11g | net carbs: 7g | fiber: 4g

Beef Chuck Roast with Broccoli

1 Leaner | 2 Greens | 1 Healthy Fat | 4 Condiments
Prep time: 15 minutes | Cook time: 28 minutes | Serves 4

1 tablespoon olive oil
1 pound (454 g) beef chuck roast, trimmed and cut into thin strips
Salt and ground black pepper, as required
1 yellow onion, chopped
2 garlic cloves, minced
Pinch of red pepper flakes, crushed
½ cup beef broth
2 tablespoons low-sodium soy sauce
1 tablespoon Erythritol
1 tablespoon arrowroot starch
1½ tablespoons cold water
¾ pound (340 g) broccoli florets
2 tablespoons water
2 tablespoons fresh cilantro, chopped

1. Add the oil in Instant Pot and select "Sauté". Then add the beef, salt and black pepper and cook for about 5 minutes.
2. Transfer the beef into a bowl.
3. Now, add the onion and cook for about 4-5 minutes.
4. Add the garlic and red pepper flakes and cook for about 1 minute.
5. Press "Cancel" and stir in beef broth, soy sauce and Erythritol and stir well.
6. Secure the lid and turn to "Seal" position.
7. Cook on "Manual" with "High Pressure" for about 12 minutes.
8. Press "Cancel" and carefully do a "Quick" release.
9. Meanwhile, in a small bowl, dissolve arrowroot starch in cold water.
10. Remove the lid and select "Sauté".
11. Add arrowroot mixture in Instant Pot, stirring continuously and cook for about 4-5 minutes or until desired thickness.
12. Meanwhile, in a large microwave-safe bowl, add broccoli and 2 tablespoons of water and microwave on High for about 3-4 minutes.
13. Add the broccoli in Instant Pot and stir well.
14. Press "Cancel" and serve with the garnishing of cilantro.

Per Serving
calories: 498 | fat: 36g | protein: 34g | carbs: 11g | net carbs: 8g | fiber: 3g

Balsamic Beef with Tomatoes

1 Leaner | 3 Greens | 1 Healthy Fat | 4 Condiments
Prep time: 15 minutes | Cook time: 25 minutes | Serves 4

1 tablespoon olive oil
1 onion, sliced thinly
2 garlic cloves, minced
2 tablespoons balsamic vinegar
1 pound (454 g) beef stew meat, trimmed and cut into 2-inch cubes
1 cup tomatoes, chopped
1 bay leaf
½ teaspoon dried oregano, crushed
½ teaspoon dried basil, crushed
Salt and ground black pepper, as required
2 green bell peppers, seeded and cut into 8 slices
2 tablespoons fresh parsley, chopped

1. Add the oil in Instant Pot and select "Sauté". Then add the onion and garlic and cook for about 2-3 minutes.
2. Add the vinegar and scrape the brown bits from the bottom.
3. Press "Cancel" and stir in beef, tomatoes, bay leaves, herbs, salt and black pepper.
4. Secure the lid and turn to "Seal" position.
5. Cook on "Manual" with "High Pressure" for about 15 minutes.
6. Press "Cancel" and carefully do a "Natural" release.
7. Remove the lid and select "Sauté".
8. Stir in bell peppers and cook for about 4-5 minutes or until desired doneness.
9. Press "Cancel" and stir in parsley.
10. Serve hot.

Per Serving
calories: 288 | fat: 11g | protein: 36g | carbs: 9g | net carbs: 2g | fiber: 7g

Cinnamon Beef with Green Beans

1 Leaner | 3 Greens | 1 Healthy Fat | 4 Condiments
Prep time: 15 minutes | Cook time: 30 minutes | Serves 4

Spice Blend:
1 tablespoon ground cinnamon
¾ teaspoon ground nutmeg
¼ teaspoon ground allspice
Salt and ground black pepper, as required

Beef Mixture:
1 pound (454 g) beef chuck roast, trimmed and cut in 2-inch chunks
¾ pound (340 g) fresh green beans, trimmed and cut in 2-inch pieces
1 medium onion, chopped
2 ounces (57 g) canned tomato sauce
1 cup chicken broth

1. For spice blend: in a bowl, add all the ingredients and mix well.
2. In the pot of Instant Pot, place the spice blend and remaining all ingredients and stir to combine.
3. Secure the lid and turn to "Seal" position.
4. Select "Meat/Stew" and just use the default time of 30 minutes.
5. Press "Cancel" and do a "Natural" release.
6. Remove the lid and serve hot.

Per Serving
calories: 469 | fat: 32g | protein: 33g | carbs: 11g | net carbs: 6g | fiber: 5g

Beef and Kale Casserole with Scallion

1 Leaner | 2 Greens | 1 Healthy Fat | 2 Condiments
Prep time: 15 minutes | Cook time: 29 minutes | Serves 4

2 tablespoons olive oil
2 cups fresh kale, trimmed and chopped
1⅓ cups scallion, sliced
8 egg, beaten
1½ cups cooked beef, shredded
Salt and ground black pepper, as required

1. Add the oil in the Instant Pot and select "Sauté". Then add the kale and scallion and cook for about 3-4 minutes.
2. Press "Cancel" and transfer the kale mixture into a bowl.
3. Add eggs and beef and mix well.
4. Transfer the mixture into a lightly greased baking dish.
5. In the bottom of Instant Pot, arrange a steamer trivet and pour 1½ cups of water.
6. Place the baking dish on top of trivet.
7. Secure the lid and turn to "Seal" position.
8. Cook on "Manual" with "High Pressure" for about 25 minutes.
9. Press "Cancel" and carefully do a "Quick" release.
10. Remove the lid and serve immediately.

Per Serving
calories: 345 | fat: 20g | protein: 34g | carbs: 7g | net carbs: 5g | fiber: 2g

Beef and Veggie Soup with Oregano

1 Leaner | 4 Greens | 1 Healthy Fat | 3 Condiments
Prep time: 15 minutes | Cook time: 15 minutes | Serves 4

2 teaspoons olive oil
1 pound (454 g) sirloin steak, trimmed and cubed
1 small carrot, peeled and chopped
1 bell pepper, seeded and chopped
1 celery stalk, chopped
1 onion, chopped
8 ounces (227 g) fresh mushrooms, sliced
2 cups beef broth
1½ cups water
1 cup tomatoes, crushed
1½ tablespoons fresh oregano, chopped
1 bay leaf
2 teaspoon garlic powder
Salt and ground black pepper, as required

1. Add the oil in an Instant Pot Mini and select "Sauté". Now, add the steak and cook for about 4-5 minutes or until browned.
2. Add the carrots, bell pepper, celery, and onion and cook for about 2-3 minutes.
3. Add the mushrooms and cook for about 4-5 minutes.
4. Press "Cancel" and stir in the remaining ingredients.
5. Secure the lid and turn to "Seal" position.
6. Select "Soup" and just use the default time of 15 minutes.
7. Press "Cancel" and do a "Quick" release.
8. Remove the lid and serve hot.

Per Serving
calories: 298 | fat: 11g | protein: 40g | carbs: 10g | net carbs: 7g | fiber: 3g

Beef and Bok Choy Soup with Cilantro

1 Leaner | 3 Greens | 1 Healthy Fat | 3 Condiments
Prep time: 15 minutes | Cook time: 23 minutes | Serves 4

2 tablespoons olive oil
½ onion, sliced
2 garlic cloves, minced
1 teaspoon fresh ginger, minced
1 pound (454 g) beef tenderloin, trimmed and cut into chunks
2 tablespoons balsamic vinegar
2 tablespoons low-sodium soy sauce
Salt and ground black pepper, as required
3 cups water
3 cups bok choy, chopped
2 tablespoons fresh cilantro, chopped

1. Add the oil in an Instant Pot and select "Sauté". Now, add the onion, garlic and ginger and cook for about 2-3 minutes.
2. Press "Cancel" and stir in the remaining ingredients except for bok choy and cilantro.
3. Secure the lid and turn to "Seal" position.
4. Cook on "Manual" with "High Pressure" for about 20 minutes.
5. Press "Cancel" and do a "Natural" release for about 10 minutes. Then allow a "Quick" release.
6. Remove the lid and mix in the bok choy.
7. Immediately, secure the lid and turn to "Seal" position for about 10 minutes.
8. Serve immediately with the garnishing of cilantro.

Per Serving
calories: 314 | fat: 18g | protein: 34g | carbs: 4g | net carbs: 3g | fiber: 1g

Beef and Carrot Chili with Cumin

1 Leaner | 4 Greens | 1 Healthy Fat | 4 Condiments
Prep time: 15 minutes | Cook time: 40 minutes | Serves 4

1 tablespoon olive oil
1 pound (454 g) ground beef
½ green bell pepper, seeded and chopped
1 small onion, chopped
1 medium carrots, peeled and chopped
2 tomatoes, chopped finely
1 jalapeño pepper, chopped

Salt and ground black pepper, as required
1 tablespoon fresh parsley, chopped
1 tablespoon Worcestershire sauce
4 teaspoons red chili powder
1 teaspoon paprika
1 teaspoon ground cumin

1. Add the oil in Instant Pot and select "Sauté". Then add the beef and cook for about 5 minutes or until browned completely.
2. Press "Cancel" and stir in remaining ingredients.
3. Secure the lid and turn to "Seal" position.
4. Select "Soup" and just use the default time of 35 minutes.
5. Press "Cancel" and do a "Natural" release.
6. Remove the lid and serve hot.

Per Serving
calories: 287 | fat: 11g | protein: 36g | carbs: 9g | net carbs: 6g | fiber: 3g

Beef and Carrot Curry with Cilantro

1 Leaner | 3 Greens | 1 Healthy Fat | 3 Condiments
Prep time: 15 minutes | Cook time: 33 minutes | Serves 4

2 tablespoons olive oil
1¼ pounds (567 g) beef stew meat, cut into 1-inch pieces
Salt and ground black pepper, as required
1 cup onion, chopped
1 tablespoon fresh ginger, minced
2 teaspoons garlic, minced
1 jalapeño pepper, chopped finely
1 tablespoon curry powder
1 teaspoon red chili powder
1 teaspoon ground cumin
2 cups beef broth
1½ cups carrots, peeled and cut into 1-inch pieces
1 cup unsweetened coconut milk
¼ cup fresh cilantro, chopped

1. Add the oil in an Instant Pot Mini and select "Sauté". Now, add the beef, salt and black pepper and cook for about 4-5 minutes or until browned completely.
2. With a slotted spoon, transfer the beef into a bowl.
3. In the pot, add the onion, ginger, garlic and jalapeño pepper and cook for about 4-5 minutes.
4. Press "Cancel" and stir in the beef, spices and broth.
5. Secure the lid and turn to "Seal" position.
6. Cook on "Manual" with "High Pressure" for about 15 minutes.
7. Press "Cancel" and do a "Quick" release.
8. Remove the lid and mix in the carrots.
9. Secure the lid and turn to "Seal" position.
10. Cook on "Manual" with "High Pressure" for about 5 minutes.
11. Press "Cancel" and do a "Natural" release for about 10 minutes. Then do a "Quick" release.
12. Remove the lid and mix in the coconut milk.
13. Now, select "Sauté" and cook for about 2-3 minutes.
14. Press "Cancel" and stir in the cilantro.
15. Serve immediately.

Per Serving
calories: 399 | fat: 18g | protein: 47g | carbs: 10g | net carbs: 7g | fiber: 3g

Beef and Veggie Curry with Cilantro

1 Leaner | 3 Greens | 1 Healthy Fat | 4 Condiments
Prep time: 15 minutes | Cook time: 40 minutes | Serves 4

1 tablespoon olive oil
¾ pound (340 g) beef brisket, cubed into 1½-inch size
1 tablespoon curry paste
½ pound (227 g) cauliflower florets
1 large carrot, peeled and chopped
1 small yellow onion, chopped
¾ cup unsweetened coconut milk
1 tablespoon fresh lime juice
1 tablespoon low-sodium soy sauce
1 tablespoon fish sauce
¼ cup fresh cilantro, chopped

1. Add the oil in Instant Pot and select "Sauté". Then add curry paste and cook for about 1 minute.
2. Add the beef and cook for about 4-5 minutes.
3. Press "Cancel" and stir in remaining ingredients except cilantro.
4. Secure the lid and turn to "Seal" position.
5. Select "Meat" and just use the default time of 35 minutes.
6. Press "Cancel" and carefully do a "Natural" release for about 10 minutes. Then do a "Quick" release.
7. Remove the lid and serve hot with the garnishing of cilantro.

Per Serving
calories: 340 | fat: 27g | protein: 15g | carbs: 10g | net carbs: 6g | fiber: 4g

Spiced Beef Meatballs with Mushroom Sauce

1 Leaner | 3 Greens | 1 Healthy Fat | 5 Condiments
Prep time: 105 minutes | Cook time: 22 minutes | Serves 4

1 pound (454 g) ground beef
1½ tablespoons dried onion, minced
3 tablespoons fresh parsley, minced
1 teaspoons dried sage
½ teaspoon ground nutmeg
½ teaspoon garlic powder
Salt and ground black pepper, as required
8 ounces (227 g) fresh button mushrooms, sliced
1 medium onion, chopped
⅓ cup beef broth
2 tablespoons low-sodium soy sauce
2 tablespoons arrowroot powder
½ cup unsweetened coconut milk

1. In a large bowl, add the beef, dried onion, parsley, sage, nutmeg, garlic powder, salt and black pepper and mix until well combined.
2. Make 1-inch meatballs from the mixture.
3. In the pot of Instant Pot, place the mushrooms, onion, broth and soy sauce and stir to combine.
4. Arrange the meatballs on top of the mushroom mixture.
5. Secure the lid and turn to "Seal" position.
6. Select "Meat/Stew" and just use the default time of 20 minutes.
7. Press "Cancel" and carefully do a "Quick" release.
8. Meanwhile, in a small bowl, dissolve the arrowroot powder in coconut milk.
9. Remove the lid and select "Sauté".
10. Add the arrowroot powder mixture and gently, stir to combine.
11. Cook for about 1-2 minutes.
12. Press "Cancel" and serve hot.

Per Serving
calories: 266 | fat: 8g | protein: 38g | carbs: 9g | net carbs: 7g | fiber: 2g

Balsamic Beef Meatballs with Spinach

1 Leaner | 2 Greens | 1 Healthy Fat | 4 Condiments
Prep time: 15 minutes | Cook time: 15 minutes | Serves 4

Sauce:
⅓ cup low-sodium soy sauce
2 tablespoons balsamic vinegar
1 tablespoon maple syrup
1 tablespoon olive oil
2 teaspoons fresh ginger, grated
2 garlic cloves, minced
1 tablespoon arrowroot starch
¼ teaspoon ground black pepper

Meatballs:
1 pound (454 g) extra-lean ground beef
1 egg
1 tablespoons olive oil

For Serving:
4 cups fresh baby spinach

1. For sauce: in a large bowl, add all ingredients and mix until well combined. Set aside.
2. For meatballs: in a bowl, add the beef and egg and mix well.
3. Make 1-inch meatballs from the mixture.
4. Add the oil in the Instant Pot and select "Sauté". Then add the meatballs and cook for about 4-5 minutes or until browned from all sides.
5. Press "Cancel" and place sauce over meatballs.
6. Secure the lid and turn to "Seal" position.
7. Cook on "Manual" with "High Pressure" for about 10 minutes.
8. Press "Cancel" and do a "Natural" release.
9. Remove the lid and transfer the meatballs onto serving plates.
10. Divide the spinach onto plates and serve immediately.

Per Serving
calories: 319 | fat: 15g | protein: 38g | carbs: 7g | net carbs: 6g | fiber: 1g

Beef and Tomato Chili with Cumin

1 Leaner | 2 Greens | 1 Healthy Fat | 4 Condiments
Prep time: 15 minutes | Cook time: 27 minutes | Serves 4

1 tablespoon avocado oil
1 yellow onion, chopped
1 small red bell pepper, seeded and chopped
Salt, as required
2 garlic cloves, minced
1½ pounds (680 g) lean ground beef
2 tablespoons red chili powder
1 tablespoon ground cumin
1 tablespoon dried oregano, crushed
2 cups tomatoes, chopped
½ cup chicken broth
2 tablespoons fresh lemon juice

1. Add the oil in Instant Pot and select "Sauté". Then add the onion, bell pepper and a pinch of salt and cook for about 3 minutes.
2. Stir in the garlic and cook for about 1 minute.
3. Add the beef and salt and cook for about 5-7 minutes.
4. Add the spices and thyme and cook for about 1 minute.
5. Press "Cancel" and stir in tomatoes and broth.
6. Secure the lid and turn to "Seal" position.
7. Cook on "Manual" with "High Pressure" for about 15 minutes.
8. Press "Cancel" and do a "Natural" release.
9. Remove the lid and stir in lemon juice.
10. Serve hot.

Per Serving
calories: 324 | fat: 15g | protein: 33g | carbs: 10g | net carbs: 7g | fiber: 3g

Pork and Mushrooms with Tomato Sauce

1 Leaner | 2 Greens | 1 Healthy Fat | 2 Condiments
Prep time: 15 minutes | Cook time: 25 minutes | Serves 4

1 tablespoon olive oil
2 garlic cloves, minced
4 (6-ounce / 170-g) bone-in pork chops
Salt and ground black pepper, as required
1 medium onion, chopped
1½ cups fresh mushrooms, chopped roughly
1 cup tomato sauce
½ cup water

1. Add the oil in Instant Pot and select "Sauté". Then add the garlic and cook for about 1 minute.
2. Add the pork chops, salt and black pepper and cook for about 5 minutes or until browned completely.
3. Press "Cancel" and stir in the mushrooms, tomato sauce and water.
4. Secure the lid and turn to "Seal" position.
5. Cook on "Manual" with "High Pressure" for about 15 minutes.
6. Press "Cancel" and carefully do a "Quick" release.
7. Remove the lid and serve hot

Per Serving
calories: 392 | fat: 15g | protein: 55g | carbs: 7g | net carbs: 5g | fiber: 2g

Pork, Bell Pepper and Tomato Stew

1 Leaner | 4 Greens | 1 Healthy Fat | 3 Condiments
Prep time: 15 minutes | Cook time: 25 minutes | Serves 4

1 tablespoon olive oil
1 small yellow onion, chopped
1 celery stalk, chopped
1 tablespoon garlic, minced
1¼ pounds (567 g) beef tenderloin, trimmed and cubed into 2-inch size
1 cup fresh tomatoes, chopped finely
2 tablespoons fresh lemon juice

1 teaspoon dried oregano, crushed
1 teaspoon dried basil, crushed
2 bay leaves
Salt and ground black pepper, as required
½ cup chicken broth
2 large green bell peppers, seeded and cut into 8 slices
2 tablespoons fresh parsley, minced

1. Add the oil in Instant Pot and select "Sauté". Then add the onion and garlic and cook for about 2 minutes.
2. Press "Cancel" and stir in the remaining ingredients except for bell peppers and parsley.
3. Cook on "Manual" with "High Pressure" for about 15 minutes.
4. Press "Cancel" and carefully do a "Natural" release for about 10 minutes. Then do a "Quick" release.
5. Remove the lid and select "Sauté".
6. Stir in bell peppers and cook for about 6-8 minutes.
7. Press "Cancel" and serve immediately with the garnishing of parsley.

Per Serving
calories: 361 | fat: 17g | protein: 43g | carbs: 8g | net carbs: 5g | fiber: 3g

Cod and Cherry Tomatoes with Olives

1 Leaner | 3 Greens | 1 Healthy Fat | 2 Condiments
Prep time: 15 minutes | Cook time: 8 minutes | Serves 4

1 pound (454 g) cherry tomatoes, halved
2 to 3 fresh thyme sprigs
4 cod fillets
1 cup black Kalamata olives
2 tablespoons capers
2 tablespoons olive oil, divided
1 garlic clove, pressed
Salt and ground black pepper, as required

1. Arrange the steamer basket in the bottom of Instant Pot and pour 2 cups of water.
2. Line the bottom of a heat-proof bowl with some cherry tomatoes, followed by thyme sprigs.
3. Arrange the cod fillets on top, followed by the remaining cherry tomatoes, garlic.
4. Drizzle with 1 tablespoon of olive oil and sprinkle with a pinch of salt and black pepper.
5. Place the bowl in steamer basket.
6. Secure the lid and turn to "Seal" position.
7. Cook on "Manual" with "Low Pressure" for about 8 minutes.
8. Press "Cancel" and carefully do a "Quick" release.
9. Remove the lid and divide the cod filets and tomatoes onto the serving plates.
10. Top each fillet with olives and capers and sprinkle with some black pepper.
11. Drizzle with remaining oil and serve.

Per Serving
calories: 258 | fat: 12g | protein: 32g | carbs: 7g | net carbs: 4g | fiber: 3g

Cod Fillets and Peas with Jalapeño

1 Leaner | 2 Greens | 1 Healthy Fat | 3 Condiments
Prep time: 15 minutes | Cook time: 3 minutes | Serves 4

2 garlic cloves, chopped
2 tablespoons fresh cilantro leaves
1 jalapeño pepper, chopped
1 teaspoon garam masala powder
¼ teaspoons red chili powder
1 tablespoon fresh lemon juice
1 cup chicken broth
4 (4-ounce / 113-g) cod fillets
Salt and ground black pepper, as required
½ pound (227 g) frozen peas

1. In a food processor, add garlic, cilantro, jalapeño and spices and pulse until finely chopped.
2. Transfer the garlic mixture into a bowl with broth and lemon juice and mix well.
3. In the bottom of Instant Pot, arrange a steamer trivet and pour 1 cup of water.
4. Place the fish fillets on top of trivet.
5. Secure the lid and turn to "Seal" position.
6. Cook on "Manual" with "High Pressure" for about 2 minutes.
7. Press "Cancel" and carefully do a "Quick" release.
8. Remove the lid and transfer the fish onto a platter.
9. Place the peas on top of trivet,
10. Secure the lid and turn to "Seal" position.
11. Cook on "Manual" with "High Pressure" for about 1 minute.
12. Press "Cancel" and carefully do a "Quick" release.
13. Remove the lid and transfer the peas onto platter with salmon.
14. Top with garlic puree and serve.

Per Serving
calories: 150 | fat: 2g | protein: 25g | carbs: 9g | net carbs: 6g | fiber: 3g

Cod and Bell Peppers with Capers

1 Leaner | 3 Greens | 1 Healthy Fat | 2 Condiments
Prep time: 15 minutes | Cook time: 4 minutes | Serves 4

¼ cup water
4 (4-ounce / 113-g) frozen cod fillets
12 cherry tomatoes
12 to 14 black olives
2 tablespoons capers
⅓ cup bell peppers, seeded and sliced
2 tablespoons olive oil
Salt, as required
Pinch of red pepper flakes

1. In the pot of Instant Pot, pour the water.
2. Place the fish fillets in water and top with tomatoes, followed by the olives, capers and red peppers.
3. Drizzle with olive oil and sprinkle with salt and red pepper flakes.
4. Secure the lid and turn to "Seal" position.
5. Cook on "Manual" with "High Pressure" for about 4 minutes.
6. Press "Cancel" and do a "Natural" release for about 8 minutes, then do a "Quick" release.
7. Remove the lid and transfer the fish mixture onto serving plates.
8. Serve hot.

Per Serving
calories: 181 | fat: 10g | protein: 21g | carbs: 3g | net carbs: 2g | fiber: 1g

Cod Fillets with Fresh Kale

1 Leaner | 3 Greens | 1 Healthy Fat | 2 Condiments
Prep time: 15 minutes | Cook time: 22 minutes | Serves 4

2 tablespoons olive oil
1 small onion, chopped finely
1 garlic clove, minced
1 medium carrot, peeled and chopped
1 cup canned sugar-free chopped tomatoes with juice
2 tablespoons fresh parsley, chopped
1½ cups water
1 pound (454 g) frozen cod fillets
Salt and freshly ground black pepper, as required
2 cups fresh kale, trimmed and chopped

1. Add the oil in the Instant Pot and select "Sauté". Then add the onion and garlic and cook for about 3 minutes.
2. Add the carrots, tomatoes, parsley and water and cook for about 3-4 minutes.
3. Press "Cancel" and arrange a steamer basket on top.
4. Place cod fillets into steamer basket and sprinkle with salt and black pepper.
5. Secure the lid and turn to "Seal" position.
6. Cook on "Manual" with "High Pressure" for about 6 minutes.
7. Press "Cancel" and carefully do a Quick release.
8. Remove the lid and carefully, transfer the fish fillets onto a platter.
9. With an immersion blender, puree the carrot mixture.
10. Select "Sauté" and stir in kale and cook for about 5 minutes.
11. Stir in fish fillets and cook for about 3-4 minutes.
12. Press "Cancel" and serve hot.

Per Serving
calories: 191 | fat: 8g | protein: 22g | carbs: 9g | net carbs: 7g | fiber: 1g

Garlic Salmon with Spinach and Carrot

1 Leaner | 3 Greens | 1 Healthy Fat | 3 Condiments
Prep time: 10 minutes | Cook time: 9 minutes | Serves 4

6 garlic cloves, minced and divided
½ teaspoons lemon zest, grated
1 teaspoon ground cumin
¼ teaspoons paprika
¼ teaspoons red chili powder
Salt and ground black pepper, as required
4 (5-ounce / 142-g) (1-inch thick) skin-on center-cut salmon fillets
½ pound (227 g) carrot, peeled and chopped
4 tablespoons olive oil, divided
1 cup water
4 cups fresh spinach

1. In a small bowl, mix together 2 garlic cloves, lemon zest and spices.
2. Rub the salmon fillets with garlic mixture evenly.
3. In the bottom of Instant Pot, place the carrot, 2 tablespoons of oil, salt, black pepper and water.
4. Arrange a steamer trivet over the potatoes.
5. Place salmon fillets on top of trivet, skin-side down.
6. Secure the lid and turn to "Seal" position.
7. Cook on "Manual" with "High Pressure" for about 3 minutes.
8. Press "Cancel" and carefully do a "Quick" release.
9. Remove the lid and transfer the salmon fillets onto a plate.
10. Remove the steamer trivet.
11. Now select "Sauté" and cook for about 1-2 minutes.
12. Add the remaining garlic and cook for about 1-2 minutes, stirring occasionally.
13. Stir in the remaining 2 tablespoons of oil, salt and black pepper.
14. Stir in spinach and cook for about 1-2 minutes.
15. Press "Cancel" and transfer the spinach mixture onto serving plates.
16. Top with salmon fillets and serve.

Per Serving
calories: 347 | fat: 23g | protein: 30g | carbs: 9g | net carbs: 6g | fiber: 2g

Salmon Fillets with Zucchini

1 Leaner | 3 Greens | 1 Healthy Fat | 3 Condiments
Prep time: 15 minutes | Cook time: 6 minutes | Serves 4

1 pound (454 g) skin-on salmon fillets
Salt and ground black pepper, as required
1 fresh parsley sprig
1 fresh dill sprig
3 teaspoons coconut oil, melted and divided
½ lemon, sliced thinly
1 carrot, peeled and julienned
1 zucchini, peeled and julienned
1 red bell pepper, seeded and julienned

1. Season the salmon fillets with salt and black pepper evenly.
2. In the bottom of Instant Pot, arrange a steamer trivet and place herb sprigs and 1 cup of water.
3. Place the salmon fillets on top of trivet, skin side down.
4. Drizzle salmon fillets with 2 teaspoons of coconut oil and top with lemon slices.
5. Secure the lid and turn to "Seal" position.
6. Select "Steam" and just use the default time of 3 minutes.
7. Press "Cancel" and do a "Natural" release.
8. Meanwhile, for sauce: in a bowl, add remaining ingredients and mix until well combined.
9. Remove the lid and transfer the salmon fillets onto a platter.
10. Remove the steamer trivet, herbs and cooking water from pot. With paper towels, pat dry the pot.
11. Place the remaining coconut oil in the Instant Pot and select "Sauté". Then add the veggies and cook or about 2-3 minutes.
12. Press "Cancel" and transfer the veggies onto platter with salmon.
13. Serve immediately.

Per Serving
calories: 204 | fat: 11g | protein: 23g | carbs: 6g | net carbs: 4g | fiber: 2g

Salmon and Cauliflower Soup

1 Leaner | 4 Greens | 1 Healthy Fat | 2 Condiments
Prep time: 15 minutes | Cook time: 21 minutes | Serves 4

1 pound (454 g) salmon fillets
1 tablespoon olive oil
1 cup carrots, peeled and chopped
½ cup celery stalk, chopped
¼ cup yellow onion, chopped
1 cup cauliflower, chopped
3 cups chicken broth
Salt and ground black pepper, as required
¼ cup fresh parsley, chopped

1. In the bottom of Instant Pot, arrange a steamer trivet and pour 1 cup of water.
2. Place the salmon fillets on top of trivet in a single layer.
3. Secure the lid and turn to "Seal" position.
4. Cook on "Manual" with "High Pressure" for about 7-8 minutes.
5. Press "Cancel" and carefully do a "Quick" release.
6. Remove the lid and transfer the salmon onto a plate. Cut the salmon into bite sized pieces.
7. Remove the water and trivet from Instant Pot.
8. Add the oil in Instant Pot and select "Sauté". Then add the carrot, celery and onion and cook for about 5 minutes or until browned completely.
9. Press "Cancel" and stir in the cauliflower and broth.
10. Secure the lid and turn to "Seal" position.
11. Cook on "Manual" with "High Pressure" for about 8 minutes.
12. Press "Cancel" and do a "Natural" release.
13. Remove the lid and stir in salmon pieces and black pepper until well combined.
14. Serve immediately with the garnishing of parsley.

Per Serving
calories: 233 | fat: 12g | protein: 27g | carbs: 6g | net carbs: 4g | fiber: 2g

Shrimp Lettuce Wraps with Radishes

1 Leaner | 3 Greens | 1 Healthy Fat | ½ Condiment
Prep time: 15 minutes | Cook time: 3 minutes | Serves 4

1 pound (454 g) fresh shrimp, peeled and deveined
1 cup radishes, trimmed and julienned
1 cup carrot, peeled and shredded
Salt and ground black pepper, as required
8 large butter lettuce leaves

1. In the pot of Instant Pot, place shrimp and enough water to cover.
2. Secure the lid and turn to "Seal" position.
3. Cook on "Manual" with "High Pressure" for about 3 minutes.
4. Press "Cancel" and carefully do a "Quick" release.
5. Remove the lid and with tongs, transfer the shrimp into a bowl.
6. Set aside to cool slightly.
7. In the bowl of shrimp, add radishes, carrot, salt and black pepper and toss to coat well.
8. Arrange lettuce leaves onto each serving plate.
9. Place the shrimp mixture in each leaf evenly and serve immediately.

Per Serving
calories: 152 | fat: 2g | protein: 26g | carbs: 6g | net carbs: 5g | fiber: 1g

Shrimp and Green Bean Chili

1 Leaner | 1 Greens | 1 Healthy Fat | 3 Condiments
Prep time: 15 minutes | Cook time: 2 minutes | Serves 4

2 tablespoons fresh lemon juice
1 teaspoon red chili powder
1 teaspoon garam masala powder
1 teaspoon ground cumin
Salt and ground black pepper, as required
1 pound (454 g) medium frozen shrimp, peeled and deveined
¾ pound (340 g) green beans, trimmed
1 tablespoon olive oil

1. In a small bowl, mix together lemon juice and spices.
2. In the bottom of Instant Pot, arrange a steamer trivet and pour 1 cup of water.
3. Arrange green beans on top of trivet in a single layer and top with shrimp.
4. Drizzle with oil and sprinkle with spice mixture.
5. Secure the lid and turn to "Seal" position.
6. Select "Steam" and just use the default time of 2 minutes.
7. Press "Cancel" and do a "Natural" release.
8. Remove the lid and serve hot.

Per Serving
calories: 197 | fat: 6g | protein: 28g | carbs: 9g | net carbs: 5g | fiber: 4g

Shrimp and Cod Stew

2 Leaner | 3 Greens | 1 Healthy Fat | 3 Condiments
Prep time: 20 minutes | Cook time: 14 minutes | Serves 4

2 tablespoons extra-virgin olive oil
1 small onion, sliced thinly
1 small green bell pepper, seeded and sliced thinly
1 cup tomatoes, chopped
2 garlic cloves, minced
¼ cup fresh cilantro, chopped and divided
2 bay leaves
1 teaspoon paprika
Salt and ground black pepper, as required
½ cup fish broth
¾ pound (340 g) shrimp, peeled and deveined
¾ pound (340 g) cod fillets, cut into 2-inch chunks

1. Add the oil in Instant Pot and select "Sauté". Then add the onion, bell pepper, tomatoes, garlic, 2 tablespoons of cilantro, bay leaves, paprika, salt and black pepper and cook for about 3-4 minutes.
2. Press "Cancel" and stir in the broth.
3. Submerge the shrimps into the vegetable mixture and top with the cod pieces.
4. Secure the lid and turn to "Seal" position.
5. Cook on "Manual" with "High Pressure" for about 10 minutes.
6. Press "Cancel" and do a "Natural" release for about 10 minutes. Then do a "Quick" release.
7. Remove the lid and serve hot with the garnishing of remaining cilantro.

Per Serving
calories: 263 | fat: 10g | protein: 36g | carbs: 8g | net carbs: 6g | fiber: 2g

Curried Tofu and Spinach

1 Leaner | 2 Greens | 1 Healthy Fat | 3 Condiments
Prep time: 15 minutes | Cook time: 13 minutes | Serves 4

3 tablespoons olive oil, divided
2 cups firm tofu, pressed, drained and cubed
1 teaspoon cumin seeds
1 onion, chopped
1 teaspoon fresh ginger, chopped
5 garlic cloves, chopped
1 tomato, chopped
1 teaspoon garam masala powder
1 teaspoon ground coriander
½ teaspoons cayenne pepper
Salt, as required
1 pound (454 g) fresh spinach

1. Add 2 tablespoons of oil in the Instant Pot and select "Sauté". Then add the tofu and sear for about 5 minutes.
2. Transfer the tofu into a bowl.
3. In the pot, add the remaining oil and cumin seeds and cook for about 1 minute.
4. Add the onion, ginger, garlic and red chilies and cook for about 3 minutes.
5. Stir in tomato and spices and cook for about 1-2 minutes.
6. Press "Cancel" and stir in spinach.
7. Secure the lid and turn to "Seal" position.
8. Cook on "Manual" with "High Pressure" for about 2 minutes.
9. Press "Cancel" and do a "Natural" release.
10. Remove the lid and with an immersion blender, blend the mixture until smooth.
11. Stir in tofu and secure the lid for about 5 minutes.
12. Serve hot.

Per Serving
calories: 228 | fat: 17g | protein: 14g | carbs: 10g | net carbs: 5g | fiber: 5g

Tofu and Veggies Curry with Scallions

1 Leaner | 3 Greens | 1 Healthy Fat | 3 Condiments
Prep time: 15 minutes | Cook time: 12 minutes | Serves 4

2 tablespoons olive oil
3 tablespoons green curry paste
1 ((14-ounce / 397-g) can coconut milk
14 ounces (397 g) firm tofu, pressed and cubed
1 carrot, peeled and sliced
1 red bell pepper, seeded and cut into 1-inch pieces
1 cup broccoli, chopped
2 scallions, cut into 2-inch pieces
1 tablespoon fresh lemon juice

1. Add the oil in Instant Pot and select "Sauté". Then add the curry paste and sauté for about 30 seconds.
2. Add the coconut milk and stir well.
3. Press "Cancel" and stir in tofu and vegetables.
4. Secure the lid and turn to "Seal" position.
5. Cook on "Manual" with "Low Pressure" for about 2 minutes.
6. Press "Cancel" and carefully do a "Quick" release.
7. Remove the lid and stir in remaining ingredients.
8. Serve hot.

Per Serving
calories: 247 | fat: 20g | protein: 10g | carbs: 10g | net carbs: 7g | fiber: 3g

Cheddar Broccoli Casserole

1 Lean | 3 Greens | 1½ Condiments
Prep time: 5 minutes | Cook time: 45 minutes | Serves 4

6 cups small broccoli florets
9 eggs
1 cup unsweetened almond milk
¼ teaspoon salt
¼ teaspoon cayenne pepper
¼ teaspoon ground pepper
Cooking spray
4 ounces (113 g) shredded, reduced-fat Cheddar cheese

1. Preheat the oven to 375°F (190°C).
2. Place the broccoli with 2 to 3 tablespoons water in a large microwave-safe dish. Microwave on High for 3 to 4 minutes or until softened. Transfer the broccoli to a colander to drain off any excess liquid. Set aside.
3. In a medium bowl, whisk together the eggs, milk, salt, cayenne pepper, and ground pepper to combine.
4. Lightly grease a baking dish with cooking spray and add the broccoli. Scatter the cheese all over the broccoli, then pour the egg mixture over top.
5. Bake in the preheated oven for 40 to 45 minutes, or until a toothpick inserted into the center comes out clean and the top is lightly browned.
6. Let rest for 5 minutes before slicing and serving.

Per Serving
calories: 423 | fat: 29g | protein: 31g | carbs: 8g | net carbs: 7g | fiber: 1g

Asparagus and Crab Frittata with Basil

1 Leanest | 3 Greens | 2 Healthy Fats | 3 Condiments
Prep time: 8 minutes | Cook time: 30 minutes | Serves 4

2 pounds (907 g) asparagus, woody ends trimmed and cut into bite-sized pieces
2½ tablespoons extra-virgin olive oil, divided
1 teaspoon salt
2 teaspoons sweet paprika
½ teaspoon black pepper
1 pound (454 g) lump crab meat
4 cups liquid egg substitute
¼ cup chopped basil
1 tablespoon finely chopped chives

1. Preheat the oven to 375°F (190°C). Line a baking sheet with parchment paper.
2. Toss the asparagus with 2 tablespoons of olive oil, salt, paprika, and black pepper until evenly coated. Spread the asparagus onto the prepared baking sheet. Bake in the preheated oven for about 10 minutes until crisp-tender.
3. Meanwhile, combine the crab meat, liquid egg substitute, basil, and chives in a mixing bowl and stir until well incorporated.
4. Heat the remaining ½ tablespoon of olive oil in an ovenproof skillet over medium heat. Carefully pour the crab mixture into the skillet with the cooked asparagus, and gently stir to mix well. Cook until the eggs start to bubble.
5. Put the skillet in the oven and bake, or until the eggs are completely cooked and golden brown, about 15 to 20 minutes.
6. Cool for 5 minutes and serve.

Per Serving
calories: 554 | fat: 8g | protein: 72g | carbs: 57g | net carbs: 32g | fiber: 25g

Cheese Zucchini Manicotti with Spinach

1 Lean | 3 Greens | 1 Condiment
Prep time: 10 minutes | Cook time: 25 minutes | Serves 4

1½ cups part-skim ricotta cheese
1 cup frozen spinach, thawed and patted dry
1½ cups reduced-fat shredded Mozzarella cheese, divided
1 egg, lightly beaten
¼ cup grated Parmesan cheese
⅛ teaspoon salt
Pinch nutmeg
2 large zucchini, sliced into ⅛-inch-thick slices
1 cup low-sugar tomato sauce

1. Preheat the oven to 375°F (190°C).
2. Mix together the ricotta, spinach, ½ cup of Mozzarella, beaten egg, Parmesan, salt, and nutmeg in a medium mixing bowl and stir to combine.
3. On a clean work surface, layer three slices of zucchini parallel to each other. Place a large spoonful of ricotta mixture on one end of the zucchini slices and roll up. Arrange the stuffed zucchini in a lightly greased baking dish. Pour the tomato sauce over top of the zucchini and scatter with the remaining 1 cup of Mozzarella.
4. Bake in the preheated oven for 25 minutes until the cheese melts.
5. Remove from the oven and rest for 5 minutes before serving.

Per Serving
calories: 329 | fat: 18g | protein: 27g | carbs: 13g | net carbs: 11g | fiber: 2g

Spicy Pork and Tomatillo Stew

1 Lean | 3 Greens | 3 Condiments
Prep time: 15 minutes | Cook time: 20 minutes | Serves 4

1 pound (454 g) tomatillos, trimmed and chopped
8 large romaine or green lettuce leaves, divided
2 serrano chilies, seeds and membranes removed, chopped
2 scallions, chopped
2 cloves garlic
½ teaspoon dried oregano
1½ pounds (680 g) boneless pork loin, cut into bite-sized cubes
¼ teaspoon salt
¼ teaspoon pepper
1 cup sliced radishes
¼ cup chopped cilantro
1 jalapeño, seeds and membranes removed, thinly sliced
4 lime wedges

1. Place the tomatillos, 4 lettuce leaves, serrano chilies, scallions, garlic, and oregano in a blender and purée until smooth.
2. Add the pork and tomatillo mixture into a medium pot (the pork should be covered by 1-inch of tomatillo mixture; if not, add the water until it is). Sprinkle with the salt and pepper. Cover and bring to a simmer over low heat, about 20 minutes.
3. Meanwhile, finely shred the remaining 4 lettuce leaves.
4. Garnish the stew with the radishes, cilantro, shredded lettuce, jalapeño slices, and lime wedges, then serve.

Per Serving
calories: 493 | fat: 10g | protein: 53g | carbs: 56g | net carbs: 36g | fiber: 20g

Barbecued Pork with Veggie Slaw

1 Lean | 3 Greens | 3 Condiments
Prep time: 10 minutes | Cook time: 1 hour 10 minutes | Serves 4

1 (1½-pound / 680-g) pork tenderloin, cut in half
Cooking spray
1 (12-ounce / 340-g) can diet root beer
½ cup sugar-free barbecue sauce

Slaw:
3 cups shredded red cabbage
3 cups shredded green cabbage
½ cup low-fat plain Greek yogurt
1 tablespoon apple cider vinegar
1 teaspoon Dijon mustard
2 teaspoons lemon juice
¼ teaspoon celery salt
Pinch stevia

1. Grease the bottom of the Instant Pot with cooking spray. Set the Instant Pot to Sauté and brown the pork on all sides, about 3 minutes per side.
2. Pour in the beer and mix well.
3. Secure the lid. Select the Manual mode and set the cooking time for 60 minutes at High Pressure.
4. Meanwhile, stir together all the slaw ingredients in a medium bowl until combined. Set aside.
5. When the timer beeps, perform a natural pressure release for 10 minutes, then release any remaining pressure. Carefully remove the lid.
6. Transfer the pork to a large bowl and shred the meat. Add the barbecue sauce and toss well. Serve the pulled pork with the slaw on the side.

Per Serving
calories: 280 | fat: 5g | protein: 26g | carbs: 22g | net carbs: 19g | fiber: 3g

Garlic Pork Chops with Chard

1 Lean | 3 Greens | 3 Condiments
Prep time: 5 to 10 minutes | Cook time: 28 minutes | Serves 4

1½ pounds (680 g) boneless pork chops
½ teaspoon salt, divided
¼ teaspoon pepper, divided
1 teaspoon dried thyme
Cooking spray
¼ cup low-sodium chicken broth
1 (8-ounce / 227-g) package sliced baby bella mushrooms
4 cloves garlic, minced
⅛ teaspoon crushed red pepper flakes
2 (10-ounce / 283-g) bags Swiss or rainbow chard, sliced and washed
¼ cup freshly grated Parmesan cheese

1. Preheat the oven to 450°F (235°C).
2. Season pork chops with ¼ teaspoon of salt, ⅛ teaspoon of pepper, and thyme.
3. Lightly grease a large skillet and heat over medium high heat. Add the chops and light brown each side for 3 to 4 minutes. Remove from heat and set aside.
4. Pour the chicken broth into the same skillet. Sauté mushrooms with garlic and red pepper flakes until just tender.
5. Arrange the chard in a large casserole dish, and season with remaining salt and pepper. Add mushroom mixture and the pork chops. Sprinkle with the Parmesan cheese.
6. Bake in the preheated oven for 18 to 20 minutes, or until the internal temperature of pork reaches 145°F (63°C).
7. Serve warm.

Per Serving
calories: 248 | fat: 6g | protein: 41g | carbs: 4g | net carbs: 3g | fiber: 1g

Beef and Spinach Bibimbap

1 Leaner | 3 Greens | 1 Healthy Fat | 2 Condiments
Prep time: 10 minutes | Cook time: 12 minutes | Serves 4

1 teaspoon olive oil
5 cups baby spinach
1 teaspoon toasted sesame oil
¼ teaspoon salt
1 pound (454 g) 95 to 97% lean ground beef
1 tablespoon reduced-sodium soy sauce
2 tablespoons chili garlic sauce
2 cups riced cauliflower
1 cup thinly sliced cucumber
4 hard-boiled eggs
½ cup chopped green onions
1 tablespoon sesame seeds

1. Heat the olive oil in a skillet over medium high heat until it shimmers. Add the baby spinach and sauté for 2 to 3 minutes until just wilted. Drizzle with the sesame oil and season with salt.
2. Remove the spinach from the skillet and set aside.
3. Place the ground beef in the same skillet and cook until fully browned. Stir in the chili garlic sauce and soy sauce and cook for 1 minute. Remove the skillet from the heat and set aside.
4. Place the riced cauliflower with 1 tablespoon water in a large microwave-safe dish. Microwave on High for 3 to 4 minutes or until tender.
5. Divide ½ cup of riced cauliflower into each bowl. Top each bowl evenly with the spinach, beef, and sliced cucumber. Place an egg on top of each bowl. Serve garnished with the green onions and green onions.

Per Serving
calories: 495 | fat: 32g | protein: 41g | carbs: 8g | net carbs: 5g | fiber: 3g

Turkey Bacon Cheeseburger Bites

1 Lean | 1 Green | 3 Condiments
Prep time: 10 minutes | Cook time: 18 minutes | Serves 4

1 pound (454 g) lean ground beef
¼ cup finely chopped yellow onion
1 tablespoon Worcestershire sauce
1 tablespoon yellow mustard
1 clove garlic, minced
½ teaspoon salt
Cooking spray

4 ultra-thin slices Cheddar cheese, each cut into 6 equal-sized rectangular pieces
3 pieces cooked turkey bacon, each cut into 8 equal-sized rectangular pieces
24 dill pickle chips
4 to 6 large green leaf lettuce leaves, torn into 24 (total) small square-shaped pieces
12 cherry tomatoes, sliced in half

1. Preheat the oven to 400°F (205°C). Line a baking sheet with aluminum foil.
2. In a medium mixing bowl, stir together the ground beef, onion, Worcestershire sauce, mustard, garlic, and salt until well mixed. Shape the mixture into 24 small meatballs. Arrange the meatballs on the prepared baking sheet and spray them with cooking spray.
3. Bake in the preheated oven for about 15 minutes until cooked through.
4. Place a piece of cheese on top of each meatball and bake for an additional 2 to 3 minutes, or until the cheese is melted. Remove from the oven and let cool.
5. Assemble the bites: On a toothpick, layer a cheese-covered meatball, piece of bacon, pickle chip, piece of lettuce, and cherry tomato half, in that order. Serve immediately.

Per Serving
calories: 492 | fat: 24g | protein: 41g | carbs: 22g | net carbs: 7g | fiber: 13g

Beef and Broccoli with Cauliflower Rice

1 Lean | 3 Greens | 2½ Condiments
Prep time: 10 minutes | Cook time: 15 minutes | Serves 4

4 cups cauliflower rice
Cooking spray
1½ pounds (680 g) flank steak, thinly sliced
2 cups broccoli florets
½ cup chicken or beef broth
1 cup diced scallions
⅓ cup reduced sodium soy sauce
1 teaspoon minced fresh ginger
2 cloves garlic, minced
½ teaspoon red pepper flakes

1. Heat a lightly greased skillet over medium-high heat. Add the cauliflower rice and cook for about 3 to 5 minutes, until tender. Remove the cauliflower rice from the skillet and set aside.
2. Lightly grease the skillet with cooking spray and add the beef. Cook over medium-high heat for about 4 to 5 minutes until cooked through, flipping the slices halfway through.
3. Add the broccoli and broth to the skillet with the beef. Continue to cook until the broccoli turns bright green and just softened.
4. Add the remaining ingredients to the skillet and stir to combine. Cook for an additional 1 to 2 minutes.
5. Remove from the heat and serve over cauliflower rice.

Per Serving
calories: 325| fat: 9g | protein: 46g | carbs: 15g | net carbs: 11g | fiber: 4g

Cod and Zucchinis with Basil

1 Leanest | 3 Greens | 2 Healthy Fats | 3 Condiments
Prep time: 15 minutes | Cook time: 40 minutes | Serves 4

2 garlic cloves
4 scallions, chopped with green and white parts separated
2½ tablespoons olive oil, divided
2½ cups diced canned tomatoes, with their juice
¼ teaspoon dried oregano
3 small zucchinis (about 12 ounces / 340 g), sliced lengthwise into ⅛-inch-thick slices
1¾ pounds (794 g) cod fillets, cut into 12 equal-sized pieces
½ teaspoon kosher salt
½ teaspoon ground black pepper, divided
⅓ cup reduced-fat crumbled feta cheese
1 cup chopped fresh whole basil leaves

1. In a saucepan, cook the garlic and white parts of scallions in 1 tablespoon of olive oil until fragrant, about 2 minutes.
2. Add the tomatoes with their juice and oregano. Bring to a gentle simmer for 20 minutes or until thickened.
3. Remove from the heat and stir in the green parts of scallions. Set aside.
4. Preheat the oven to 425°F (220°C).
5. Lay the zucchini slices in an ovenproof casserole dish and top with the cod fillets. Sprinkle with the salt and ¼ teaspoon of black pepper. Drizzle with the remaining olive oil. Scatter the cooked tomatoes and feta cheese on top.
6. Bake in the preheated oven for 20 minutes, or until the cod reaches an internal temperature of 145°F (63°C).
7. Serve topped with the basil leaves and remaining ¼ teaspoon of black pepper.

Per Serving
calories: 314 | fat: 15g | protein: 48g | carbs: 6g | net carbs: 5g | fiber: 1g

Parmesan Asparagus and Salmon

1 Lean | 3 Greens | 3 Condiments
Prep time: 5 minutes | Cook time: 15 to 20 minutes | Serves 4

1½ pounds (680 g) salmon, skin-on
Cooking spray
2 teaspoons salt-free lemon pepper seasoning
½ teaspoon salt
Lemon slices, for garnish
¼ cup grated Parmesan cheese
½ teaspoon garlic powder
1½ pounds (680 g) asparagus, woody ends trimmed

1. Preheat the oven to 400°F (205°C). Line a baking sheet with aluminum foil and spray it with cooking spray.
2. Put the salmon in the center of baking sheet and spritz the salmon lightly with cooking spray. Sprinkle with the lemon pepper seasoning and salt. Scatter the lemon slices on top.
3. Combine the Parmesan cheese and garlic powder in a small bowl. Arrange the asparagus spears around the salmon. Lightly spritz with cooking spray and scatter with the Parmesan cheese mixture.
4. Bake in the preheated oven for about 15 to 20 minutes, or until the salmon is cooked through.
5. Serve hot.

Per Serving
calories: 324 | fat: 14g | protein: 40g | carbs: 8g | net carbs: 4g | fiber: 4g

Salmon Florentine with Spinach

1 Lean | 3 Greens | 3 Condiments
Prep time: 15 minutes | Cook time: 20 minutes | Serves 4

½ cup chopped green onions
1 teaspoon olive oil
2 garlic cloves, minced
1 (12-ounce / 340-g) package frozen chopped spinach, thawed and patted dry
1½ cups chopped cherry tomatoes
¼ teaspoon crushed red pepper flakes
¼ teaspoon pepper
¼ teaspoon salt
½ cup part-skim ricotta cheese
4 (5½-ounce / 156-g) wild salmon fillets
Cooking spray

1. Preheat the oven to 350°F (180°C).
2. In a medium skillet, cook the onions in the olive oil for about 2 minutes, or until they begin to soften.
3. Add the minced garlic and cook for another 1 minute. Add the spinach, tomatoes, red pepper flakes, pepper and salt. Cook, stirring, for 2 minutes.
4. Remove from heat and let cool for 10 minutes. Stir in the ricotta cheese.
5. Put a quarter of the spinach mixture on top of each salmon fillet. Arrange the fillets on a lightly greased rimmed baking sheet. Bake in the preheated oven until the salmon is cooked through, for 15 minutes.
6. Cool for 5 minutes before serving.

Per Serving
calories: 657| fat: 91g | protein: 27g | carbs: 6g | net carbs: 4g | fiber: 2g

Peppery Salmon with Cilantro

1 Lean | 3 Greens | 3 Condiments
Prep time: 15 minutes | Cook time: 32 minutes | Serves 4

4 cups fresh cilantro, divided
2 tablespoons fresh lemon juice
2 tablespoons hot red pepper sauce
1 teaspoon cumin
½ teaspoon salt, divided
½ cup water
4 (7-ounce / 198-g) raw salmon fillets
2 cups sliced red bell pepper
2 cups sliced green bell pepper
2 cups sliced yellow bell pepper
⅛ teaspoon ground black pepper
Cooking spray

1. In a food processor, combine half of the cilantro, lemon juice, hot red pepper sauce, cumin, ¼ teaspoon of salt, and water. Pulse until creamy. Transfer the marinade to a resealable plastic bag.
2. Dunk the salmon into the marinade. Seal the bag and shake to make sure the salmon is coated well.
3. Put the bag in the refrigerator. Refrigerate for an hour, turning bag occasionally.
4. Preheat the oven to 400°F (205°C).
5. Arrange the pepper slices in a greased baking dish. Sprinkle with black pepper and remaining salt.
6. Bake in the preheated oven for 20 minutes, flipping the pepper slices once.
7. Remove the bag from the refrigerator. Discard the marinade. Dust the salmon with remaining cilantro.
8. Place salmon on top of pepper slices, and bake for an additional 12 minutes or until tender.
9. Serve immediately.

Per Serving
calories: 57 | fat: 1g | protein: 2g | carbs: 15g | net carbs: 12g | fiber: 3g

Cajun Shrimp with Cheesy Cauliflower Rice

1 Leanest | 3 Greens | 2 Healthy Fats | 3 Condiments
Prep time: 10 minutes | Cook time: 15 minutes | Serves 2

1 pound (454 g) raw, peeled and deveined shrimp
½ tablespoon Cajun seasoning
Cooking spray
¼ cup chicken broth
1 tablespoon lemon juice
1 tablespoon butter
2½ cups finely riced cauliflower
½ cup unsweetened almond or cashew milk
¼ teaspoon salt
⅓ cup reduced-fat shredded Cheddar cheese
2 tablespoons sour cream
¼ cup thinly sliced scallions

1. Add the shrimp and Cajun seasoning into a large, resealable plastic bag. Seal the bag and toss to coat well.
2. Grease a skillet with cooking spray and heat over medium heat.
3. Add the shrimp and cook each side for about 2 to 3 minutes. Add chicken broth and lemon juice, scraping any bits off of the bottom of the pan, and let simmer for 1 minute. Remove from the heat and set aside.
4. In a separate skillet, melt the butter over medium heat.
5. Add the riced cauliflower and cook for 5 minutes. Add milk and salt and cook for an additional 5 minutes.
6. Remove from heat and stir in sour cream and cheese until melted.
7. Serve the shrimp over cauliflower grits and sprinkle with the scallions.

Per Serving
calories: 752 | fat: 45g | protein: 42g | carbs: 88g | net carbs: 56g | fiber: 32g

Old Bay Shrimp Lettuce Wraps

1 Leanest | 3 Greens | 2 Healthy Fats | 3 Condiments
Prep time: 15 minutes | Cook time: 6 minutes | Serves 4

2 pounds (907 g) raw shrimp, peeled and deveined
1 tablespoon Old Bay blackened seasoning
4 teaspoons olive oil, divided
6 ounces (170 g) avocado
1 cup plain Greek yogurt
2 tablespoons lime juice, divided
1½ cups diced tomato
¼ cup diced green bell pepper
¼ cup chopped cilantro
1 jalapeño pepper, chopped and deseeded
¼ cup chopped red onion
12 large romaine lettuce leaves

1. Place shrimp and Old Bay seasoning in a resealable plastic bag. Shake to coat well.
2. Heat 2 teaspoons of olive oil in a skillet and add the shrimp. Cook for 5 minutes on both sides or until shrimp are pink and cooked through. You may need to work in batches to avoid overcrowding.
3. Combine the avocado, Greek yogurt, and 1 tablespoon of lime juice in a food processor. Pulse until smooth.
4. Stir the tomatoes, green bell pepper, cilantro, jalapeño pepper, onion, and remaining tablespoon of lime juice in a medium bowl.
5. Divide the shrimp, avocado mixture, and tomato mixture among the lettuce leaves.
6. Serve immediately.

Per Serving
calories: 711 | fat: 19g | protein: 70g | carbs: 38g | net carbs: 7g | fiber: 31g

Oregano Chicken Thighs and Asparagus

1 Lean| 3 Greens | 2 Condiments
Prep time: 5 minutes | Cook time: 40 minutes | Serves 4

1¾ pounds (794 g) bone-in, skinless chicken thighs
2 tablespoons lemon juice
2 tablespoons minced fresh oregano
2 cloves garlic, minced
¼ teaspoon pepper
¼ teaspoon salt
2 pounds (907 g) asparagus, trimmed

1. Preheat the oven to 350°F (180°C).
2. Toss all the ingredients except the asparagus in a mixing bowl until combined.
3. Roast the chicken thighs in the preheated oven for about 40 minutes, or until it reaches an internal temperature of 165°F (74°C).
4. When cooked, remove the chicken thighs from the oven and set aside to cool.
5. Meanwhile, steam the asparagus in the microwave to the desired doneness.
6. Serve the asparagus with roasted chicken thighs.

Per Serving
calories: 748 | fat: 44g | protein: 42g | carbs: 38g | net carbs: 33g | fiber: 5g

Mozzarella Chicken Cauliflower Skillet

1 Lean | 3 Greens | 1 Condiment
Prep time: 10 minutes | Cook time: 10 minutes | Serves 4

2 teaspoons olive oil
1½ cups sliced mushrooms
1 (12-ounce / 340-g) bag frozen riced cauliflower
2 cloves garlic, minced
½ cup chicken broth
1 (12-ounce / 340-g) can shredded chicken breast, drained
8 ounces (227 g) reduced-fat shredded Mozzarella cheese
½ teaspoon dried oregano
2 scallions, chopped

1. In a skillet over medium heat, cook the mushrooms, cauliflower, and garlic in the olive oil for 3 to 4 minutes.
2. Pour in the chicken broth and bring to a boil.
3. Once it starts to boil, add the chicken breast, reduce the heat, and let simmer for 4 to 5 minutes, or until the vegetables are tender and chicken is heated through.
4. Stir in the Mozzarella cheese and oregano. Serve topped with the scallions.

Per Serving
calories: 482 | fat: 13g | protein: 27g | carbs: 38g | net carbs: 17g | fiber: 21g

Chicken and Bell Pepper Lettuce Wraps

1 Leaner | 3 Greens | 1 Healthy Fat | 3 Condiments
Prep time: 10 minutes | Cook time: 25 to 30 minutes | Serves 2

1 pound (454 g) chicken breast, thinly sliced into strips
2 bell peppers, thinly sliced into strips
2 teaspoons olive oil
2 teaspoons fajita seasoning
Juice of half a lime
6 leaves from a romaine heart
¼ cup nonfat plain Greek yogurt (optional)

1. Preheat the oven to 400°F (205°C).
2. Combine all the ingredients except for lettuce leaves and yogurt in a large, resealable plastic bag. Shake well to coat chicken and vegetables evenly with oil and seasoning.
3. Spread contents of the bag evenly on a foil-lined baking sheet. Bake in the preheated oven for 25 to 30 minutes, or until the chicken is cooked through.
4. Serve over the lettuce leaves, topped with the yogurt if desired.

Per Serving
calories: 230 | fat: 13g | protein: 24g | carbs: 3g | net carbs: 2g | fiber: 1g

Balsamic Chicken with Mozzarella

1 Leaner | 1 Green | 1 Healthy Fat | 3 Condiments
Prep time: 10 minutes | Cook time: 15 minutes | Serves 4

2 teaspoons olive oil
2 garlic cloves, minced
2 cups halved grape tomatoes
3 tablespoons balsamic vinegar
¼ teaspoon salt
¼ teaspoon pepper
½ cup fresh basil leaves, torn into small pieces
4 (4-ounce / 113-g) boneless, skinless chicken breasts, butterflied then pounded very thin (⅛ to ¼-inch thick)
2 cups reduced-fat shredded Mozzarella cheese

1. Heat the olive oil in a large skillet over medium high heat. Add garlic and stir for 1 minute. Add tomatoes, balsamic vinegar, salt, and pepper. Cover and cook for 8 to 10 minutes, or until tomatoes are tender.
2. Remove from the heat and stir in the basil.
3. Grill or sauté the chicken breasts over medium-high heat for a few minutes on each side until cooked through.
4. Transfer the chicken breasts to a baking sheet. Top the chicken with tomato mixture and Mozzarella cheese. Broil for 2 to 5 minutes, or until cheese melts.
5. Cool for 5 minutes before serving.

Per Serving
calories: 363 | fat: 8g | protein: 29g | carbs: 23g | net carbs: 4g | fiber: 19g

Queso Chicken with Cheddar

1 Leaner | 3 Greens | 1 Healthy Fat | 1 Condiment
Prep time: 10 minutes | Cook time: 20 minutes | Serves 4

12 ounces (340 g) shredded, cooked chicken breast
1½ cups reduced-fat shredded sharp Cheddar cheese
¾ cup low-fat plain Greek yogurt
4 tablespoons reduced-fat cream cheese, softened
1 cup diced tomatoes with green chilies
½ cup chopped cilantro (optional)
1 (1-pound / 454-g) bag mini sweet peppers, halved lengthwise, stems and seeds removed
2½ cups celery sticks (about 13 ounces / 369 g)

1. Preheat the oven to 350°F (180°C).
2. Combine all ingredients except the bell peppers and celery sticks in a large bowl, then pour into a lightly greased casserole dish.
3. Bake in the preheated oven for 20 minutes until heated through.
4. Serve hot with halved mini sweet peppers and celery sticks.

Per Serving
calories: 623 | fat: 32g | protein: 37g | carbs: 47g | net carbs: 44g | fiber: 3g

Arroz Con Pollo with Olives

1 Leaner | 3 Greens | 1 Healthy Fat | 1 Condiment
Prep time: 5 minutes | Cook time:20 minutes | Serves 4

1¾ pounds (794 g) boneless, skinless chicken breasts
¼ teaspoon salt
¼ teaspoon pepper
2 cloves garlic, minced
1 scallion, minced
4 cups cauliflower rice
1½ cups halved cherry tomatoes
½ cup green beans, cut into ¼-inch pieces
40 green pitted olives

1. Preheat the oven to 350°F (180°C).
2. Season chicken breasts with salt and pepper, and place on a lightly greased baking sheet.
3. Roast in the preheated oven until the internal temperature reaches 165°F (74°C), about 20 minutes. Once cooked, remove from oven and set aside to cool.
4. Meanwhile, combine all of the remaining ingredients in a pot. Simmer on low for 8 to 10 minutes, stirring occasionally.
5. When finished, slice the chicken and serve with cauliflower rice.

Per Serving
calories: 423 | fat: 29g | protein: 31g | carbs: 8g | net carbs: 7g | fiber: 1g

Chicken and Cauliflower Risotto

1 Leaner | 3 Greens | 1 Healthy Fat | 2 Condiments
Prep time: 10 minutes | Cook time: 30 minutes | Serves 4

2 pounds (907 g) boneless, skinless chicken breasts
¼ teaspoon salt
¼ teaspoon ground black pepper
2 tablespoons butter, melted
1¼ pounds (567 g) riced cauliflower
¼ pound (113 g) asparagus, chopped
½ cup chicken stock
4 tablespoons nutritional yeast

1. Preheat the oven to 350°F (180°C).
2. Place the chicken in a casserole dish and season with salt and pepper.
3. Pour melted butter over, and roast in the preheated oven for 30 minutes or until an internal temperature reaches at least 165°F (74°C). Remove from oven and allow to cool.
4. Meanwhile, combine the cauliflower rice, asparagus, and chicken stock in a pot and simmer over medium heat for 6 minutes or until soft.
5. Remove the cauliflower and asparagus from the stovetop and stir in the nutritional yeast.
6. Serve with roasted chicken breast.

Per Serving
calories: 532 | fat: 19g | protein: 29g | carbs: 60g | net carbs: 52g | fiber: 8g

Cheese Cauliflower Soup with Bacon

1 Lean | 3 Greens | 3 Condiments
Prep time: 15 minutes | Cook time: 15 minutes | Serves 4

1 teaspoon olive oil
¼ cup diced onion
½ cup diced celery
2 cloves garlic, minced
4 cups chopped cauliflower florets
1 medium zucchini, chopped
2 cups chicken broth
1 bay leaf
¼ teaspoon salt
¼ teaspoon pepper
1 (5.3-ounce / 150-g) container low-fat plain Greek yogurt
1½ cups reduced-fat shredded Cheddar cheese, divided
12 ounces (340 g) cooked boneless, skinless
    chicken breast, diced
2 slices turkey bacon, cooked and chopped
Chopped chives, for garnish (optional)

1. Heat the olive oil in a large saucepan over medium heat.
2. Add the onion and cook for 2 minutes, or until translucent. Add the celery and garlic and cook for another 2 to 3 minutes.
3. Add the cauliflower, zucchini, chicken broth, bay leaf, salt, and pepper, Cover and bring to a boil, then reduce heat and allow to simmer until vegetables are tender, about 8 minutes.
4. Remove from heat and discard the bay leaf. Purée the mixture with an immersion blender. Slowly mix in the yogurt and 1 cup of the cheese, then add the chicken breast.
5. Garnish with the remaining ½ cup of cheese, bacon, and chives. Serve immediately.

Per Serving
calories: 365 | fat: 16g | protein: 26g | carbs: 29g | net carbs: 25g | fiber: 4g

Chicken with Broccoli and Bell Peppers

1 Leaner | 3 Greens | 1 Healthy Fat | 3 Condiments
Prep time: 15 minutes | Cook time: 13 minutes | Serves 4

2 pounds (907 g) raw, boneless, skinless chicken breast, cut into strips
½ cup light lime vinaigrette dressing
1 teaspoon garlic and herb seasoning blend
2 teaspoons onion powder
1½ cups chopped yellow bell pepper
1½ cups chopped red bell pepper
3 cups chopped raw broccoli
½ ounce (14 g) pine nuts, toasted
Cooking spray

1. Coat the chicken breast strips with the dressing in a large bowl. Sprinkle with seasoning blend and onion powder. Let marinate for 1 hour in the refrigerator.
2. Sauté the peppers and broccoli in a greased skillet for 5 minutes or until tender. Set them aside.
3. Add the marinated chicken, and cook for 8 minutes or until well browned.
4. Transfer the cooked chicken on a large serving plate and add the peppers, broccoli, and toasted pine nuts.
5. Serve immediately.

Per Serving
calories: 679 | fat: 6g | protein: 42g | carbs: 14g | net carbs: 12g | fiber: 2g

Cheese-Stuffed Mushrooms with Cilantro

1 Lean | 3 Greens | 2 Condiments
Prep time: 5 minutes | Cook time: 15 to 19 minutes | Serves 2

4 large portobello mushroom caps, stemmed
1 tablespoon lemon juice
1 tablespoon soy sauce
1 teaspoon olive oil, divided
2 cups reduced-fat shredded Mozzarella cheese
½ cup chopped fresh tomato
½ teaspoon Italian seasoning
1 clove garlic, minced
1 tablespoon chopped fresh cilantro

1. Preheat the oven to 400°F (205°C).
2. Using a spoon, scoop out interior of mushroom caps to create "bowls".
3. In a small bowl, combine lemon juice, soy sauce, and half of olive oil. Brush both sides of the mushroom caps with the mixture.
4. Place the mushroom caps onto a foil-lined baking sheet, and bake until softened, about 10 to 12 minutes.
5. Meanwhile, in a medium bowl, combine Mozzarella, tomatoes, Italian seasoning, garlic, and remaining half of olive oil.
6. Divide the cheese mixture evenly among the mushroom caps, and bake for 5 to 7 minutes more, or until cheese is melted.
7. Serve topped with the cilantro.

Per Serving
calories: 423 | fat: 29g | protein: 31g | carbs: 8g | net carbs: 7g | fiber: 1g

Cheddar Spaghetti Squash Gratin

1 Lean | 3 Greens | 3 Condiments
Prep time: 10 minutes | Cook time: 1 hour | Serves 2

1 (2½-pounds / 1.1-kg) spaghetti squash
Cooking spray
2 eggs, lightly beaten
1 cup reduced-fat shredded Cheddar cheese
½ cup low-fat plain Greek yogurt
2 cloves garlic, minced
½ tablespoon fresh thyme
¼ teaspoon salt
¼ teaspoon pepper
¼ cup reduced-fat grated Parmesan cheese

1. Preheat the oven to 400°F (205°C). Line a baking sheet with parchment paper.
2. Halve the squash and scoop out the seeds. Place the squash face-side down on the prepared baking sheet and bake for about 30 minutes, or until squash is easily pierced with a fork.
3. Remove from the oven and let cool, then scoop out spaghetti strands and place in a large bowl.
4. Lightly grease a casserole dish with cooking spray. In a medium bowl, combine the remaining ingredients except for the Parmesan cheese. Stir mixture into the spaghetti squash strands. Spread into the greased casserole dish. Top with the Parmesan cheese and press down to moisten. Bake uncovered for an additional 30 minutes.
5. Cool for 5 minutes before serving.

Per Serving
calories: 394 | fat: 16g | protein: 31g | carbs: 31g | net carbs: 25g | fiber: 4g

Classic Huevos Rancheros

1 Leanest | 3 Greens | 2 Healthy Fats | 2½ Condiments
Prep time: 5 to 10 minutes | Cook time: 10 minutes | Serves 1

1 teaspoon olive oil, divided
½ cup sliced jalapeño
½ cup diced tomato
½ cup diced bell pepper
¼ teaspoon garlic powder
¼ teaspoon onion powder
1 teaspoon hot pepper sauce (optional)
2 cups liquid egg substitute
⅛ teaspoon salt
¼ teaspoon pepper
1½ ounces (43 g) sliced avocado
½ cup fresh cilantro

1. Heat ½ teaspoon olive oil in a skillet over medium heat.
2. Add the jalapeño, tomato, bell pepper, garlic powder, onion powder, and hot pepper sauce (if desired) and sauté for 5 to 7 minutes.
3. Meanwhile, whisk liquid egg substitute with salt and pepper in a medium bowl.
4. In a separate skillet, heat the remaining ½ teaspoon olive oil over medium heat. Add the egg mixture to hot olive oil and sauté, stirring frequently, until cooked.
5. Serve eggs topped with sautéed vegetables, sliced avocado, and fresh cilantro.

Per Serving
calories: 468 | fat: 12g | protein: 53g | carbs: 39g | net carbs: 33g | fiber: 6g

Bell Pepper Casserole

1 Lean | 3 Greens | 3 Condiments
Prep time: 5 minutes | Cook time: 50 minutes | Serves 4

3 large eggs
12 ounces (340 g) low-fat plain Greek yogurt
½ cup thinly sliced onion
1 clove garlic, minced
1 teaspoon olive oil
¼ teaspoon salt
1 teaspoon cumin
½ teaspoon dry mustard
½ teaspoon coriander
¼ teaspoon cayenne pepper
1 (20-ounce / 567-g) bag frozen chopped bell peppers, thawed
8 ounces (227 g) reduced-fat shredded Cheddar or Mozzarella cheese

1. Preheat the oven to 375°F (190°C).
2. Beat together the eggs and yogurt in a bowl. Set aside.
3. In a medium skillet over medium heat, cook the onion and garlic in olive oil with spices, until the onion is translucent.
4. Add peppers and continue to cook over low heat, 4 to 5 minutes if using frozen and 8 to 10 if using fresh.
5. Spread half the pepper mixture in a deep casserole dish, and top with half the cheese, repeat the layers. Pour the egg mixture over top.
6. Cover and bake for 30 minutes, then uncover and bake for an additional 15 minutes.
7. Serve warm.

Per Serving
calories: 207 | fat: 10g | protein: 20g | carbs: 8g | net carbs: 8g | fiber: 0g

Cauliflower Curry with Cilantro

3 Greens | 1 Healthy Fat | 3 Condiments
Prep time: 8 minutes | Cook time: 25 to 35 minutes | Serves 4

6 cups cauliflower florets
4 teaspoons coconut oil, melted
1 tablespoon lemon juice
2 teaspoons curry powder
1 teaspoon garlic powder
½ teaspoon turmeric
½ teaspoon cayenne
½ teaspoon salt
¼ cup chopped fresh cilantro, for garnish

1. Preheat the oven to 450°F (235°C).
2. In a large bowl, toss cauliflower with coconut oil, lemon juice, curry powder, garlic powder, turmeric, cayenne, and salt.
3. Spread cauliflower onto a large, foil-lined baking sheet in a single layer, and roast for about 25 to 35 minutes, stirring and turning over occasionally, or until tender and golden brown.
4. Serve garnished with the fresh cilantro.

Per Serving
calories: 88 | fat: 5g | protein: 3g | carbs: 10g | net carbs: 6g | fiber: 4g

Green Bean and Mushroom Casserole

¼ Leaner | 3 Greens | ½ Healthy Fat | 3 Condiments
Prep time: 10 minutes | Cook time: 40 minutes | Serves 4

1 (16-ounce / 454-g) bag frozen whole green beans
Cooking spray
2 cups chopped mushrooms
¼ cup diced yellow onion
1 clove garlic, minced
¾ cup nonfat plain Greek yogurt
¼ cup reduced-fat sour cream
1 teaspoon cornstarch
½ packet stevia
½ teaspoon salt
½ teaspoon pepper
½ cup reduced-fat shredded Cheddar cheese
2 tablespoons grated Parmesan cheese

1. Preheat the oven to 350°F (180°C).
2. Microwave the green beans according to package directions.
3. Lightly grease a skillet with cooking spray, and heat over medium heat.
4. Cook the mushrooms, onion, and garlic until tender, about 5 to 7 minutes.
5. Combine the mushroom mixture with green beans in a large bowl, and let cool.
6. Meanwhile, whisk together the yogurt, sour cream, cornstarch, stevia, salt, and pepper in a small bowl. Toss vegetables in sauce mixture until evenly coated. Add Cheddar cheese and stir until well combined.
7. Spread into a lightly greased baking dish and top with Parmesan cheese. Bake until topping is golden brown, about 30 to 35 minutes.
8. Remove from the oven and serve warm.

Per Serving
calories: 97 | fat: 2g | protein: 7g | carbs: 10g | net carbs: 8g | fiber: 2g

Cheese Broccoli Egg Bites

1 Leaner | 3 Greens | 1 Healthy Fat | 2 Condiments
Prep time: 5 minutes | Cook time: 25 to 30 minutes | Serves 4

6 cups steam-in-bag frozen broccoli
¼ cup thinly sliced scallions
4 large eggs
2 cups 1% cottage cheese
1¼ cup shredded Mozzarella cheese
¼ cup Parmesan cheese
2 teaspoons olive oil
1 teaspoons garlic powder
¼ teaspoon salt
Cooking spray

1. Preheat the oven to 375°F (190°C).
2. Cook broccoli according to package directions. Once cooled, add broccoli to a food processor and blend until finely chopped. Add scallions, eggs, cottage cheese, Mozzarella, Parmesan, olive oil, garlic powder, and salt to broccoli, and blend until well combined.
3. Scoop mixture into 20 to 24 slots of two lightly greased muffin tins. Bake in the preheated oven for 25 to 30 minutes, or until golden brown.
4. Serve warm.

Per Serving
calories: 269 | fat: 13g | protein: 29g | carbs: 8g | net carbs: 6g | fiber: 2g

Cheddar Beef and Lettuce

1 Lean | 3 Greens | 3 Condiments | 1 Healthy Fat
Prep time: 5 minutes | Cook time: 15 minutes | Serves 2

2 tablespoons chopped white onion
10 ounces (284 g) ground lean beef
4 tablespoons Thousand Island dressing
¼ teaspoon white vinegar
¼ teaspoon onion powder
5 cups green lettuce, shredded
2 ounces (57 g) dill pickle slices
4 tablespoons Cheddar cheese, grated
1 teaspoon sesame seeds
Cooking spray, as required

Per Serving
calories: 369 | fat: 19g | protein: 36g | carbs: 13g | net carbs: 11g | fiber: 2g

1. Put the chopped onion in the air fryer basket and spray some cooking oil.
2. Set the temperature to 300°F (150°C) and fry for 3 minutes.
3. Keep shaking the pan intermittently until the onion become wilt.
4. Transfer it to a plate.
5. Now add the lean beef in the air fryer basket and spray some cooking oil.
6. Set the temperature to 400°F (205°C) and cook for 5 minutes.
7. After 5 minutes, shake the basket and spray some more cooking oil.
8. Again, air fry for another 5 minutes.
9. Now prepare the dressing by mixing onion powder, Thousand Island dressing, and vinegar.
10. On the serving plate, place the lettuce and top it with cooked beef and scatter the cooked onion.
11. Sprinkle the grated cheese over it and top it with pickle slices.
12. Finally, scatter the dressing and sprinkle the sesame seeds.
13. Serve hot.

Zucchini Breadsticks with Mozzarella

1 Lean | 3 Greenss | 2 Condiments | 1 Optional Snack
Prep time: 10 minutes | Cook time: 35 minutes | Serves 2

2 cups shredded zucchini
1 large egg
2 packets Sea Salt Crackers, finely ground
1¾ cups low-fat Mozzarella, grated
½ teaspoon Italian seasoning
1 cup canned fire-roasted tomatoes, diced
1 clove garlic
½ teaspoon garlic salt
¼ teaspoon salt

1. Preheat the air fryer to 450°F (235°C).
2. Put the shredded zucchini in a think dish towel and squeeze the water as much as possible.
3. Place the squeezed zucchini in a bowl and crumble.
4. Add egg, one-third of grated Mozzarella, Italian seasoning and combine it well.
5. Spread a parchment paper in the air fryer baking tray and place the zucchini mixture in square shape or rectangular shape.
6. Place the baking tray into the air fryer and bake for about 25 minutes under 450°F (235°C).
7. While the baking is in progress, let us make the marinara sauce.
8. In a blender, place the diced tomatoes, salt, garlic, and blitz until they become a smooth puree.
9. After 25 minutes, check the baking consistency, and if done correctly, reduce the temperature to 400°F (205°C).
10. Drizzle the remaining shredded Mozzarella cheese and garlic salt on top of the crust.
11. Continue baking for another 10 minutes until the cheese starts to melt.
12. Stop backing and transfer the crust into a plate and allow it cool.
13. Cut into breadstick shape and serve with marinara sauce.

Per Serving
calories: 466 | fat: 28g | protein: 38g | carbs: 17g | net carbs: 13g | fiber: 4g

Grilled Chicken Breast and Veggies

1 Lean | 3 Greenss | 3 Condiments | 1 Healthy Fat
Prep time: 15 minutes | Cook time: 20 minutes | Serves 2

¾ pound (340 g) chicken breast, skinless and boneless
¼ teaspoon salt
¼ teaspoon pepper
½ cup Kabocha squash, cubed
½ cup zucchini, finely chopped
½ cup summer squash, finely chopped
½ cup broccoli, finely chopped
4 cherry tomatoes, halved
4 radishes, thinly sliced
½ cup red cabbage, finely chopped

Green Dressing:
¼ cup low-fat Greek yogurt
½ cup fresh basil, chopped
1 clove garlic
2 tablespoons lemon juice
¼ teaspoon ground pepper
¼ teaspoon salt

1. Preheat air fryer to 360°F (182°C).
2. Season chicken with pepper and salt in a shallow bowl.
3. Place the chicken in the air fryer and roast for 12-15 minutes.
4. When the internal chicken temperature reaches 165°F (74°C), remove it on a chopping board and cut it into bite-size.
5. Now in a baking tray, place the chopped yellow summer squash, kabocha squash, broccoli, and zucchini.
6. Cook it in the air fryer for 5 minutes until they become tender.
7. Now prepare the green dressing by combining the green dressing in a blender until they become a smooth puree.
8. To serve, place the veggies in a serving plate and place the sliced cherry tomatoes, radishes, chopped cabbages, and chicken.
9. Top it with green dressing.

Per Serving
calories: 336 | fat: 16g | protein: 29g | carbs: 10g | net carbs: 8g | fiber: 2g

Cheese Zucchini with Spinach

1 Lean | 3 Greens | 1 Condiment
Prep time: 10 minutes | Cook time: 25 minutes | Serves 2

½ cup spinach
1 large zucchini
½ cup Ricotta, skimmed
1 egg
¾ cup Mozzarella cheese, grated, divided
¼ cup Parmesan cheese, shredded
¼ cup low-sugar tomato sauce
⅛ teaspoon salt
⅛ teaspoon nutmeg
Cooking oil, as required

1. Preheat air fryer to 375°F (190°C).
2. Julien zucchini into thin slices and keep ready to use.
3. Combine egg, ricotta, half of shredded Mozzarella, spinach, Parmesan, nutmeg, and salt in a medium bowl.
4. Place a parchment paper in the baking tray and spray some cooking oil on it.
5. Layer the zucchini slices in two sets, overlapping one another on a plate.
6. Place the ricotta mixture at the end of the zucchini slice and roll-up.
7. Now place the rolled-up zucchini on the parchment paper.
8. On top of the zucchini, pour the tomato sauce.
9. Sprinkle grated cheese over it and bake for 25 minutes.
10. Serve hot.

Per Serving
calories: 296 | fat: 29g | protein: 16g | carbs: 7g | net carbs: 5g | fiber: 2g

Chicken with Lettuce Salad

1 Lean | 3 Greens | 3 Condiments | 1 Healthy Fat
Prep time: 15 minutes | Cook time: 25 minutes | Serves 2

Chicken:
¾ pound (340 g) chicken breast, boneless and skinless
¾ tablespoon butter, melted
¼ teaspoon ground pepper
¼ teaspoon salt

Salad:
3 cups lettuce, roughly chopped
½ cup green cucumber, sliced
8 ounces (227 g) cherry tomatoes, halved
5 Kalamata olives, pitted
¼ cup low-fat Feta cheese
1 tablespoon lemon juice
¼ teaspoon pepper
¼ teaspoon salt

1. Wash the chicken and pat dry.
2. Preheat the air fryer to 355°F (179°C).
3. Season the chicken with salt, pepper, butter, and allow it to marinate for 15 minutes.
4. Place the marinated chicken in the air fryer grill and roast for 25 minutes until the chicken's internal temperature reaches 160°F (70°C).
5. After cooking, remove it on a cutting board and allow it to settle down the heat.
6. Now combine all the salad ingredients in a large bowl and toss well.
7. Slice the chicken and place it over the salad.
8. Serve hot.

Per Serving
calories: 481 | fat: 25g | protein: 22g | carbs: 22g | net carbs: 18g | fiber: 4g

Chicken Burgers with Cucumber Salad

1 Lean | 3 Greens | 3 Condiments | 1 Healthy Fat
Prep time: 15 minutes | Cook time: 10 minutes | Serves 2

Chicken Burgers:
½ pound (227 g) 95% lean ground chicken
1 ounce (28 g) low-fat Feta
1 egg
½ cup fresh spinach, chopped
5 Kalamata olives, pitted and chopped
½ tablespoon cornstarch
1 teaspoon oregano, dried
1 clove garlic, chopped
¼ teaspoon salt
¼ teaspoon ground pepper
1 teaspoon olive oil
1 tomato, sliced
1 lettuce head, cut into pieces
Cooking spray, as required

Salad:
1 small cucumber
½ tablespoon mint, fresh, chopped
½ tablespoon dill, fresh, finely chopped
1 teaspoon lemon juice
1 garlic clove, minced
½ cup low-fat Greek yogurt

1. In a large bowl, wash the minced chicken, and using a sieve, drain the minced chicken until the water completely drains out.
2. Cut half of the cucumber into small pieces and slice the remaining half into thin slices. Keep both in a separate bowl.
3. Add all the salad ingredients in the bowl, which has the cucumber cut into small pieces, and refrigerate it.
4. Combine egg, feta, olives, spinach, cornstarch, chopped garlic, salt, oregano, and pepper in a large bowl.
5. Add minced chicken into the bowl and mix it well.
6. Make 2 burger patties out of it.
7. Spray some cooking oil on a towel and rub on the air fryer grill.
8. Place the burgers on the grill.
9. Set the temperature to 160°F (70°C), grill it for 10 minutes, and flip the sides after 5 minutes.
10. Take out salad from the refrigerator and transfer to a serving plate.
11. Place the burger on the salad and dress it with the sliced tomatoes and cucumber.

Per Serving
calories: 528 | fat: 32g | protein: 44g | carbs: 14g | net carbs: 11g | fiber: 3g

Shrimp and Cucumber with Avocado Sauce

1 Lean | 1⅔ Greens | 3 Condiments | 2 Healthy Fats
Prep time: 5 minutes | Cook time: 12 minutes | Serves 2

15 ounces (425 g) cooked shrimp
1 cup cucumber, sliced
1½ teaspoons olive oil

Sauce:
1 tablespoon Creole seasoning
4 ounces (113 g) avocado sauce
½ cup green onion, sliced
2 tablespoons fresh cilantro, finely chopped
1 tablespoon lemon juice
¼ teaspoon salt
½ teaspoon cayenne

1. In a large bowl, put the shrimps, olive oil, and toss well.
2. Place the marinated shrimps in the air fryer.
3. Set the temperature to 400°F (205°C) and air fry for 12 minutes by intermittently shaking the air fryer basket.
4. For preparing the sauce, in a large bowl, combine all the sauce ingredients.
5. On a serving plate, arrange the sliced cucumber and top it with avocado sauce.
6. On top, place the air fried shrimps.
7. Enjoy the shrimp bites.

Per Serving
calories: 356 | fat: 14g | protein: 45g | carbs: 9g | net carbs: 4g | fiber: 5g

Blackened Shrimp Lettuce Wraps

1 Lean | 3 Greens | 3 Condiments | 2 Healthy Fats
Prep time: 15 minutes | Cook time: 14 minutes | Serves 2

1 pound (454 g) raw shrimps, peeled, deveined
½ tablespoon blackened seasoning
2 teaspoons olive oil, divided
½ cup Greek yogurt
3 ounces (85 g) avocado sauce
2 tablespoons lime juice

¾ cup tomato, sliced
¼ cup bell pepper, green, diced
¼ cup onion, red, chopped
¼ cup cilantro, chopped
1 jalapeño pepper, deseeded and chopped
6 large lettuce leaves

1. Wash the shrimps thoroughly and pat dry.
2. In a large bowl, put the shrimps, blackened seasoning, half of the olive oil and combine well to marinate.
3. Apply some oil to the air fryer basket.
4. Layer the marinated shrimps on the air fryer basket.
5. Set the temperature to 400°F (205°C) and air fry for 14 minutes by flipping the side intermittently for an even frying experience.
6. For making the avocado sauce, in a blender, put avocado sauce, Greek yogurt, 1 tablespoon lime juice, and blend to become a smooth puree.
7. For making the tomato salsa, toss bell pepper, tomatoes, jalapeno pepper, cilantro, onion, and remaining 1 tablespoon lime juice in a large bowl.
8. Spread the lettuce leaves and evenly place shrimps and avocado sauce.
9. Place the tomato salsa on top of it.
10. Enjoy your shrimp lettuce wrap.

Per Serving

calories: 683 | fat: 17g | protein: 68g | carbs: 78g | net carbs: 30g | fiber: 48g

Chicken with Cauliflower Risotto

1 Lean | 3 Greens | 2 Condiments | 1 Healthy Fat
Prep time: 10 minutes | Cook time: 38 minutes | Serves 2

1 pound (454 g) chicken breast, skinless and boneless
¼ teaspoon ground pepper
¼ teaspoon salt
1 tablespoon butter, softened
2¾ cups cauliflower, finely grated
¼ cup asparagus, chopped
¼ cup chicken stock
2 tablespoons large flake nutritional yeast

1. Wash the chicken breast and pat dry.
2. Preheat the air fryer to 350°F (180°C).
3. In a large bowl, marinate the chicken with salt and pepper.
4. Place the marinated chicken on the air fryer pan and pour the softened butter on top of the chicken.
5. Air fry the chicken for 30 minutes until the internal meat temperature reaches 165°F (74°C).
6. After cooking, remove it from the air fryer and keep aside.
7. Now in a large bowl, combine the chopped asparagus, grated cauliflower, and the chicken stock.
8. Transfer it into the air fryer tray and cook for 8 minutes until they become tender.
9. After that, remove it from the air fryer and transfer it into a bowl.
10. Add the yeast and stir to combine the risotto.
11. Slice the chicken and serve on a plate along with cauliflower asparagus risotto.

Per Serving

calories: 528 | fat: 27g | protein: 55g | carbs: 13g | net carbs: 8g | fiber: 5g

Paprika Turkey and Cabbage

1 Lean | 3 Greens | 3 Condiments | 2 Healthy Fats
Prep time: 10 minutes | Cook time: 36 minutes | Serves 2

¾ pound (340 g) lean ground turkey
1½ cups cabbage, finely chopped
1 green onion, finely shredded
⅛ cup roasted pine nuts, chopped
1 teaspoon paprika
1 teaspoon salt, divided
1 teaspoon coarsely crushed pepper, divided
½ teaspoon olive oil
½ pound (227 g) small fennel bulb
1 tablespoon Parmesan cheese, grated

1. Wash turkey and drain using a colander.
2. Preheat air fryer at 400°F (205°C) for 10 minutes.
3. Combine minced turkey meat, shredded cabbage, pine nuts, half of the salt, minced onion, and half pepper in a large bowl.
4. In the air fryer tray, spread a parchment paper and place the turkey meat mix and make that into a 7" x 4" size loaf shape.
5. Place the tray in the air fryer oven.
6. At 400°F (205°C), bake the meatloaf for 30 minutes until the meat's internal temperature becomes 165°F (74°C).
7. After cooking, remove and keep ready to use it.
8. Now start working on the fennel.
9. Remove the fennel stalks and chop the fennel bulbs into halves lengthwise.
10. Cut the halves again and remove the core.
11. Slightly apply some olive oil to the air fryer basket.
12. Place the chopped fennel bulbs onto it and air fry for 6 minutes at 350°F (180°C) until they become tender and become slightly brown.
13. Once they become tender, transfer them into a serving plate.
14. Drizzle the remaining salt, pepper, and give a gentle toss.
15. Now slice the air fried turkey loaf and place it on top of the fried fennel.
16. Drizzle shredded Parmesan cheese on top and serve hot.

Per Serving

calories: 403 | fat: 22g | protein: 36g | carbs: 17g | net carbs: 11g | fiber: 6g

Cauliflower Curry with Cilantro

3 Greens | 3 Condiments | 1 Healthy Fat
Prep time: 5 minutes | Cook time: 35 minutes | Serves 2

3 cups cauliflower florets
2 teaspoons coconut oil
1 tablespoon lemon juice
2 teaspoons curry powder
1 teaspoon garlic, ground
¼ teaspoon ground cayenne
¼ teaspoon turmeric powder
¼ teaspoon salt
¼ cup fresh cilantro, coarsely chopped
Cooking spray, as required

1. Put the cauliflower florets in the large bowl.
2. Pour lemon juice, coconut oil, and toss to mix.
3. Add curry powder, turmeric powder, garlic powder, salt, cayenne powder, and gently toss to mix all the ingredients on the cauliflower florets.
4. Line aluminum foil on the air fryer tray and spray some cooking oil.
5. Spread the cauliflower on the air fryer baking tray.
6. Set the temperature to 450°F (235°C), and air fry them for 35 minutes until the florets turn tender and golden brown.
7. After cooking, transfer it to a serving bowl.
8. Garnish with fresh chopped cilantro and serve hot.

Per Serving
calories: 91 | fat: 5g | protein: 4g | carbs: 10g | net carbs: 5g | fiber: 5g

Cheese Spaghetti Squash with Eggs

1 Lean | 3 Greens | 3 Condiments
Prep time: 5 minutes | Cook time: 1hr and 5 minutes |
    Serves 2

1 medium spaghetti squash
3 eggs
1½ cups Cottage cheese
5 packets zero-calorie sugar substitute
¼ teaspoon ground cinnamon
¼ teaspoon salt
⅛ teaspoon ground nutmeg
Cooking spray, as required

1. Cut the squash into half and remove the seeds.
2. Line the air fryer baking with foil paper and bake the squash face down at 375°F (190°C) for 30 minutes.
3. After 30 minutes, remove it from the air fryer allow to settle down the heat.
4. Scoop the spaghetti strands (3 cups) into a bowl.
5. Add all the remaining ingredients into the bowl and combine it well.
6. Spray some cooking oil in the casserole and spread the spaghetti mixture.
7. Place it in the air fryer and bake for 35 minutes at 375°F (190°C) until its edge become golden.
8. After that, remove from the air fryer and allow it to settle down the heat.
9. Serve hot.

Per Serving
calories: 373 | fat: 31g | protein: 32g | carbs: 12g | net carbs: 11g | fiber: 1g

Salmon with Maple Mustard Glaze

1 Lean | 3 Condiments | 2 Healthy Fats
Prep time: 5 minutes | Cook time: 20 minutes | Serves 2

¾ pound (340 g) salmon fillet, cut into 4 equal parts
¼ cup fish broth
¼ cup pancake syrup
1 tablespoon grainy mustard
½ tablespoon low-sodium soy sauce
½ teaspoon ground pepper
Cooking oil spray, as required.

1. Wash and pat dry the salmon fillet.
2. In the air fryer tray, spray some cooking oil and arrange the fillets.
3. Combine maple syrup, soy sauce, butter, and mustard in a small bowl.
4. Pour the mix over the salmon fillets.
5. Drizzle some pepper ground on top.
6. Select the bake option in the air fryer and set the temperature to 425°F (220°C).
7. Set the timer to 20 minutes and start cooking.
8. It must be ready, and check with a fork if it flakes.
9. Serve hot.

Per Serving
calories: 326 | fat: 12g | protein: 36g | carbs: 15g | net carbs: 14g | fiber: 1g

Italian Chicken Bake

1 Lean | 2 Greens | 3 Condiments | 1 Healthy Fat
Prep time: 5 minutes | Cook time: 30 minutes | Serves 2

10 ounces (284 g) shredded chicken
½ teaspoon garlic, ground
½ teaspoon Italian seasoning
1 cup low-carb tomato sauce
4 tablespoons cream cheese
½ cup low-fat plain Greek yogurt
¼ cup Parmesan cheese, grated
Cooking spray, as required

1. Wash the shredded chicken and drain suing sieve.
2. Preheat the air fryer at 350°F (180°C) for 10 minutes.
3. Spray some cooking oil in the bottom of the air fryer tray.
4. Put the shredded chicken in the air fryer tray.
5. In a small bowl, mix all the ingredients except the tomato sauce.
6. Pour the mixture over the chicken.
7. On top, scatter the shredded Parmesan cheese.
8. Bake for 30 minutes until the bubble starts.
9. Remove it from the air fryer and serve hot.

Per Serving
calories: 370 | fat: 17g | protein: 39g | carbs: 14g | net carbs: 12g | fiber: 2g

Baked Broccoli with Cheddar

1 Lean | 3 Greens | 1½ Condiments
Prep time: 5 minutes | Cook time: 51 minutes | Serves 2

3 cups small broccoli florets
3 tablespoons water
4 eggs
½ cup unsweetened almond milk
¼ teaspoon ground pepper
¼ teaspoon salt
¼ teaspoon ground cayenne pepper
2 ounces (57 g) low-fat Cheddar cheese, grated
Cooking spray, as required

1. In the air fryer tray, pour 3 tablespoons of water and place the broccoli into it.
2. Set the temperature to 390°F (199°C) and air fry for 6 minutes.
3. Transfer the cooked broccoli into a bowl and discard the excess water.
4. In a mixing bowl, combine almond milk, eggs, and other seasonings.
5. Spray some cooking on the baking tray.
6. Now arrange the cooked broccoli in the baking tray.
7. Scatter the grated cheese over the broccoli and pour the egg-almond mixture on the broccoli.
8. Re-set the temperature to 345°F (174°C) and select the bake option.
9. Set the timer to 45 minutes and bake until the center becomes firm.
10. Remove it from the air fryer when the top turns to light brown.
11. Serve hot.

Per Serving
calories: 395 | fat: 36g | protein: 28g | carbs: 10g | net carbs: 8g | fiber: 2g

Mustard Honey Chicken Nuggets

1 Lean | 1 Fueling | 2 Condiments
Prep time: 5 minutes | Cook time: 20 minutes | Serves 2

12 ounces (340 g) chicken breast, skinless, boneless, cubed
1 egg, beaten
2 sachets Honey Mustard and Onion sticks
¼ cup low-fat plain Greek yogurt
2 teaspoons spicy brown mustard
¼ teaspoon garlic, ground
Cooking spray, as required

1. Wash chicken and pat dry.
2. Crush the honey mustard and onion sticks into breadcrumb consistency in a shallow bowl.
3. Preheat the air fryer to 400°F (205°C).
4. Keep the beaten egg and crushed honey mustard and onion stick in two separate shallow bowls.
5. Line a foil paper in the air fryer baking tray and lightly grease it with cooking spray.
6. Take boneless chicken cub one by one, dip in the honey and dredge in the honey mustard and onion stick powder and layer it on the tray.
7. Repeat the entire chicken cubes.
8. Bake the chicken for 20 minutes by flipping intermittently until the meat's internal temperature reaches 165°F (74°C).
9. While the baking is in progress, mix garlic powder, Greek yogurt, and mustard in a small bowl to make the dip.
10. Serve the nugget with the dip.

Per Serving
calories: 380 | fat: 21g | protein: 41g | carbs: 3g |
net carbs: 3g | fiber: 0g

Salmon Burgers with Cucumber Salad

1 Lean | 3 Greens | 3 Condiments | ½ Snack
Prep time: 10 minutes | Cook time: 13 minutes | Serves 2

Salmon Burgers:
5 ounces (142 g) canned pink salmon, boneless
1 egg
1½ tablespoons light mayonnaise
½ teaspoon lemon juice
1 tablespoon onion, finely grated
¼ teaspoon dried parsley
¼ teaspoon ground pepper
10 ounces (284 g) multigrain crackers, crushed
Cooking spray, as required

Salad:
3 cups cucumber, peeled and sliced
3 ounces (85 g) low-fat plain Greek yogurt
2 tablespoons apple cider vinegar
1 tablespoon fresh dill
¼ teaspoon pepper
¼ teaspoon salt

1. Drain the salmon thoroughly
2. Beat the egg in a small bowl.
3. Combine mayonnaise, egg, onion, lemon juice, pepper, and parsley in a medium bowl to become a smooth paste.
4. Put the salmon and crushed cracked into it and gently fold the mixture.
5. Make the mixture into two patties.
6. Spray some cooking on the air fryer baking tray and place the patties onto it.
7. Set the temperature to 375°F (190°C) and bake for 13 minutes by flipping sides intermittently.
8. While the cooking is going on, in a medium bowl, gently mix vinegar, yogurt, dill, pepper, and salt.
9. Add the sliced cucumber into it and gently mix.
10. Serve the salmon burger along with the salad.

Per Serving
calories: 980 | fat: 42g | protein: 32g | carbs: 94g | net carbs: 90g | fiber: 4g

Roasted Veggies and Tofu

1 Lean | 3 Greens | 3 Condiments
Prep time: 10 minutes | Cook time: 12 minutes | Serves 2

¾ cup cauliflower florets
¾ cup broccoli florets
¾ cup red cabbage, coarsely chopped
1 large bell pepper, cored, cut into lengthwise
¼ teaspoon ground pepper
¼ teaspoon salt
1 pound (454 g) tofu, cut into ½» cut cubes
1 tablespoon powdered peanut butter
1½ tablespoons water
¼ tablespoon Sambal
Cooking spray, as required

1. Wash all the veggies and pat dry.
2. Preheat the air fryer to 375°F (190°C).
3. Layer all the vegetables in the air fryer baking tray and lightly spray with cooking oil.
4. Drizzle pepper and salt over it.
5. Bake the veggies for 12 minutes by flipping intermittently, until they get caramelized and tender.
6. Once cooked, remove it to a bowl.
7. In the air fryer baking tray, layer the tofu cubes and air fry at 375°F (190°C) for 15 minutes by flipping intermittently.
8. For making the peanut sauce, combine peanut powder, sambal, and water in a small bowl.
9. In a serving bowl, place the tofu topped with air-fried veggies.
10. Pour sauce on top of the veggies and serve.

Per Serving
calories: 673| fat: 47g | protein: 42 | carbs: 33g | net carbs: 22g | fiber: 11g

Cucumber and Beef Burger Lettuce Wraps

1 Lean | 3 Greens | 3 Condiments
Prep time: 25 minutes | Cook time: 8 minutes | Serves 2

½ pound (227 g) lean beef, minced
1 teaspoon salt, divided
½ teaspoon ground black pepper, divided
1 teaspoon garlic, crushed, divided
½ scallion, finely minced
½ tablespoon capers, finely minced

1½ ounces (43 g)low-fat Feta cheese, shredded
½ pound (227 g) green cucumber
¼ cup low-fat plain Greek yogurt
4 lettuce leaves, large
Cooking spray, as required

1. Wash and drain the minced beef thoroughly using a sieve.
2. In a large bowl, combine beef with half of the crushed garlic, pepper, and salt.
3. Fold in the shredded feta into the beef mixture to make 4 equal size patties and keep it ready.
4. Grate the cucumber, add the remaining salt, and combine it.
5. Put the grated cucumber in a sieve and allow it to drain for 10 minutes.
6. Now transfer it into a clean cotton towel and squeeze the water maximum.
7. Transfer the squeezed grated cucumber into a medium bowl.
8. Add the remaining salt, garlic, pepper, and also add the yogurt.
9. Combine it very well.
10. In the air fry tray, spray some cooking oil.
11. Place the patties on the fryer tray and broil at 375°F (190°C) for 8 minutes by flipping sides intermittently until the meat's internal temperature reaches 165°F (74°C).
12. Serve the burger on lettuce leaves toping with cucumber tzatziki.

Per Serving
calories: 262 | fat: 11g | protein: 32g | carbs: 7g | net carbs: 5g | fiber: 2g

Mozzarella Cauliflower Rolls

¼ Lean | 2 Greens | 3 Condiments
Prep time: 5 minutes | Cook time: 30 minutes | Serves 2

2 cups cauliflower, riced
¼ cup almond flour
1 egg
¼ cup low-fat Mozzarella cheese, grated
1 tablespoon fresh rosemary, finely chopped
¼ teaspoon salt
Cooking spray, as required

1. In a large bowl, mix all the ingredients.
2. Line the air fryer baking tray with foiled baking paper.
3. Spray cooking slightly on the foil sheet.
4. Make 6 even shaped biscuits with the mixture and place on the baking liner.
5. Set the temperature to 390°F (199°C) and bake for 30 minutes until it turns golden brown.
6. Serve hot.

Per Serving
calories: 145 | fat: 8g | protein: 11g | carbs: 6g | net carbs: 4g | fiber: 2g

Lobster Lettuce Roll

1 Leaner | 3 Greens | 1 Condiment | 2 Healthy Fats
Prep time: 10 minutes | Cook time: 4 minutes | Serves 2

6 ounces (170 g) lobster meat, cooked
1 small Romaine lettuce
½ tablespoon butter, melted
½ cup low-fat plain Greek yogurt
1 tablespoon mayonnaise with olive oil base
1 small stalk celery, smartly diced
1 teaspoon lemon juice
½ tablespoon fresh chives, chopped
¼ teaspoon Old Bay seasoning
¼ teaspoon ground pepper
⅛ teaspoon salt

1. Preheat the air fryer to 375°F (190°C).
2. Cut the romaine hearts in lengthwise to half.
3. Make some lobster filling in boat shape by removing some inner leaves of romaine hearts.
4. Apply some butter inside portion of the boat-shaped romaine leaves.
5. Place the coated lettuce in the air fryer tray and select broil at 375°F (190°C) for 3-4 minutes to get slightly charred and have the flavor of lettuce.
6. Mix all the ingredients, except the lobster meat, in a large bowl.
7. Now fold in all the lobster gently until the mix gets coated on the lobster.
8. Distribute the coated lobster in the boat-shaped lettuce evenly.
9. Serve and enjoy.

Per Serving
calories: 362 | fat: 9g | protein: 35g | carbs: 37g | net carbs: 22g | fiber: 15g

Salmon with Cucumber and Tomato Salad

1 Lean | 3 Greens | 3 Condiments
Prep time: 10 minutes | Cook time: 10 minutes | Serves 2

¾ pound (340 g) salmon
2 cups cucumber, sliced
8 ounces (227 g) cherry tomatoes, cut into halves
⅛ cup cider vinegar
⅛ cup fresh dill, chopped
⅛ teaspoon salt
⅛ teaspoon ground pepper
½ tablespoon Za'atar
2 lemons, cut into wedges

1. Set the air temperature to 355°F (179°C) and preheat.
2. Put cucumber, tomatoes, vinegar, dill, salt, and pepper in a medium bowl and toss to mix well.
3. Rub Za'atar on the salmon and allow it to season for 3-4 minutes.
4. Line the baking tray of the air fryer with a foil baking paper.
5. Place the seasoned salmon on it without overlapping.
6. Broil it for 10 minutes flipping sides halfway through.
7. Serve hot with salad.
8. Top it with lemon wedges.

Per Serving
calories: 348 | fat: 36g | protein: 12g | carbs: 33g | net carbs: 31g | fiber: 2g

Broiled Beef Steak with Broccoli

1 Lean | 1 Green | 3 Condiments
Prep time: 10 minutes | Cook time: 11 minutes | Serves 2

16 ounces (454 g) lean rib-eye steak
6 cups broccoli
Marinade:
¼ cup beef broth
2 tablespoons lime juice
2 teaspoons ground cumin
2 teaspoons ground coriander
1 clove garlic, minced
2 tablespoons cooking oil

1. Wash the steak and drain the water thoroughly.
2. Mix all the marinade ingredients in a blender by slowly adding oil.
3. Place the steak in a dish and pour the marinade over it.
4. Refrigerate for 6-8 hours for marination.
5. Place the marinated steaks in the air fryer grill tray.
6. Set the temperature to 400°F (205°C) and broil for 7 minutes, flipping sides halfway through and applying the remaining marinade mix.
7. After cooking, transfer it to a serving plate.
8. Now air fry broccoli for 4 minutes, shaking intermittently for even air frying.
9. Serve the steaks along with broccoli.

Per Serving
calories: 762 | fat: 62g | protein: 45g | carbs: 9g | net carbs: 5g | fiber: 4g

Shrimp-Stuffed Eggplant

1 Lean | 3 Greens | 3 Condiments | 2 Healthy Fats
Prep time: 10 minutes | Cook time: 33 minutes |
Serves 2

1 large eggplant
¼ teaspoon salt, divided
Cooking spray, as required
½ pound (227 g) shrimp, peeled and deveined
¼ teaspoon ground black pepper
1 cup cauliflower, riced
1 scallion, without the head, finely chopped
¼ cup low-fat plain Greek yogurt
¼ cup Parmesan cheese, shredded

1. Wash eggplant and cut into 4 rounds.
2. Remove the flesh and make it into a cup shape.
3. Chop the flesh and keep ready to use.
4. Rub inside with half portion of the salt.
5. Put in the air fryer grill tray and bake for 18 minutes at 450°F (235°C).
6. After baking, keep it aside.
7. Now season the shrimp with pepper and the remaining salt.
8. Place it in the air fryer grill tray and spray some cooking oil.
9. Broil it for 5 minutes by flipping sides halfway through the cooking, until it turns to pink.
10. After that, remove and keep it aside.
11. In the air fry tray, put the chopped eggplant flesh, cauliflower rice, scallions, and air fry or 3-4 minutes until they become tender.
12. Transfer the air fried veggies into a bowl and add the fried shrimps into it.
13. Add yogurt and combine to mix.
14. Now scoop the mix into the eggplant cup.
15. Top it with grated Parmesan cheese.
16. Put it in the air fryer baking grill and bake for 15 minutes at 450°F (235°C).
17. Serve hot.

Per Serving
calories: 433 | fat: 52g | protein: 42g | carbs: 23g | net carbs: 14g | fiber: 9g

Cheese Broccoli Bites with Scallions

1 Lean | 3 Greens | 2 Condiments | 1 Healthy Fat
Prep time: 5 minutes | Cook time: 40 minutes | Serves 2

3 cups frozen broccoli
¼ cup scallions, thinly sliced
2 eggs
1 cup Cottage cheese
¾ cup Mozzarella cheese, grated
¼ cup Parmesan cheese, shredded
1 teaspoon olive oil
½ teaspoon garlic powder
⅛ teaspoon salt
2 cups water
Cooking spray, as required

1. Preheat the air fryer to 375°F (190°C).
2. Place the broccoli in an air fryer, save bowl, and pour water.
3. Air fryer it for 10 minutes until the broccoli becomes tender.
4. Drain the water and transfer the broccoli into the blender.
5. Blitz it until it chopped well.
6. Now add cottage cheese, scallions, Parmesan, Mozzarella, eggs, olive oil, salt, and garlic into the blender.
7. Pulse it until it gets mixed well.
8. Transfer it to 12 muffin tins evenly after greasing them.
9. Place it in the air fryer and bake for 30 minutes until the filling becomes firm and its top turns to a golden brown.
10. After baking, remove them from the air fryer.
11. Allow it to settle down the heat, and serve.

Per Serving
calories: 428 | fat: 22g | protein: 44g | carbs: 19g | net carbs: 11g | fiber: 8g

Chicken-Stuffed Pepper Nachos

1 Lean | 3 Greens | 1 Condiment | 1 Heavy Fat
Prep time: 10 minutes | Cook time: 13 minutes | Serves 2

¼ cup jalapeño pepper, diced
12 bell peppers, halved, cored
6 ounces (170 g) chicken breast, canned in low sodium water
3 ounces (85 g) avocado, mashed
¼ cup low-fat plain Greek yogurt
1 cup low-fat Cheddar cheese, divided
½ teaspoon chili powder
¼ cup scallions, chopped
Cooking oil spray, as required

1. Drain the chicken thoroughly.
2. Put the diced jalapeno pepper in the air fryer tray and spray some cooking spray oil.
3. Air fry it at 390°F (199°C) for 2-3 minutes until they become tender.
4. Transfer them to a large bowl, add chicken, yogurt, avocado, half portion of cheese, jalapeno, chili powder, and combine to mix.
5. In the air fryer tray, arrange the bell pepper and fill the chicken mixture.
6. Top them with the remaining cheese.
7. Bake it for 10 minutes until the cheese starts to melt.
8. Serve with garnished scallion.

Per Serving
calories: 556| fat: 29g | protein: 44g | carbs: 33g | net carbs: 27g | fiber: 6g

Cheddar Herb Pizza Bites with Basil

1 Fueling | ¼ Lean | ½ Green | 2 Condiments | ½ Healthy Fat
Prep time: 5 minutes | Cook time: 10 minutes | Serves 2

2 sachets Optavia Buttermilk Cheddar Herb Biscuit
½ cup unsweetened almond milk
1 teaspoon olive oil
½ cup basil leaves, julienned
2 ounces (57 g) Mozzarella stick, cut into 6 small pieces
1 medium tomato, sliced
1 tablespoon balsamic vinegar
Cooking spray, as required

1. Preheat the air fryer to 450°F (235°C).
2. Combine the Buttermilk Cheddar Herb Biscuit, olive oil, and almond milk in a large bowl until they become a smooth paste.
3. Take 6 muffin tin and spray lightly with cooking oil.
4. Distribute the mixture evenly into the muffin tin.
5. Place the muffin tin on the air fryer grill tray, topped with Mozzarella and sliced tomato.
6. Sprinkle basil on top and bake for 10 minutes, until the biscuit mixture becomes brown and cheese starts to bubble.
7. Drop balsamic vinegar on top before serving.

Per Serving
calories: 306 | fat: 13g | protein: 10g | carbs: 34g | net carbs: 30g | fiber: 4g

Cauliflower Egg Muffins with Tomatoes

1 Lean | 3 Greens | 1 Healthy Fat | 1
    Condiment
Prep time: 10 minutes | Cook time: 25
    minutes | Serves 2

Egg Muffins:
4 eggs
1 cup liquid egg whites
¼ cup low-fat plain Greek yogurt
¼ teaspoon salt
Cooking spray

Tomato Mix:
6 ounces (170 g) cauliflower rice, frozen
1 ounce (28 g) low-fat Mozzarella cheese
1 cup cherry tomatoes
2 cups water

1. Thaw the frozen cauliflower rice for 10 minutes.
2. Preheat the air fryer to 375°F (190°C).
3. Cook the cauliflower rice in the air fryer by adding 2 cups of water for 10 minutes.
4. Drain the water using a sieve and keep aside ready.
5. In a large bowl, combine Greek yogurt, egg whites, eggs, cheese, and salt.
6. Add all the vegetables to the bowl mix to combine well.
7. Take 12 muffin tins and lightly spray with cooking oil.
8. Transfer the mixture evenly into the muffin tins.
9. Place them in the air fryer and bake for 25 minutes until the center portion becomes hard.
10. Do a toothpick test by inserting it in the center and check if it comes out clean.
11. After that, remove it from the air fryer and allow it to settle down the heat before serving.
12. Enjoy your muffin.

Per Serving
calories: 457 | fat: 23g | protein: 38g | carbs: 24g | net carbs: 20g | fiber: 4g

Cheese-Stuffed Mushrooms

1 Lean | 3 Greens | 2 Condiments
Prep time: 15 minutes | Cook time: 17
    minutes | Serves 2

4 large portabella mushroom caps
1 tablespoon soy sauce
1 tablespoon lemon juice
1 teaspoon olive oil, divided
2 cups low-fat Mozzarella cheese, grated
½ cup fresh tomato, diced
1 clove garlic, finely grated
1 tablespoon fresh cilantro, chopped

1. Make bowls by scooping the flesh from the interior of the mushroom caps.
2. Set the air fryer temperature to 390°F (199°C) and preheat.
3. Mix the soy sauce, lemon juice, and half a portion of olive oil in a small bowl.
4. Marinate the mixture on the mushroom cap both inside and outside.
5. Line foil coated baking paper in the air fryer tray.
6. Place the marinated mushroom cap in the tray and bake for 10 minutes until they become tender.
7. Now combine tomatoes, Mozzarella, garlic, remaining olive oil, and Italian seasoning in a medium bowl.
8. Fill the mushroom caps with the mixture evenly.
9. Bake it in the air fryer for 7 minutes, until the cheese starts to melt.
10. Sprinkle cilantro on top and serve.

Per Serving
calories: 477 | fat: 32g | protein: 39g | carbs: 6g | net carbs: 5g | fiber: 1g

Kale Egg Muffins with Bell Pepper

1 Lean | 3 Greens | 1 Healthy Fat | 1 Condiment
Prep time: 10 minutes | Cook time: 25 minutes | Serves 2

Egg Muffins:
4 eggs
1 cup liquid egg whites
¼ cup low-fat plain Greek yogurt
¼ teaspoon salt
Cooking spray

Bell Pepper Mix:
6 ounces (170 g) red bell pepper, cored and chopped
5 ounces (142 g) kale, frozen, chopped
1 ounce (28 g) Goat cheese

1. Thaw the frozen cauliflower rice for 10 minutes.
2. Preheat the air fryer to 375°F (190°C).
3. In a large bowl, combine Greek yogurt, egg whites, eggs, cheese, and salt.
4. Add all the vegetables to the bowl mix to combine well.
5. Take 12 muffin tins and lightly spray with cooking oil.
6. Transfer the mixture evenly into the muffin tins.
7. Place them in the air fryer and bake for 25 minutes until the center portion becomes hard.
8. Do a toothpick test by inserting it in the center and check if it comes out clean.
9. After that, remove it from the air fryer and allow it to settle down the heat before serving.
10. Enjoy your muffin.

Per Serving
calories: 469 | fat: 25g | protein: 40g | carbs: 21g | net carbs: 17g | fiber: 4g

Oregano Chicken and Asparagus

1 Lean | 3 Greens | 2 Condiments
Prep time: 5 minutes | Cook time: 44 minutes | Serves 2

½ pound (227 g) chicken breast, boneless and skinless
1 tablespoon lemon juice
1 clove garlic, minced
1 tablespoon fresh oregano, minced
¼ teaspoon ground black pepper
¼ teaspoon salt
1 pound (454 g) asparagus, ends trimmed
1 cup water

1. Soak, wash, and pat dry chicken.
2. Put the chicken in a large bowl and marinate with pepper, lemon juice, salt, garlic, and oregano.
3. Place the marinated chicken in the air fry grill tray.
4. Broil at 345°F (174°C) for 40 minutes until the meat's internal temperature reaches 160°F (70°C).
5. After broiling, remove it from the air fryer and set aside.
6. Now place the asparagus in the air fry ray and pour 1 cup water.
7. Air fry at 345°F (174°C) for 4 minutes until the asparagus becomes tender.
8. Remove it from the air fryer and drain the water.
9. Slice the chicken and serve along with asparagus.

Per Serving
calories: 247 | fat: 10g | protein: 28g | carbs: 10g | net carbs: 5g | fiber: 5g

Chicken with Mushrooms

1 Leaner | 3 Greens | 1 Healthy Fat | 3 Condiments
Prep time: 15 minutes | Cook time: 30 minutes | Serves 4

2 tablespoons extra-virgin olive oil
4 (6-ounce/ 170 g) bone-in, skin-on chicken thighs
1 (4-ounce/ 113 g) package sliced fresh mushrooms
3 celery stalks, chopped
½ of onion, chopped
2 garlic cloves, minced
1 (14-ounce/ 397 g) can stewed tomatoes
2 tablespoons tomato paste
2 teaspoons Herbes de Provence
¾ cup water
Pinch of red pepper flakes
Ground black pepper, as required

1. Add the oil in Instant Pot and select "Sauté". Then add the chicken thighs and cook for about 5 to 6 minutes per side.
2. With a slotted spoon, transfer chicken thighs onto a plate.
3. In the pot, add the mushrooms, celery and onion and cook for about 5 minutes.
4. Add the garlic and cook for about 2 minutes.
5. Press "Cancel" and stir in the chicken, tomatoes, tomato paste, Herbes de Provence and water.
6. Secure the lid and turn to "Seal" position.
7. Cook on "Manual" with "High Pressure" for about 11 minutes.
8. Press "Cancel" and carefully do a "Quick" release.
9. Remove the lid and stir in red pepper flakes and black pepper.
10. Serve hot.

Per Serving
calories: 430 | fat: 24.7g | protein: 52.1g | carbs: 9.2g | net carbs: 6.8g | fiber: 2.4g

Chicken with Olives

1 Leaner | 2 Greens | 1 Healthy Fat | 3 Condiments
Prep time: 15 minutes | Cook time: 21 minutes | Serves 4

For spice blend
½ teaspoon paprika
½ teaspoon ground ginger
½ teaspoon ground cumin
½ teaspoon ground coriander
¼ teaspoons ground turmeric
¼ teaspoons ground cinnamon
¼ teaspoons ground allspice
¼ teaspoons kosher salt

For chicken
1 tablespoon olive oil
1 small red onion, sliced
2 garlic cloves, chopped
½ cup low-sodium chicken broth
¾ cup green olives, pitted
½ of lemon, seeded and sliced thinly
1½ pounds boneless, skinless
  chicken thighs
2 tablespoons fresh parsley, chopped

1. For spice blend: in a small bowl, mix together all ingredients. Set aside.
2. Add the oil in Instant Pot and select "Sauté". Then add the onion and garlic and cook for about 5 minutes.
3. Stir in the spice blend and cook for about 1 minute.
4. Add the broth and scrape up the browned bits from bottom.
5. Press "Cancel" and stir in the olives, raisins, lemon slices, and chicken thighs.
6. Secure the lid and turn to "Seal" position.
7. Select "Poultry" and just use the default time of 15 minutes.
8. Press "Cancel" and carefully do a "Quick" release.
9. Remove the lid and serve hot.

Per Serving
calories: 398 | fat: 19g | protein: 50.2g | carbs: 4.7g | net carbs: 3.1g | fiber: 1.6g

Chicken with Olives & Bell Peppers

1 Leaner | 3 Greens | 1 Healthy Fat | 3 Condiments
Prep time: 15 minutes | Cook time: 25 minutes | Serves 4

2 tablespoons extra-virgin olive oil
1 pound (454 g) chicken breast, cut into bite-sized pieces
1 lemon, peeled and sliced very thinly
¼ cup green olives, pitted
2 bell peppers, seeded and cut into long, wide, strips
1 onion, quartered
2 garlic cloves, chopped
2 tablespoons tomato paste
1 tablespoon Dijon Mustard
1 teaspoon ground cumin
1 teaspoon ground turmeric
½ teaspoons ground ginger
½ teaspoons ground cinnamon
Salt and ground black pepper, as required

1. Add the oil in Instant Pot and select "Sauté". Then add the chicken pieces and cook for about 3 to 5 minutes or browned from all sides.
2. Press "Cancel" and stir in the remaining ingredients.
3. Secure the lid and turn to "Seal" position.
4. Cook on "Manual" with "High Pressure" for about 20 minutes.
5. Press "Cancel" and carefully do a "Quick" release.
6. Remove the lid and serve hot.

Per Serving
calories: 243 | fat: 11.3g | protein: 25.7g | carbs: 9g | net carbs: 6.7g | fiber: 2.3g

Chicken with Broccoli

1 Leaner | 2 Greens | 1 Healthy Fat | 3 Condiments
Prep time: 10 minutes | Cook time: 23 minutes | Serves 4

2 tablespoons olive oil
4 (4-ounce/ 113 g) skinless, boneless chicken breasts
Salt and ground black pepper, as required
1 medium onion, chopped
1 garlic clove, minced
2 cups chicken broth
1½ tablespoons arrowroot starch
4 tablespoons water, divided
1 cup low-fat cheddar cheese, shredded
4 cups small broccoli florets

1. Add the oil in Instant Pot and select "Sauté". Then add the chicken breasts and cook for about 4 to 5 minutes.
2. With a slotted spoon, transfer the chicken breasts into a plate.
3. Add the onion and cook for about 2 to 3 minutes.
4. Add the garlic and cook for about 1 minute.
5. Press "Cancel" and stir in the cooked chicken and broth.
6. Secure the lid and turn to "Seal" position.
7. Cook on "Manual" with "High Pressure" for about 5 minutes.
8. Press "Cancel" and carefully do a "Quick" release.
9. Remove the lid and with tongs, transfer chicken breasts onto a cutting board.
10. With a sharp knife, cut chicken into desired sized pieces.
11. Meanwhile, in a small bowl, dissolve arrowroot starch in 1½ tablespoons of water.
12. Now, select "Sauté" of Instant Pot.
13. Add the arrowroot starch mixture, stirring continuously.
14. Add the cheddar cheese and cook until melted completely, stirring continuously.
15. Meanwhile, in a large microwave-safe bowl, add broccoli and 2 tablespoons of water.
16. Microwave on High for about 3 to 4 minutes.
17. Add the chopped chicken and broccoli in Instant Pot and stir well.
18. Cook for about 4 to 5 minutes.
19. Press "Cancel" and serve hot.

Per Serving
calories: 380 | fat: 21.4g | protein: 37.8g | carbs: 10g | net carbs: 7g | fiber: 3g

Chicken with Cabbage

1 Leaner | 2 Greens | 1 Healthy Fat | 2½ Condiments
Prep time: 10 minutes | Cook time: 8 minutes | Serves 4

1 tablespoon olive oil
1 small yellow onion, chopped
1 jalapeño pepper, seeded and chopped
2 cups cooked chicken, chopped
1½ pounds cabbage, sliced into thin strips
½ cup chicken broth
½ tablespoon fresh lemon juice
Salt and freshly ground black pepper, as required

1. Add the oil in Instant Pot and select "Sauté". Then add the onion and cook for about 3 minutes.
2. Add chicken and cook for about 2 minutes.
3. Press "Cancel" and stir in the chicken, cabbage and broth.
4. Secure the lid and turn to "Seal" position.
5. Cook on "Manual" with "High Pressure" for about 3 minutes.
6. Press "Cancel" and carefully do a Quick release.
7. Remove the lid and stir in lemon juice, salt and black pepper.
8. Serve hot.

Per Serving
calories: 192 | fat: 6g | protein: 23.3g | carbs: 10g | net carbs: 5.3g | fiber: 4.7g

Chicken with Mushrooms & Zucchini

1 Leaner | 3 Greens | 1 Healthy Fat | 2 Condiments
Prep time: 10 minutes | Cook time: 17 minutes | Serves 4

1 tablespoon olive oil
12 ounces (340 g) boneless, skinless chicken breasts, cubed
12 ounces (340 g) fresh mushrooms, sliced
½ cup onion, chopped
2 garlic cloves, minced
1 medium zucchini, cut into ½-inch slices
2 tablespoons fresh basil, chopped
Salt and freshly ground black pepper, to taste
1 cup tomatoes, chopped
1 cup chicken broth

1. Add the oil in Instant Pot and select "Sauté". Then add the chicken cubes and cook for about 4 to 5 minutes.
2. Add the mushrooms, onion and garlic and cook for about 5 minutes.
3. Add the zucchinis, basil, salt and black pepper and cook for about 1 to 2 minutes.
4. Press "Cancel" and stir in the tomatoes and broth.
5. Secure the lid and turn to "Seal" position.
6. Cook on "Manual" with "High Pressure" for about 5 minutes.
7. Press "Cancel" and do a "Natural" release.
8. Remove the lid and serve hot.

Per Serving
calories: 244 | fat: 10.6g | protein: 29.8g | carbs: 8.3g | net carbs: 6g | fiber: 2.33g

Chicken & Mushroom Stew

1 Leaner | 3 Greens | 1 Healthy Fat | 3 Condiments
Prep time: 15 minutes | Cook time: 19 minutes | Serves 4

2 tablespoons olive oil
4 (5-ounce/ 142 g) skinless chicken thighs
¾ pound (340 g) fresh cremini mushrooms, stemmed and quartered
1 small onion, chopped
1 tablespoon tomato paste
3 garlic cloves, minced
¼ cup green olives, pitted and halved
1 cup fresh cherry tomatoes
½ cup chicken broth
Salt and ground black pepper, as required
2 tablespoons fresh parsley, chopped

1. Add the oil in Instant Pot and select "Sauté". Then add the chicken thighs and cook for about 2 to 3 minutes per side.
2. Transfer chicken thighs onto a plate.
3. In the Instant pot, add mushrooms and onion and cook for about 4 to 5 minutes.
4. Add tomato paste and garlic and cook for about 1 minute.
5. Press "Cancel" and stir in the chicken, olives, tomatoes and broth.
6. Secure the lid and turn to "Seal" position.
7. Cook on "Manual" with "High Pressure" for about 10 minutes.
8. Press "Cancel" and carefully do a "Quick" release.
9. Remove the lid and stir in salt, black pepper and parsley.
10. Serve hot.

Per Serving
calories: 282 | fat: 24.0g | protein: 10.1g | carbs: 6.9g | net carbs: 2.8g | fiber: 4.1g

Chicken, Bell Pepper & Carrot Curry

1 Leaner | 3 Greens | 1 Healthy Fat | 4 Condiments
Prep time: 15 minutes | Cook time: 12 minutes | Serves 4

1 (14-ounce/ 397 g) can unsweetened coconut milk
2 tablespoons Thai red curry paste
1 pound boneless chicken breasts, cut into thin bite-size pieces
1 cup carrots, peeled and sliced
1½ cups green bell pepper, seeded and cubed
½ cup onion, sliced
¼ cup chicken broth
2 tablespoon fish sauce
1 tablespoon fresh lime juice
12 fresh basil leaves, chopped
Salt and ground black pepper, as required

1. Add the oil in Instant Pot and select "Sauté". Then add half of coconut milk and curry paste and cook for about 1 to 2 minutes.
2. Press "Cancel" and stir in remaining coconut milk, chicken, carrot, bell pepper, onion and broth.
3. Secure the lid and turn to "Seal" position.
4. Cook on "Manual" with "High Pressure" for about 5 minutes.
5. Press "Cancel" and carefully do a "Quick" release.
6. Remove the lid and select "Sauté".
7. Stir in the remaining ingredients and cook for about 4 to 5 minutes.
8. Stir in the salt and black pepper and press "Cancel".
9. Serve hot.

Per Serving
calories: 282 | fat: 24.0g | protein: 10.1g | carbs: 6.9g | net carbs: 2.8g | fiber: 4.1g

Chicken & Veggie Casserole

1 Leaner | 3 Greens | 1 Healthy Fat | 4 Condiments
Prep time: 10 minutes | Cook time: 40 minutes | Serves 4

½ cup unsweetened almond milk
½ cup almond flour
8 large eggs
Salt and ground black pepper, as required
1 cup cooked chicken, chopped
1 medium zucchini, chopped
1 medium green bell pepper, seeded and chopped
1 cup part-skim mozzarella cheese, shredded

1. In a baking dish, add milk, flour, eggs, salt and black pepper and beat until well combined.
2. Add the chicken, vegetables and cheese and stir to combine.
3. In the bottom of Instant Pot, arrange a steamer trivet and pour 1 cup of water.
4. With a piece of foil, cover the baking dish and place on top of trivet.
5. Secure the lid and turn to "Seal" position.
6. Cook on "Manual" with "High Pressure" for about 30 minutes.
7. Press "Cancel" and do a "Natural" release for about 10 minutes. Then do a "Quick" release.
8. Remove the lid and serve immediately.

Per Serving
calories: 328 | fat: 20.4g | protein: 25.7g | carbs: 7.7g | net carbs: 5.1g | fiber: 2.6g

Chickens, Cauliflower & Peas Curry

1 Leaner | 3 Greens | 1 Healthy Fat | 2 Condiments
Prep time: 20 minutes | Cook time: 20 minutes | Serves 4

1½ pounds skinless, boneless chicken thighs, cubed
Salt, as required
½ tablespoon olive oil
½ of onion, chopped
1 teaspoon ginger root, minced
3 garlic cloves, minced
1 teaspoon ground cumin
1 teaspoon ground coriander
½ teaspoon garam masala
½ teaspoon ground turmeric
½ teaspoon cayenne pepper
¼ teaspoon red pepper flakes, crushed
1 (14-ounce/ 397 g) can diced tomatoes, drained
2 cups cauliflower florets
½ cup frozen peas
½ cup full-fat coconut milk
¼ cup fresh cilantro leaves, chopped

1. Season the chicken with 1 teaspoon of salt. Keep aside.
2. Add the oil in Instant Pot and select "Sauté". Then add the onion, ginger, garlic and spices and cook for about 2 to 3 minutes.
3. Add tomatoes and with an immersion blender, blend until smooth.
4. Press "Cancel" and stir in the chicken.
5. Secure the lid and turn to "Seal" position.
6. Cook on "Manual" with "High Pressure" for about 15 minutes.
7. Press "Cancel" and carefully do a "Quick" release.
8. Remove the lid and stir in the cauliflower and peas.
9. Secure the lid and turn to "Seal" position.
10. Cook on "Manual" with "High Pressure" for about 2 minutes.
11. Press "Cancel" and carefully do a "Quick" release.
12. Remove the lid and stir in coconut milk.
13. Serve hot with the garnishing of cilantro.

Per Serving
calories: 345 | fat: 15.7g | protein: 40.9g | carbs: 10g | net carbs: 7g | fiber: 3g

Chicken Chili

1 Leaner | 2 Greens | 1 Healthy Fat | 3 Condiments
Prep time: 10 minutes | Cook time: 20 minutes | Serves 4

3 (5-ounce/ 142 g) chicken breasts
1 carrot, peeled and chopped
1 celery stalk, chopped
1 medium yellow onion, chopped
2 garlic cloves, chopped
1 teaspoon dried oregano
1 teaspoon ground cumin
Salt and ground black pepper, as required
½ cup unsweetened coconut milk
1 cup chicken broth

1. In the pot of Instant Pot, add all ingredients and stir to combine.
2. Secure the lid and turn to "Seal" position.
3. Select "Poultry" and just use the default time of 20 minutes.
4. Press "Cancel" and do a "Natural" release.
5. Remove the lid and with a slotted spoon, transfer the chicken breasts into a bowl.
6. With 2 forks, shred chicken breasts and then return into the pot.
7. Serve immediately.

Per Serving
calories: 306 | fat: 15.6g | protein: 33.4g | carbs: 7.1g | net carbs: 5.2g | fiber: 1.9g

Ground Turkey with Mushrooms

1 Leaner | 3 Greens | 1 Healthy Fat | 2½ Condiments
Prep time: 15 minutes | Cook time: 13 minutes | Serves 4

2 tablespoons olive oil
10 ounces (283 g) fresh mushrooms, trimmed and chopped finely
1 carrot, peeled and chopped finely
1 small onion, chopped finely
2 garlic cloves, chopped finely
1 pound (454 g) 93% lean ground turkey
½ cup chicken broth
1 (14-ounce/ 397 g) can crushed tomatoes
1 bay leaf
1 teaspoon dried thyme
Salt and ground black pepper, as required

1. Add the oil in Instant Pot and select "Sauté". Then add the
2. Add chopped vegetables and cook for about 4-5 minutes.
3. Add the ground turkey and cook for about 8-10 minutes, breaking up with a wooden spoon.
4. Add the broth and scrape the brown bits from the bottom.
5. Press "Cancel" and stir in the remaining ingredients.
6. Secure the lid and turn to "Seal" position.
7. Cook on "Manual" with "High Pressure" for about 20 minutes.
8. Press "Cancel" and carefully do a "Natural" release for about 10 minutes. Then do a "Quick" release.
9. Remove the lid and serve hot.

Per Serving
calories: 335 | fat: 20.1g | protein: 35.2g | carbs: 9.9g | net carbs: 7.2g | fiber: 2.7g

Ground Turkey Stew

1 Leaner | 3 Greens | 1 Healthy Fat | 4 Condiments
Prep time: 15 minutes | Cook time: 27 minutes | Serves 4

1 tablespoon olive oil
1 pound ground turkey
1½ cups carrots, peeled and chopped
1 cup frozen peas
2 garlic cloves, minced
1 teaspoon dried oregano
1 teaspoon dried basil
½ teaspoon dried thyme
Salt, as required
3 cups chicken broth
2 tablespoons arrowroot starch
2 tablespoons water

1. Add the oil in Instant Pot and select "Sauté". Now, add the ground turkey and cook for about 8 to 10 minutes or until browned completely.
2. Press "Cancel" and stir in the remaining ingredients except arrowroot starch and water.
3. Secure the lid and turn to "Seal" position.
4. Cook on "Manual" with "High Pressure" for about 15 minutes.
5. Press "Cancel" and do a "Natural" release.
6. Meanwhile, in a small bowl, dissolve arrowroot starch in water.
7. Remove the lid and select "Sauté".
8. Add the arrowroot mixture and stir until smooth.
9. Cook for about 1 to 2 minutes.
10. Press "Cancel" and serve hot.

Per Serving
calories: 345 | fat: 17.1g | protein: 37.2g | carbs: 11g | net carbs: 7g | fiber: 4g

Beef with Broccoli

1 Leaner | 2 Greens | 1 Healthy Fat | 4 Condiments
Prep time: 15 minutes | Cook time: 32 minutes | Serves 4

1 tablespoon olive oil
1 pound (454 g) beef chuck roast, trimmed and cut into thin strips
Salt and ground black pepper, as required
1 yellow onion, chopped
2 garlic cloves, minced
Pinch of red pepper flakes, crushed
½ cup beef broth

2 tablespoons low-sodium soy sauce
1 tablespoon Erythritol
1 tablespoon arrowroot starch
1½ tablespoons cold water
¾ pound (340 g) broccoli florets
2 tablespoons water
2 tablespoons fresh cilantro, chopped

1. Add the oil in Instant Pot and select "Sauté". Then add the beef, salt and black pepper and cook for about 5 minutes.
2. Transfer the beef into a bowl.
3. Now, add the onion and cook for about 4 to 5 minutes.
4. Add the garlic and red pepper flakes and cook for about 1 minute.
5. Press "Cancel" and stir in beef broth, soy sauce and Erythritol and stir well.
6. Secure the lid and turn to "Seal" position.
7. Cook on "Manual" with "High Pressure" for about 12 minutes.
8. Press "Cancel" and carefully do a "Quick" release.
9. Meanwhile, in a small bowl, dissolve arrowroot starch in cold water.
10. Remove the lid and select "Sauté".
11. Add arrowroot mixture in Instant Pot, stirring continuously and cook for about 4 to 5 minutes or until desired thickness.
12. Meanwhile, in a large microwave-safe bowl, add broccoli and 2 tablespoons of water and microwave on High for about 3 to 4 minutes.
13. Add the broccoli in Instant Pot and stir well.
14. Press "Cancel" and serve with the garnishing of cilantro.

Per Serving
calories: 498 | fat: 35.6g | protein: 33.6g | carbs: 11g | net carbs: 8g | fiber: 3g

Beef with Bell Peppers

1 Leaner | 3 Greens | 1 Healthy Fat | 4 Condiments
Prep time: 15 minutes | Cook time: 13 minutes | Serves 4

1 tablespoon olive oil
1 onion, sliced thinly
2 garlic cloves, minced
2 tablespoons balsamic vinegar
1 pound (454 g) beef stew meat, trimmed and cut into 2-inch cubes
1 cup tomatoes, chopped
1 bay leaf
½ teaspoon dried oregano, crushed
½ teaspoon dried basil, crushed
Salt and ground black pepper, as required
2 green bell pepper, seeded and cut into 8 slices
2 tablespoons fresh parsley, chopped

1. Add the oil in Instant Pot and select "Sauté". Then add the onion and garlic and cook for about 2 to 3 minutes.
2. Add the vinegar and scrape the brown bits from the bottom.
3. Press "Cancel" and stir in beef, tomatoes, bay leaves, herbs, salt and black pepper.
4. Secure the lid and turn to "Seal" position.
5. Cook on "Manual" with "High Pressure" for about 15 minutes.
6. Press "Cancel" and carefully do a "Natural" release.
7. Remove the lid and select "Sauté".
8. Stir in bell peppers and cook for about 4 to 5 minutes or until desired doneness.
9. Press "Cancel" and stir in parsley.
10. Serve hot.

Per Serving
calories: 288 | fat: 10.9g | protein: 35.9g | carbs: 9g | net carbs: 2.3g | fiber: 6.7g

Beef with Mushrooms

1 Leaner | 3 Greens | 1 Healthy Fat | 4 Condiments
Prep time: 15 minutes | Cook time: 67 minutes | Serves 4

For Beef
¾ pound (340 g) beef chuck roast, trimmed and cubed into 2-inch size
2 garlic cloves, minced
½ tablespoon mixed dried herbs, crushed (of your choice)
Salt and freshly ground white pepper, as required
1 tablespoon olive oil
1 medium yellow onion, chopped
¾ cup beef broth
1 tablespoons fresh lemon juice
1 medium carrot, peeled and cut into 1-inch pieces

For Mushroom Gravy
2 tablespoons olive oil
4 ounces (113 g) cremini mushrooms, sliced
½ teaspoon dried thyme, crushed
¼ cup beef broth
1 tablespoon fresh lemon juice

1. For beef in a bowl, add beef, garlic, mixed herbs, salt and white pepper and toss to coat well.
2. Add the oil in Instant Pot and select "Sauté". Then add the onion and cook for about 4 to 5 minutes.
3. Add the broth and lemon juice and cook for about 1 to 2 minutes scraping the brown bits from the bottom.
4. Press "Cancel" and place the beef over the onion, followed by broth.
5. Secure the lid and turn to "Seal" position.
6. Cook on "Manual" with "High Pressure" for about 40 minutes.
7. Press "Cancel" and carefully do a "Quick" release.
8. Remove the lid and stir in the carrot.
9. Select "Sauté" and cook for about 10 minutes.
10. Transfer the beef mixture into a large bowl and cover with a piece of foil to keep warm.
11. For gravy: Add the oil in Instant Pot and select "Sauté". Then add the mushrooms, thyme and wine and cook for about 10 minutes.
12. Press "Cancel" and place mushroom gravy over beef mixture.
13. Serve immediately.

Per Serving
calories: 443 | fat: 34.9g | protein: 25.9g | carbs: 6.2g | net carbs: 4.8g | fiber: 1.4g

Beef & Kale Casserole

1 Leaner | 2 Greens | 1 Healthy Fat | 2 Condiments
Prep time: 10 minutes | Cook time: 29 minutes | Serves 4

2 tablespoons olive oil
2 cups fresh kale, trimmed and chopped
1 ⅓ cups scallion, sliced
8 egg, beaten
1½ cups cooked beef, shredded
Salt and ground black pepper, as required

1. Add the oil in the Instant Pot and select "Sauté". Then add the kale and scallion and cook for about 3 to 4 minutes.
2. Press "Cancel" and transfer the kale mixture into a bowl.
3. Add eggs and beef and mix well.
4. Transfer the mixture into a lightly greased baking dish.
5. In the bottom of Instant Pot, arrange a steamer trivet and pour 1½ cups of water.
6. Place the baking dish on top of trivet.
7. Secure the lid and turn to "Seal" position.
8. Cook on "Manual" with "High Pressure" for about 25 minutes.
9. Press "Cancel" and carefully do a "Quick" release.
10. Remove the lid and serve immediately.

Per Serving
calories: 345 | fat: 20.2g | protein: 34.2g | carbs: 6.6g | net carbs: 5.2g | fiber: 1.4g

Beef & Mushroom Soup

1 Leaner | 4 Greens | 1 Healthy Fat | 3 Condiments
Prep time: 15 minutes | Cook time: 28 minutes | Serves 4

2 teaspoons olive oil
1 pound (454 g) sirloin steak, trimmed and cubed
1 small carrot, peeled and chopped
1 bell pepper, seeded and chopped
1 celery stalk, chopped
1 onion, chopped
8 ounces (227 g) fresh mushrooms, sliced
2 cups beef broth
1½ cups water
1 cup tomatoes, crushed
1½ tablespoons fresh oregano, chopped
1 bay leaf
2 teaspoon garlic powder
Salt and ground black pepper, as required

1. Add the oil in an Instant Pot Mini and select "Sauté". Now, add the steak and cook for about 4 to 5 minutes or until browned.
2. Add the carrots, bell pepper, celery, and onion and cook for about 2 to 3 minutes.
3. Add the mushrooms and cook for about 4 to 5 minutes.
4. Press "Cancel" and stir in the remaining ingredients.
5. Secure the lid and turn to "Seal" position.
6. Select "Soup" and just use the default time of 15 minutes.
7. Press "Cancel" and do a "Quick" release.
8. Remove the lid and serve hot.

Per Serving
calories: 298 | fat: 10.6g | protein: 39.9g | carbs: 10g | net carbs: 6.7g | fiber: 3.3g

Beef & Bok Choy Soup

1 Leaner | 3 Greens | 1 Healthy Fat | 3 Condiments
Prep time: 15 minutes | Cook time: 43 minutes | Serves 4

2 tablespoons olive oil
½ onion, sliced
2 garlic cloves, minced
1 teaspoon fresh ginger, minced
1 pound (454 g) beef tenderloin, trimmed and cut into chunks
2 tablespoons balsamic vinegar
2 tablespoons low-sodium soy sauce
Salt and ground black pepper, as required
3 cups water
3 cups bok choy, chopped
2 tablespoons fresh cilantro, chopped

1. Add the oil in an Instant Pot and select "Sauté". Now, add the onion, garlic and ginger and cook for about 2 to 3 minutes.
2. Press "Cancel" and stir in the remaining ingredients except for bok choy and cilantro.
3. Secure the lid and turn to "Seal" position.
4. Cook on "Manual" with "High Pressure" for about 20 minutes.
5. Press "Cancel" and do a "Natural" release for about 10 minutes. Then allow a "Quick" release.
6. Remove the lid and mix in the bok choy.
7. Immediately, secure the lid and turn to "Seal" position for about 10 minutes.
8. Serve immediately with the garnishing of cilantro.

Per Serving
calories: 314 | fat: 17.5g | protein: 34.4g | carbs: 3.8g | net carbs: 2.9g | fiber: 0.9g

Ground Beef & Green Beans Soup

1 Leaner | 2 Greens | 1 Healthy Fat | 3 Condiments
Prep time: 10 minutes | Cook time: 38 minutes | Serves 4

1 tablespoon olive oil
1 pound (454 g) lean ground beef
1 medium onion, chopped
1 tablespoon garlic, minced
2 teaspoons dried thyme, crushed
1 teaspoon ground cumin
2 cups fresh tomatoes, chopped finely
½ pound (226 g) fresh green beans, trimmed and cut into
    1-inch pieces
4 cups beef broth
Salt and ground black pepper, as required

1. Add the oil in Instant Pot and select "Sauté". Then add the beef and cook for about 5 minutes or until browned completely.
2. Add onion, garlic, thyme, cumin and cook for about 3 minutes.
3. Press "Cancel" and stir in the tomatoes, beans and broth.
4. Secure the lid and turn to "Seal" position.
5. Cook on "Manual" with "Low Pressure" for about 30 minutes.
6. Press "Cancel" and carefully do a "Quick" release.
7. Remove the lid and stir in the salt and black pepper.
8. Serve immediately.

Per Serving
calories: 327 | fat: 12.3g | protein: 30.3g | carbs: 11g | net carbs: 7g | fiber: 4g

Ground Beef & Spinach Soup

1 Leaner | 3 Greens | 1 Healthy Fat | 2 Condiments
Prep time: 10 minutes | Cook time: 30 minutes | Serves 4

1 tablespoon olive oil
1 pound (454 g) ground beef
1 onion, chopped
1 cup carrots, peeled and shredded
4 cups chicken broth
1 teaspoon ground ginger
4 cups fresh spinach, chopped
Freshly ground black pepper, as required

1. Add the oil in Instant Pot and select "Sauté". Then add the beef and cook for about 5 minutes or until browned completely.
2. Press "Cancel" and stir in the remaining ingredients.
3. Secure the lid and turn to "Seal" position.
4. Cook on "Manual" with "High Pressure" for about 25 minutes.
5. Press "Cancel" and carefully do a "Quick" release.
6. Remove the lid and serve hot.

Per Serving
calories: 310 | fat: 12.1g | protein: 40.7g | carbs: 7.6g | net carbs: 5.6g | fiber: 2g

Beef & Veggies Stew

1 Leaner | 2 Greens | 1 Healthy Fat | 4 Condiments
Prep time: 10 minutes | Cook time: 55 minutes | Serves 4

1¼ pounds (680 g) beef stew meat, cubed
2 small zucchinis, chopped
½ pound (226 g) small broccoli florets
2 garlic cloves, minced
½ cup chicken broth
1 tablespoon curry powder
1 teaspoon ground cumin
Salt and ground black pepper, as required
7 ounce (198 g) unsweetened coconut milk
2 tablespoons fresh cilantro, chopped

1. In the pot of Instant Pot, place all ingredients except coconut milk and cilantro and stir to combine.
2. Secure the lid and turn to "Seal" position.
3. Cook on "Manual" with "High Pressure" for about 45 minutes.
4. Press "Cancel" and carefully do a "Natural" release for about 10 minutes. Then do a "Quick" release.
5. Remove the lid and stir in coconut milk.
6. Serve immediately with the garnishing of cilantro.

Per Serving
calories: 389 | fat: 17.9g | protein: 46.7g | carbs: 10g | net carbs: 7g | fiber: 3g

Beef & Carrot Chili

1 Leaner | 4 Greens | 1 Healthy Fat | 4 Condiments
Prep time: 15 minutes | Cook time: 40 minutes | Serves 4

1 tablespoon olive oil
1 pound (454 g) ground beef
½ green bell pepper, seeded and chopped
1 small onion, chopped
1 medium carrots, peeled and chopped
2 tomatoes, chopped finely
1 jalapeño pepper, chopped

Salt and ground black pepper, as required
1 tablespoon fresh parsley, chopped
1 tablespoon Worcestershire sauce
4 teaspoons red chili powder
1 teaspoon paprika
1 teaspoon ground cumin

1. Add the oil in Instant Pot and select "Sauté". Then add the beef and cook for about 5 minutes or until browned completely.
2. Press "Cancel" and stir in remaining ingredients.
3. Secure the lid and turn to "Seal" position.
4. Select "Soup" and just use the default time of 35 minutes.
5. Press "Cancel" and do a "Natural" release.
6. Remove the lid and serve hot.

Per Serving
calories: 287 | fat: 11.4g | protein: 36g | carbs: 9g | net carbs: 6g | fiber: 3g

Beef & Carrot Curry

1 Leaner | 3 Greens | 1 Healthy Fat | 3 Condiments
Prep time: 15 minutes | Cook time: 43 minutes | Serves 4

2 tablespoons olive oil
1¼ pounds (568 g) beef stew meat, cut into 1-inch pieces
Salt and ground black pepper, as required
1 cup onion, chopped
1 tablespoon fresh ginger, minced
2 teaspoons garlic, minced
1 jalapeño pepper, chopped finely
1 tablespoon curry powder
1 teaspoon red chili powder
1 teaspoon ground cumin
2 cups beef broth
1½ cups carrots, peeled and cut into 1-inch pieces
1 cup unsweetened coconut milk
¼ cup fresh cilantro, chopped

1. Add the oil in an Instant Pot Mini and select "Sauté". Now, add the beef, salt and black pepper and cook for about 4 to 5 minutes or until browned completely.
2. With a slotted spoon, transfer the beef into a bowl.
3. In the pot, add the onion, ginger, garlic and jalapeño pepper and cook for about 4 to 5 minutes.
4. Press "Cancel" and stir in the beef, spices and broth.
5. Secure the lid and turn to "Seal" position.
6. Cook on "Manual" with "High Pressure" for about 15 minutes.
7. Press "Cancel" and do a "Quick" release.
8. Remove the lid and mix in the carrots.
9. Secure the lid and turn to "Seal" position.
10. Cook on "Manual" with "High Pressure" for about 5 minutes.
11. Press "Cancel" and do a "Natural" release for about 10 minutes. Then do a "Quick" release.
12. Remove the lid and mix in the coconut milk.
13. Now, select "Sauté" and cook for about 2 to 3 minutes.
14. Press "Cancel" and stir in the cilantro.
15. Serve immediately.

Per Serving
calories: 399 | fat: 18.1g | protein: 46.7g | carbs: 10g | net carbs: 7g | fiber: 3g

Beef & Cauliflower Curry

1 Leaner | 3 Greens | 1 Healthy Fat | 4 Condiments
Prep time: 15 minutes | Cook time: 28 minutes | Serves 4

1 tablespoon olive oil
¾ pound (340 g) beef brisket, cubed into 1½-inch size
1 tablespoon curry paste
½ pound (226 g) cauliflower florets
1 large carrot, peeled and chopped
1 small yellow onion, chopped
¾ cup unsweetened coconut milk
1 tablespoon fresh lime juice
1 tablespoon low-sodium soy sauce
1 tablespoon fish sauce
¼ cup fresh cilantro, chopped

1. Add the oil in Instant Pot and select "Sauté". Then add curry paste and cook for about 1 minute.
2. Add the beef and cook for about 4-5 minutes.
3. Press "Cancel" and stir in remaining ingredients except cilantro.
4. Secure the lid and turn to "Seal" position.
5. Select "Meat" and just use the default time of 35 minutes.
6. Press "Cancel" and carefully do a "Natural" release for about 10 minutes. Then do a "Quick" release.
7. Remove the lid and serve hot with the garnishing of cilantro.

Per Serving
calories: 320 | fat: 18.6g | protein: 10.1g | carbs: 28.3g | net carbs: 7.5g | fiber: 2.5g

Beef Meatballs in Veggie Gravy

1 Leaner | 3 Greens | 1 Healthy Fat | 4 Condiments
Prep time: 15 minutes | Cook time: 41 minutes | Serves 4

¾ pound (340 g) ground beef
1 teaspoon adobo seasoning
Salt and ground black pepper, as required
½ tablespoon olive oil
2 small tomatoes, chopped roughly
5 mini bell peppers, seeded and halved
1 small onion, chopped roughly
2 garlic cloves, peeled
1 teaspoon fresh ginger, minced
½ cup tomato sauce
¼ teaspoon red pepper flakes
2 tablespoons fresh parsley, chopped

1. In a bowl, add beef, adobo seasoning, salt and black pepper and mix well.
2. Make golf ball sized balls from mixture.
3. Add the oil in Instant Pot and select "Sauté". Then add the meatballs for about 3 to 4 minutes or until browned completely.
4. Press "Cancel" and transfer meatballs into a bowl.
5. In the pot, place remaining ingredients except cilantro and stir to combine.
6. Arrange meatballs on top of vegetable mixture.
7. Secure the lid and turn to "Seal" position.
8. Select "Meat/Stew" and just use the default time of 35 minutes.
9. Press "Cancel" and do a "Natural" release.
10. Remove the lid and with a slotted spoon, transfer the meatballs onto a plate.
11. With an immersion blender, blend the vegetable mixture until smooth.
12. Select "Sauté "and stir in meatballs, salt and black pepper.
13. Cook for about 2 minutes.
14. Press "Cancel" and serve hot with the garnishing of parsley.

Per Serving
calories: 219 | fat: 7.4g | protein: 27.5g | carbs: 8.8g | net carbs: 6.2g | fiber: 2.6g

Beef Meatballs in Sauce

1 Leaner | 2 Greens | 1 Healthy Fat | 4 Condiments
Prep time: 15 minutes | Cook time: 15 minutes | Serves 4

For Sauce
⅓ cup low-sodium soy sauce
2 tablespoons balsamic vinegar
1 tablespoon maple syrup
1 tablespoon olive oil
2 teaspoons fresh ginger, grated
2 garlic cloves, minced
1 tablespoon arrowroot starch
¼ teaspoon ground black pepper

For Meatballs
1 pound extra-lean ground beef
1 egg
1 tablespoons olive oil

For Serving
4 cups fresh baby spinach

1. For sauce: in a large bowl, add all ingredients and mix until well combined. Set aside.
2. For meatballs: in a bowl, add the beef and egg and mix well.
3. Make 1-inch meatballs from the mixture.
4. Add the oil in the Instant Pot and select "Sauté". Then add the meatballs and cook for about 4 to 5 minutes or until browned from all sides.
5. Press "Cancel" and place sauce over meatballs.
6. Secure the lid and turn to "Seal" position.
7. Cook on "Manual" with "High Pressure" for about 10 minutes.
8. Press "Cancel" and do a "Natural" release.
9. Remove the lid and transfer the meatballs onto serving plates.
10. Divide the spinach onto plates and serve immediately.

Per Serving
calories: 319 | fat: 15.3g | protein: 38.2g | carbs: 6.9g | net carbs: 6.1g | fiber: 0.8g

Pork Chops with Mushrooms

1 Leaner | 2 Greens | 1 Healthy Fat | 2 Condiments
Prep time: 10 minutes | Cook time: 22 minutes | Serves 4

1 tablespoon olive oil
2 garlic cloves, minced
4 (6-ounce/ 170 g) bone-in pork chops
Salt and ground black pepper, as required
1 medium onion, chopped
1½ cups fresh mushrooms, chopped roughly
1 cup tomato sauce
½ cup water

1. Add the oil in Instant Pot and select "Sauté". Then add the garlic and cook for about 1 minute.
2. Add the pork chops, salt and black pepper and cook for about 5 minutes or until browned completely.
3. Press "Cancel" and stir in the mushrooms, tomato sauce and water.
4. Secure the lid and turn to "Seal" position.
5. Cook on "Manual" with "High Pressure" for about 15 minutes.
6. Press "Cancel" and carefully do a "Quick" release.
7. Remove the lid and serve hot

Per Serving
calories: 392 | fat: 15.1g | protein: 55g | carbs: 7.2g | net carbs: 5.4g | fiber: 1.8g

Cod with Olives

1 Leaner | 3 Greens | 1 Healthy Fat | 2 Condiments
Prep time: 10 minutes | Cook time: 8 minutes |
    Serves 4

1 pound cherry tomatoes, halved
2 to 3 fresh thyme sprigs
4 cod fillets
1 cup black Kalamata olives
2 tablespoons capers
2 tablespoons olive oil, divided
1 garlic clove, pressed
Salt and ground black pepper, as required

1. Arrange the steamer basket in the bottom of Instant Pot and pour 2 cups of water.
2. Line the bottom of a heat-proof bowl with some cherry tomatoes, followed by thyme sprigs.
3. Arrange the cod fillets on top, followed by the remaining cherry tomatoes, garlic.
4. Drizzle with 1 tablespoon of olive oil and sprinkle with a pinch of salt and black pepper.
5. Place the bowl in steamer basket.
6. Secure the lid and turn to "Seal" position.
7. Cook on "Manual" with "Low Pressure" for about 8 minutes.
8. Press "Cancel" and carefully do a "Quick" release.
9. Remove the lid and divide the cod filets and tomatoes onto the serving plates.
10. Top each fillet with olives and capers and sprinkle with some black pepper.
11. Drizzle with remaining oil and serve.

Per Serving
calories: 258 | fat: 12.4g | protein: 31.8g | carbs: 7g | net carbs: 4.4g | fiber: 2.6g

Cod with Peas

1 Leaner | 2 Greens | 1 Healthy Fat | 3 Condiments
Prep time: 10 minutes | Cook time: 3 minutes | Serves 4

2 garlic cloves, chopped
2 tablespoons fresh cilantro leaves
1 jalapeño pepper, chopped
1 teaspoon garam masala powder
¼ teaspoons red chili powder
1 tablespoon fresh lemon juice
1 cup chicken broth
4 (4-ounce/ 113 g) cod fillets
Salt and ground black pepper, as required
½ pound frozen peas

1. In a food processor, add garlic, cilantro, jalapeño and spices and pulse until finely chopped.
2. Transfer the garlic mixture into a bowl with broth and lemon juice and mix well.
3. In the bottom of Instant Pot, arrange a steamer trivet and pour 1 cup of water.
4. Place the fish fillets on top of trivet.
5. Secure the lid and turn to "Seal" position.
6. Cook on "Manual" with "High Pressure" for about 2 minutes.
7. Press "Cancel" and carefully do a "Quick" release.
8. Remove the lid and transfer the fish onto a platter.
9. Place the peas on top of trivet,
10. Secure the lid and turn to "Seal" position.
11. Cook on "Manual" with "High Pressure" for about 1 minute.
12. Press "Cancel" and carefully do a "Quick" release.
13. Remove the lid and transfer the peas onto platter with salmon.
14. Top with garlic puree and serve.

Per Serving
calories: 150 | fat: 1.6g | protein: 24.6g | carbs: 9.2g | net carbs: 5.9g | fiber: 3.3g

Cod with Bell Peppers

1 Leaner | 3 Greens | 1 Healthy Fat | 2 Condiments
Prep time: 10 minutes | Cook time: 28 minutes | Serves 4

¼ cup water
4 (4-ounce/ 113 g) frozen cod fillets
12 cherry tomatoes
12 to 14 black olives
2 tablespoons capers
⅓ cup bell peppers, seeded and sliced
2 tablespoons olive oil
Salt, as required
Pinch of red pepper flakes

1. In the pot of Instant Pot, pour the water.
2. Place the fish fillets in water and top with tomatoes, followed by the olives, capers and red peppers.
3. Drizzle with olive oil and sprinkle with salt and red pepper flakes.
4. Secure the lid and turn to "Seal" position.
5. Cook on "Manual" with "High Pressure" for about 4 minutes.
6. Press "Cancel" and do a "Natural" release for about 8 minutes, then do a "Quick" release.
7. Remove the lid and transfer the fish mixture onto serving plates.
8. Serve hot.

Per Serving
calories: 181 | fat: 9.9g | protein: 20.9g | carbs: 3.4g | net carbs: 2.2g | fiber: 1.2g

Salmon with Veggies

1 Leaner | 3 Greens | 1 Healthy Fat | 3 Condiments
Prep time: 10 minutes | Cook time:6 minutes | Serves 4

1 pound skin-on salmon fillets
Salt and ground black pepper, as required
1 fresh parsley sprig
1 fresh dill sprig
3 teaspoons coconut oil, melted and divided
½ lemon, sliced thinly
1 carrot, peeled and julienned
1 zucchini, peeled and julienned
1 red bell pepper, seeded and julienned

1. Season the salmon fillets with salt and black pepper evenly.
2. In the bottom of Instant Pot, arrange a steamer trivet and place herb sprigs and 1 cup of water.
3. Place the salmon fillets on top of trivet, skin side down.
4. Drizzle salmon fillets with 2 teaspoons of coconut oil and top with lemon slices.
5. Secure the lid and turn to "Seal" position.
6. Select "Steam" and just use the default time of 3 minutes.
7. Press "Cancel" and do a "Natural" release.
8. Meanwhile, for sauce: in a bowl, add remaining ingredients and mix until well combined.
9. Remove the lid and transfer the salmon fillets onto a platter.
10. Remove the steamer trivet, herbs and cooking water from pot. With paper towels, pat dry the pot.
11. Place the remaining coconut oil in the Instant Pot and select "Sauté". Then add the veggies and cook or about 2 to 3 minutes.
12. Press "Cancel" and transfer the veggies onto platter with salmon.
13. Serve immediately.

Per Serving
calories: 204 | fat: 10.6g | protein: 23.1g | carbs: 5.7g | net carbs: 4.3g | fiber: 1.4g

Shrimp with Green Beans

1 Leaner | 1 Greens | 1 Healthy Fat | 3 Condiments
Prep time: 10 minutes | Cook time: 2 minutes | Serves 4

2 tablespoons fresh lemon juice
1 teaspoon red chili powder
1 teaspoon garam masala powder
1 teaspoon ground cumin
Salt and ground black pepper, as required
1 pound (454 g) medium frozen shrimp, peeled and deveined
¾ pound green beans, trimmed
1 tablespoon olive oil

1. In a small bowl, mix together lemon juice and spices.
2. In the bottom of Instant Pot, arrange a steamer trivet and pour 1 cup of water.
3. Arrange green beans on top of trivet in a single layer and top with shrimp.
4. Drizzle with oil and sprinkle with spice mixture.
5. Secure the lid and turn to "Seal" position.
6. Select "Steam" and just use the default time of 2 minutes.
7. Press "Cancel" and do a "Natural" release.
8. Remove the lid and serve hot.

Per Serving
calories: 197 | fat: 5.8g | protein: 27.6g | carbs: 8.5g | net carbs: 5.2g | fiber: 3.3g

Seafood Stew

2 Leaner | 3 Greens | 1 Healthy Fat | 3 Condiments
Prep time: 15 minutes | Cook time: 24 minutes | Serves 4

2 tablespoons extra-virgin olive oil
1 small onion, sliced thinly
1 small green bell pepper, seeded and sliced thinly
1 cup tomatoes, chopped
2 garlic cloves, minced
¼ cup fresh cilantro, chopped and divided
2 bay leaves
1 teaspoon paprika
Salt and ground black pepper, as required
½ cup fish broth
¾ pound (340 g) shrimp, peeled and deveined
¾ pound (340 g) cod fillets, cut into 2-inch chunks

1. Add the oil in Instant Pot and select "Sauté". Then add the onion, bell pepper, tomatoes, garlic, 2 tablespoons of cilantro, bay leaves, paprika, salt and black pepper and cook for about 3 to 4 minutes.
2. Press "Cancel" and stir in the broth.
3. Submerge the shrimps into the vegetable mixture and top with the cod pieces.
4. Secure the lid and turn to "Seal" position.
5. Cook on "Manual" with "High Pressure" for about 10 minutes.
6. Press "Cancel" and do a "Natural" release for about 10 minutes. Then do a "Quick" release.
7. Remove the lid and serve hot with the garnishing of remaining cilantro.

Per Serving
calories: 263 | fat: 9.7g | protein: 36.3g | carbs: 7.8g | net carbs: 6.1g | fiber: 1.6g

Tofu with Peas

1 Leaner | 1 Greens | 1 Healthy Fat | 3 Condiments
Prep time: 10 minutes | Cook time: 8 minutes | Serves 4

1¼ cups unsweetened coconut milk
2 tablespoons curry paste
14 ounces firm tofu, pressed, drained and cubed
1 tablespoon olive oil
½ teaspoons garam masala powder
½ teaspoons ground cumin
¼ teaspoons cayenne pepper
¼ teaspoons ground turmeric
1½ cups frozen green peas, thawed
Salt, as required

1. In a bowl add coconut milk and curry paste and mix until smooth.
2. Add the oil in Instant Pot and select "Sauté". Then add the garam masala, cumin, cayenne and turmeric and cook for about 30 seconds.
3. Stir in tofu cubes and cook for about 2 minutes.
4. Press "Cancel" and stir in the coconut milk mixture, peas and salt.
5. Secure the lid and turn to "Seal" position.
6. Cook on "Manual" with "High Pressure" for about 5 minutes.
7. Press "Cancel" and carefully do a "Quick" release.
8. Remove the lid and serve hot.

Per Serving
calories: 321 | fat: 24.8g | protein: 12.2g | carbs: 13g | net carbs: 9g | fiber: 4g

Tofu with Broccoli

1 Leaner | 1 Greens | 1 Healthy Fat | 3 Condiments
Prep time: 14 minutes | Cook time: 13 minutes | Serves 4

For Tofu
14 ounces (397 g) extra firm tofu, pressed, drained and cubed
2 tablespoons low-sodium soy sauce
2 teaspoons Sriracha
1 teaspoon olive oil
2 teaspoons balsamic vinegar

For Sauce
3 tablespoons low-sodium soy sauce
2 tablespoons water
1 tablespoon maple syrup
1 tablespoon olive oil
1 tablespoons balsamic vinegar
1 teaspoon fresh ginger, grated

For Cooking
1½ tablespoons olive oil
2 cups broccoli florets

1. For tofu: in a resealable bag, place all the ingredients.
2. Seal the bag and shake to coat well.
3. Set aside for 5 about minutes, tossing occasionally.
4. For sauce: in a medium bowl, add all the ingredients and beat until well combined.
5. Add the oil in the Instant Pot and select "Sauté". Then add the tofu and cook for about 2 minutes per side.
6. Press "Cancel" and stir in the sauce.
7. Secure the lid and turn to "Seal" position.
8. Cook on "Manual" with "High Pressure" for about 3 minutes.
9. Press "Cancel" and carefully do a "Quick" release.
10. Remove the lid and stir in the broccoli florets.
11. Secure the lid and turn to "Seal" position.
12. Cook on "Manual" with "Low Pressure" for about 1 minute.
13. Press "Cancel" and carefully do a "Quick" release.
14. Remove the lid and select "Sauté".
15. Cook for about 3 to 5 minutes.
16. Press "Cancel" and serve hot.

Per Serving
calories: 198 | fat: 9.9g | protein: 11g | carbs: 9.9g | net carbs: 6.9g | fiber: 3g

Pan-Seared Scallops

1 Leaner | 3 Greens | 1 Healthy Fat | 3 Condiments
Prep time: 10 minutes | Cook time: 7 minutes | Serves 10

2 tablespoons olive oil
3½ cups fresh baby spinach
3 pounds (1.4 kg) jumbo sea scallops
12 garlic cloves, minced
2 cups onions, chopped
Salt and black pepper, to taste

1. Warm up olive oil in a large non-stick skillet and cook scallops with salt and pepper for about 2 minutes 30 seconds on each side in it.
2. Take the scallops out of the pan and set them aside.
3. Now, add onions and garlic in the same skillet and sauté for about 3 minutes.
4. Add in spinach and cook for about 3 minutes.
5. Take out and set spinach on serving plates.
6. Top with scallops and serve.

Per Serving
calories: 170 | fat: 4.2g | protein: 24.7g | carbs: 8.7g | net carbs: 23.1g | fiber: 1.6g

Vegetable Curry

1 Leaner | 3 Greens | 1 Healthy Fat | 3 Condiments
Prep time: 10 minutes | Cook time: 27 minutes | Serves 12

2 tablespoons olive oil
6 cups fresh spinach
2 small yellow onions, chopped
2 pounds (907 g) Brussels sprouts
2 teaspoons fresh thyme, chopped
2 cups fresh mushrooms, sliced
Salt and black pepper, to taste

1. Heat oil in a non-stick skillet and sauté onions for about 4 minutes.
2. Now, sauté thyme and garlic for about 1 minute.
3. Add in mushrooms and cook for about 15 minutes.
4. Then, add in Brussels sprouts and stir properly.
5. Cook for about 3 minutes and stir in spinach.
6. Cook for about 4 minutes and stir in salt and pepper.
7. Take out and serve.

Per Serving
calories: 64 | fat: 2.7g | protein: 3.5g | carbs: 9g | net carbs: 5.4g | fiber: 3.6g

Herbed Chicken

Leaner | Greens | Healthy Fat | Condiments
Prep time: 10 minutes | Cook time: 45 minutes | Serves 12

¾ pound (340 g) skinless, boneless chicken thighs
2 teaspoons dried rosemary, crushed
6 broccoli heads, cut into florets
2 teaspoons dried oregano, crushed
8 garlic cloves, minced
½ cup extra-virgin olive oil
Salt and pepper, to taste

1. Warm up the baking oven to 375°F (190°C) and grease a baking dish.
2. Meanwhile, add chicken thighs, dried rosemary, dried oregano, garlic cloves, salt, pepper, and oil. Toss to coat well.
3. Arrange broccoli florets in the bottom of a baking dish and top them with chicken thighs.
4. Bake for 45 minutes and take out.
5. Serve and enjoy!

Per Serving
calories: 127 | fat: 9.6g | protein: 7.8g | carbs: 4g | net carbs: 2.6g | fiber: 1.4g

Filling Beef Dish

1 Leaner | 2 Greens | 1 Healthy Fat | 4 Condiments
Prep time: 10 minutes | Cook time: 10 minutes | Serves 2

1 tablespoon olive oil
1½ tablespoons low-sodium soy sauce
2 garlic cloves, minced
1 cup fresh kale, chopped
½ pound (226 g) beef sirloin steak, cut into bite-sized pieces
1 cup carrots, chopped
Salt and pepper, to taste

1. Warm up olive oil in a large skillet and sauté garlic for about 1 minute.
2. Add in beef and black pepper. Stir well.
3. Cook for about 4 minutes and add in kale, carrot and soy sauce.
4. Cook for about 5 minutes and stir in soy sauce and salt.
5. Take out and serve.

Per Serving
calories: 328 | fat: 14.1g | protein: 2.6g | carbs: 12.7g | net carbs: 10.8g | fiber: 1.9g

Asian Style Beef

1 Leaner | 2 Greens | 1 Healthy Fat | 4 Condiments
Prep time: 10 minutes | Cook time: 16 minutes | Serves 2

½ pound (226 g) sirloin steak
1 tablespoon fresh lime juice
1 tablespoon olive oil
1 tablespoon low-sodium soy sauce

1 garlic clove, minced
1 cup broccoli florets
½ Serrano pepper, seeded and chopped finely
Salt and pepper, to taste

1. Marinade the steak slices with black pepper.
2. Meanwhile, warm up oil in a skillet and fry the steak slices for about 8 minutes.
3. Take out the slices and sauté garlic and Serrano pepper for about 1 minute.
4. Add in broccoli and stir for about 3 minutes.
5. Now, stir in steak slices, soy sauce and lemon juice.
6. Cook for about 4 minutes and take out.
7. Serve and enjoy!

Per Serving
calories: 297 | fat: 14.3g | protein: 36.4g | carbs: 6g | net carbs: 4.6g | fiber: 1.4g

Citrus Fruit Salad

1 Leaner | 2 Greens | 1 Healthy Fat | 2 Condiments
Prep time: 5 minutes | Cook time: 0 minutes | Serves 2

1 orange, peeled and segmented
½ cup fresh strawberries, hulled and sliced
2 cups fresh baby arugula
1 teaspoon extra-virgin olive oil
1 tablespoon fresh lemon juice
Salt and pepper, to taste

1. Add orange, strawberries, arugula, oil, salt, and pepper in a large bowl.
2. Toss to coat well and squeeze lemon on the top.
3. Serve and enjoy!

Per Serving
calories: 82 | fat: 2.7g | protein: 1.7g | carbs: 14.5g | net carbs: 11.26g | fiber: 3.3g

High-Protein Salad

1 Leaner | 3 Greens | 1 Healthy Fat | 2 Condiments
Prep time: 10 minutes | Cook time: 0 minutes | Serves 2

2 boneless, skinless chicken breasts, shredded
1½ lettuce, torn
1 tablespoon olive oil
1½ fresh baby greens
¼ cup cherry tomatoes, halved
Salt and black pepper, to taste

1. Add each ingredient in a large bowl and toss to coat well.
2. Serve and enjoy!

Per Serving
calories: 447 | fat: 17.7g | protein: 49.6g | carbs: 24.7g | net carbs: 15.2g | fiber: 9.5g

Beef & Cabbage Stew

1 Leaner | 5 Greens | 1 Healthy Fat | 2 Condiments
Prep time: 10 minutes | Cook time: 1 hour 50 minutes | Serves 8

2 pounds beef stew meat, trimmed and cubed into 1-inch size
1 ⅓ cups hot low-sodium chicken broth
2 yellow onions, chopped
2 bay leaves
1 teaspoon Greek seasoning
Salt and ground black pepper, as required
3 celery stalks, chopped
1 (8-ounce/ 227 g) package shredded cabbage
1 (6-ounce/ 170 g) can sugar-free tomato sauce
1 (8-ounce/ 227 g) can sugar-free whole plum tomatoes, chopped roughly with liquid

1. Heat a large nonstick pan over medium-high heat and cook the beef for about 4 to 5 minutes or until browned.
2. Drain excess grease from the pan.
3. Stir in the broth, onion, bay leaves, Greek seasoning, salt and black pepper and bring to a boil.
4. Reduce the heat to low and cook, covered for about 1¼ hours.
5. Stir in the celery and cabbage and cook, covered for about 30 minutes.
6. Stir in the tomato sauce and chopped plum tomatoes and cook, uncovered for about 15 to 20 minutes.
7. Stir in the salt and remove from heat.
8. Discard bay leaves and serve hot.

Per Serving
calories: 247 | fat: 7.5g | protein: 36.5g | carbs: 7g | net carbs: 4.9g | fiber: 2.1g

Beef & Carrot Stew

1 Leaner | 2 Greens | 1 Healthy Fat | 8 Condiments
Prep time: 15 minutes | Cook time: 55 minutes | Serves 6

1½ pounds (680 g) beef stew meat, trimmed and chopped
Salt and ground black pepper, as required
1 tablespoon olive oil
1 cup homemade tomato puree
4 cups homemade low-sodium beef broth
3 carrots, peeled and sliced
2 garlic cloves, minced
½ tablespoons dried thyme
1 teaspoon dried parsley
1 teaspoon dried rosemary
1 tablespoon paprika
1 teaspoon onion powder
1 teaspoon garlic powder
3 tablespoons fresh parsley, chopped

1. In a large bowl, add the beef cubes, salt, and black pepper, and toss to coat well.
2. In a Dutch oven, heat oil over medium-high heat and cook the beef cubes for about 4 to 5 minutes or until browned.
3. Add in remaining ingredients except for parsley and stir to combine.
4. Adjust the heat to high and bring to a boil.
5. Now, adjust the heat to low and simmer, covered for about 40 to 50 minutes.
6. Stir in the salt and black pepper and remove from the heat.
7. Garnish with parsley and serve hot.

Per Serving
calories: 295 | fat: 10.5g | protein: 39g | carbs: 8g | net carbs: 5.8g | fiber: 2.2g

Baked Beef Stew

1 Leaner | 2 Greens | 1 Healthy Fat | 4 Condiments
Prep time: 15 minutes | Cook time: 2¼ hours | Serves 8

1 teaspoon ground coriander
¾ teaspoon ground cumin
½ teaspoon cayenne pepper
2 tablespoons coconut oil
3 pounds beef stew meat, cubed
Salt and ground black pepper, as required
½ yellow onion, chopped
2 garlic cloves, minced
2 cups low-sodium chicken broth
1 (15-ounce/425 g) can sugar-free diced tomatoes
1 medium head cauliflower, cut into 1-inch florets

1. Preheat your oven to 300°F (150°C).
2. In a small bowl, mix together spices. Set aside.
3. In a large ovenproof pan, heat the oil over medium heat and cook beef with salt and black pepper for about 10 minutes or until browned from all sides.
4. Transfer the beef into a bowl.
5. In the same pan, add the onion and sauté for about 3-4 minutes.
6. Add the garlic and spice mixture and sauté for about 1 minute.
7. Add the cooked beef, broth and tomatoes and bring to a gentle boil.
8. Immediately cover the pan and transfer into oven.
9. Bake for approximately 1½ hours.
10. Remove from the oven and stir in the cauliflower.
11. Bake, covered for about 30 minutes more or until cauliflower is done completely.
12. Serve hot.

Per Serving
calories: 372 | fat: 14.2g | protein: 53.4g | carbs: 5.1g | net carbs: 3.4g | fiber: 1.7g

Beef Lettuce Wraps

1 Leaner | 2 Greens | 1 Healthy Fat | 2 Condiments
Prep time: 10 minutes | Cook time: 13 minutes | Serves 2

2 tablespoons white onion, chopped
5 ounces (142 g) lean ground beef
2 tablespoons light thousand island dressing
⅛ teaspoon white vinegar
⅛ teaspoon onion powder
4 lettuce leaves
2 tablespoons low-fat cheddar cheese, shredded
1 small cucumber, julienned

1. Heat a small, lightly greased wok over medium-high heat and sauté the onion for about 2 to 3 minutes.
2. Add the beef and cook for about 8 to 10 minutes or until cooked through.
3. Remove from the heat and set aside.
4. In a bowl, add the dressing, vinegar and onion powder and mix well.
5. Arrange the lettuce leaves onto serving plates.
6. Place beef mixture over each lettuce leaf, followed by the cheese and cucumber.
7. Drizzle with sauce and serve.

Per Serving
calories: 203 | fat: 8.8g | protein: 49.6g | carbs: 5.3g | net carbs: 4.8g | fiber: 0.5g

Spicy Beef Burgers

1 Leaner | 2 Greens | 1 Healthy Fat | 5 Condiments
Prep time: 15 minutes | Cook time: 6 minutes | Serves 4

For Burgers
1-pound (454 g) lean ground beef
¼ cup fresh parsley, chopped
¼ cup fresh parsley, chopped
¼ cup fresh cilantro, chopped
1 tablespoon fresh ginger, chopped
1 teaspoon ground cumin
1 teaspoon ground coriander
½ teaspoon ground cinnamon
Salt and ground black pepper, as required

For Salad:
6 cup fresh baby arugula
2 cups cherry tomatoes, quartered
1 tablespoon fresh lemon juice
1 tablespoon extra-virgin olive oil

1. In a bowl, add the beef, ¼ cup of parsley, cilantro, ginger, spices, salt and black pepper and mix until well combined.
2. Make 4 equal-sized patties from the mixture.
3. Heat a greased grill pan over medium-high heat and cook the patties for about 3 minutes per side or until desired doneness.
4. Meanwhile, in a bowl, add arugula, tomatoes, lemon juice and oil and toss to coat well.
5. Divide the salad onto serving plates and top each with 1 patty.
6. Serve immediately.

Per Serving
calories: 274 | fat: 11.2g | protein: 36.3g | carbs: 6.4g | net carbs: 4.3g | fiber: 2.1g

Spiced Beef Meatballs

1 Leaner | 3 Greens | 1 Healthy Fat | 2 Condiments
Prep time: 15 minutes | Cook time: 30 minutes | Serves 6

For Meatballs:
½ cup carrot, peeled and grated
½ cup zucchini, grated
½ cup yellow squash, grated
Salt, as required
1 pound (454 g) lean ground beef
1 egg, beaten
¼ of a small onion, chopped finely
1 garlic clove, minced
2 tablespoons mixed fresh herbs (parsley, basil, cilantro, chopped final

For Serving:
6 cups fresh baby spinach
3 large tomatoes, sliced

1. Preheat your oven to 400°F (205°C).
2. Line a large baking sheet with parchment paper.
3. In a large colander, place the carrot, zucchini and yellow squash and sprinkle with 2 pinches of salt. Set aside for at least 10 minutes.
4. Transfer the veggies over a paper towel and squeeze out all the moisture
5. In a large mixing bowl, add squeezed vegetables, beef, egg, onion, garlic, herbs and salt and mix until well combined.
6. Shape the mixture into equal-sized balls.
7. Arrange the meatballs onto the prepared baking sheet in a single layer.
8. Bake for approximately 25 to 30 minutes or until done completely.
9. Divide the spinach and tomato slices onto serving plates.
10. Top each plate with meatballs and serve.

Per Serving
calories: 184 | fat: 5.8g | protein: 25.9g | carbs: 6.9g | net carbs: 4.5g | fiber: 2.4g

Spicy Beef Koftas

1 Leaner | 2 Greens | 1 Healthy Fat | 5 Condiments
Prep time: 10 minutes | Cook time: 10 minutes | Serves 6

1-pound (454 g) ground beef
2 tablespoons low-fat plain Greek yogurt
2 tablespoons yellow onion, grated
2 teaspoons garlic, minced
2 tablespoons fresh cilantro, minced
1 teaspoon ground coriander
1 teaspoon ground cumin
1 teaspoon ground turmeric
Salt and ground black pepper, as required
1 tablespoon olive oil
8 cups fresh salad greens

1. In a large bowl, add all the ingredients except for greens and mix until well combined.
2. Make 12 equal-sized oblong patties from the mixture.
3. In a large non-stick wok, heat the oil over medium-high heat and cook the patties for about 10 minutes or until browned from both sides, flipping occasionally.
4. Serve the Koftas with salad greens

Per Serving
calories: 193 | fat: 7,4g | protein: 24.5g | carbs: 6.6g | net carbs: 4g | fiber: 2.6g

Beef Kabobs

1 Leaner | 1 Greens | 1 Healthy Fat | 6 Condiments
Prep time: 10 minutes | Cook time: 38 minutes | Serves 6

3 garlic cloves, minced
1 tablespoon fresh lemon zest, grated
2 teaspoons fresh rosemary, minced
2 teaspoons fresh parsley, minced
2 teaspoons fresh oregano, minced
2 teaspoons fresh thyme, minced
4 tablespoons olive oil
2 tablespoons fresh lemon juice
Salt and ground black pepper, as required
2 pounds beef sirloin, cut into cubes
8 cups fresh baby greens

1. In a bowl, add all the ingredients except the beef and greens and mix well.
2. Add the beef and coat with the herb mixture generously.
3. Refrigerate to marinate for at least 20 to 30 minutes.
4. Preheat the grill to medium-high heat. Grease the grill grate.
5. Remove the beef cubes from the marinade and thread onto metal skewers.
6. Place the skewers onto the grill and cook for about 6 to 8 minutes, flipping after every 2 minutes.
7. Remove from the grill and place onto a platter for about 5 minutes before serving.
8. Serve alongside the greens.

Per Serving
calories: 240 | fat: 15g | protein: 23.7g | carbs: 2.5g | net carbs: 1.4 g | fiber: 1.1 g

Garlicky Beef Tenderloin

1 Leaner | 1 Greens | 1 Healthy Fat | 2 Condiments
Prep time: 5 minutes | Cook time: 13 minutes | Serves 19

1 (3-pound/ 1.4 kg) center-cut beef tenderloin roast
4 garlic cloves, minced
1 tablespoon fresh rosemary, minced
Salt and ground black pepper, as required
1 tablespoon olive oil
15 cups fresh spinach

1. Preheat your oven to 425°F (220°C).
2. Grease a large shallow roasting pan.
3. Place the roast into the prepared roasting pan.
4. Rub the roast with garlic, rosemary, salt, and black pepper, and drizzle with oil.
5. Roast the beef for about 45-50 minutes.
6. Remove from oven and place the roast onto a cutting board for about 10 minutes.
7. With a knife, cut beef tenderloin into desired-sized slices and serve alongside the spinach.

Per Serving
calories: 283 | fat: 15.6g | protein: 32.6g | carbs:1.9g | net carbs: 0.9g | fiber: 01g

Simple Steak

1 Leaner | 1 Greens | 1 Healthy Fat | 1 Condiments
Prep time: 5 minutes | Cook time: 5 minutes | Serves 4

1 tablespoon olive oil
4 (6-ounce/ 170 g) flank steaks
Salt and ground black pepper, as required
6 cups fresh salad greens

1. In a wok, heat the oil over medium-high heat and cook steaks with salt and black pepper for about 3 to 5 minutes per side.
2. Transfer the steaks onto serving plates and serve alongside the greens.

Per Serving
calories:284| fat: 38g | protein: 12g | carbs: 3g | net carbs: 1g | fiber: 2g

Spiced Flank Steak

1 Leaner | 1 Greens | 5 Condiments
Prep time: 10 minutes | Cook time: 30 minutes | Serves 5

½ teaspoons dried thyme, crushed
½ teaspoons dried oregano, crushed
1 teaspoon red chili powder
½ teaspoons ground cumin
¼ teaspoons garlic powder
Salt and ground black pepper, as required
1½ pounds (680 g) flank steak, trimmed
6 cups salad greens

1. In a large bowl, add the dried herbs and spices and mix well.
2. Add the steaks and rub with mixture generously.
3. Set aside for about 15 to 20 minutes.
4. Preheat the grill to medium heat. Grease the grill grate.
5. Place the steak onto the grill over medium coals and cook for about 18 to 20 minutes, flipping once halfway through.
6. Remove the steak from grill and place onto a cutting board for about 10 minutes before slicing.
7. With a knife, cut steak into desired sized slices and serve alongside the greens.

Per Serving
calories: 277 | fat: 11.5g | protein: 38.6g | carbs: 2.4g | net carbs: 1.5g | fiber: 0.9g

Simple Flank Steak

1 Leaner | 1 Greens | 1 Healthy Fat | 2 Condiments
Prep time: 10 minutes | Cook time: 4 minutes | Serves 4

For Steak:
2 tablespoons extra-virgin olive oil
4 (6-ounce/ 170 g) flank steaks
Salt and ground black pepper, as required

For Salad:
6 cups fresh baby arugula
3 tablespoons extra-virgin olive oil
2 tablespoons balsamic vinegar
Salt and ground black pepper, as required

1. In a sauté pan, heat the oil over medium-high heat and cook the steaks with salt and black pepper for about 3 to 4 minutes per side.
2. For salad, in a salad bowl, place all ingredients and toss to coat well.
3. Divide the arugula onto serving plates and top each with 1 steak.
4. Serve immediately.

Per Serving
calories: 385 | fat: 24.7 g | protein: 38.4g | carbs: 1.2g | net carbs: 0.7g | fiber: 0.5g

Steak with Green Beans

1 Leaner | 1 Greens | 1 Healthy Fat | 2 Condiments
Prep time: 10 minutes | Cook time: 13 minutes | Serves 2

For Steak:
2 (5-ounce/ 142 g) sirloin steaks, trimmed
Salt and ground black pepper, as required
1 tablespoon extra-virgin olive oil
1 garlic clove, minced

For Green Beans:
½ pound fresh green beans
½ tablespoon olive oil
½ tablespoon fresh lemon juice

1. For steak: season the steaks with salt and black pepper evenly.
2. In a cast-iron sauté pan, heat the olive oil over high heat and sauté garlic for about 15 to 20 seconds.
3. Add the steaks and cook for about 3 minutes per side.
4. Flip the steaks and cook for about 3 to 4 minutes or until desired doneness, flipping once.
5. Meanwhile, for green beans: in a pan of boiling water, arrange a steamer basket.
6. Place the green beans in steamer basket and steam, covered for about 4 to 5 minutes.
7. Carefully transfer the beans into a bowl.
8. Add olive oil and lemon juice and toss to coat well.
9. Divide green beans onto serving plates.
10. Top each with 1 steak and serve.

Per Serving
calories: 388 | fat: 18.9g | protein: 45.5g | carbs: 8.7g | net carbs: 4.8g | fiber: 3.9g

Veggie & Feta Stuffed Steak

1 Leaner | 4 Greens | 1 Healthy Fat | 2 Condiments
Prep time: 10 minutes | Cook time: 35 minutes |
  Serves 6

1 tablespoon dried oregano leaves
⅓ cup fresh lemon juice
2 tablespoons olive oil
1 (2-pound/ 907 g) beef flank steak, pounded into
    ½-inch thickness.
⅓ cup olive tapenade
1 cup frozen chopped spinach, thawed and squeezed
¼ cup feta cheese, crumbled
4 cups fresh cherry tomatoes
Salt, as required

1. In a large baking dish, add the oregano, lemon juice and oil and mix well.
2. Add the steak and coat with the marinade generously.
3. Refrigerate to marinate for about 4 hours, flipping occasionally.
4. Preheat your oven to 425°F (218°C).
5. Line a shallow baking dish with parchment paper.
6. Remove the steak from baking dish, reserving the remaining marinade in a bowl.
7. Cover the bowl of marinade and refrigerate.
8. Arrange the steak onto a cutting board.
9. Place the tapenade onto the steak evenly and top with the spinach, followed by the feta cheese.
10. Carefully roll the steak tightly to form a log.
11. With 6 kitchen string pieces, tie the log at 6 places.
12. Carefully cut the log between strings into 6 equal pieces, leaving the string in place.
13. In a bowl, add the reserved marinade, tomatoes and salt and toss to coat.
14. Arrange the log pieces onto the prepared baking dish, cut-side up.
15. Now, arrange the tomatoes around the log pieces evenly.
16. Bake for approximately 25 to 35 minutes.
17. Remove from the oven and set aside for about 5 minutes before serving.

Per Serving
calories: 395 | fat: 18.2g | protein: 48.4g | carbs: 7g | net carbs: 4.8g | fiber: 2.2g

Beef Taco Bowl

1 Leaner | 3 Greens | 5 Condiments
Prep time: 15 minutes | Cook time: 15 minutes |
  Serves 4

1 teaspoon red chili powder
1 teaspoon ground cumin
Salt and freshly ground black pepper, as required
1-pound (454 g) flank steak, trimmed
2 scallions
1 lime, cut in half
8 cups lettuce, torn
1 red bell pepper, seeded and sliced
1 cup tomato, chopped
½ cup fresh cilantro, chopped
¼ cup light sour cream

1. Preheat the grill to medium-high heat. Grease the grill grate.
2. In a small bowl, mix together the spices, salt and black pepper.
3. Rub the steak with spice mixture generously.
4. Place the steak onto the grill and cook for about 4 to 6 minutes per side or until desired doneness.
5. Remove from the grill and place the steak onto a cutting board for about 5 minutes.
6. Now, place the scallions onto the grill and cook for about 1 minute per side.
7. Place the lime halves onto the grill, cut-side down and cook for about 1 minute.
8. Remove the scallions and lime halves from the grill and place onto a plate.
9. Chop the scallions roughly.
10. With a sharp knife, cut the steak into thin slices.
11. In a bowl, place the beef slices and chopped scallions.
12. Squeeze the lime halves over steak mixture and toss to coat well.
13. Divide lettuce into serving bowls and top each with bell pepper, followed by tomato, cilantro and beef mixture.
14. Top each bowl with sour cream and serve.

Per Serving
calories: 288 | fat: 13g | protein: 33.5g | carbs: 8.7g |
net carbs: 6.3g | fiber: 2.4g

Salmon & Arugula Omelet

1 Leaner | 1 Greens | 1 Healthy Fat | 1 Condiments
Prep time: 10 minutes | Cook time: 7 minutes | Serves 4

6 eggs
2 tablespoons unsweetened almond milk
Salt and ground black pepper, as required
2 tablespoons olive oil

4 ounces (113 g) smoked salmon, cut into bite-sized chunks
2 cups fresh arugula, chopped finely
4 scallions, chopped finely

1. In a bowl, place the eggs, coconut milk, salt and black pepper and beat well. Set aside.
2. In a nonstick wok, heat the oil over medium heat.
3. Place the egg mixture evenly and cook for about 30 seconds without stirring.
4. Place the salmon, arugula and scallions on top of egg mixture evenly.
5. Reduce heat to low and cook, covered for about 4 to 5 minutes or until omelet is done completely.
6. Uncover the wok and cook for about 1 minute.
7. Carefully transfer the omelet onto a serving plate and serve.

Per Serving
calories: 210 | fat: 14.9g | protein: 14.8g | carbs: 5.2g | net carbs: 4.3g | fiber: 0.9g

Tuna Omelet

1 Leaner | 2 Greens | 1 Healthy Fat | 3 Condiments
Prep time: 15 minutes | Cook time: 5 minutes | Serves 2

4 eggs
¼ cup unsweetened almond milk
1 tablespoon scallions, chopped
1 garlic clove, minced
½ of jalapeño pepper, minced
Salt and ground black pepper, as required
1 (5-ounce/ 142 g) can water-packed tuna, drained and flaked
1 tablespoon olive oil
3 tablespoons green bell pepper, seeded and chopped
3 tablespoons tomato, chopped
¼ cup low-fat cheddar cheese, shredded

1. In a bowl, add the eggs, almond milk, scallions, garlic, jalapeño pepper, salt, and black pepper, and beat well.
2. Add the tuna and stir to combine.
3. In a large nonstick frying pan, heat oil over medium heat.
4. Place the egg mixture in an even layer and cook for about 1 to 2 minutes, without stirring.
5. Carefully lift the edges to run the uncooked portion flow underneath.
6. Spread the veggies over the egg mixture and sprinkle with the cheese.
7. Cover the frying pan and cook for about 30 to 60 seconds.
8. Remove the lid and fold the omelet in half.
9. Remove from the heat and cut the omelet into 2 portions.
10. Serve immediately.

Per Serving
calories: 340 | fat: 21.5g | protein: 33.3g | carbs: 3.4g | net carbs: 2.6g | fiber: 0.8g

Spicy Salmon

1 Leaner | 1 Greens | 1 Healthy Fat | 3 Condiments
Prep time: 10 minutes | Cook time: 8 minutes | Serves 4

4 tablespoons extra-virgin olive oil, divided
2 tablespoons fresh lemon juice
1 teaspoon ground turmeric
1 teaspoon ground cumin
Salt and ground black pepper, as required
4 (4-ounce/ 113 g) boneless, skinless salmon fillets
6 cups fresh arugula

1. In a bowl, mix together 2 tablespoons of oil, lemon juice, turmeric, cumin, salt and black pepper.
2. Add the salmon fillets and coat with the oil mixture generously. Set aside.
3. In a non-stick wok, heat the remaining oil over medium heat.
4. Place salmon fillets, skin-side down and cook for about 3 to 5 minutes.
5. Change the side and cook for about 2 to 3 minutes more.
6. Divide the salmon onto serving plates and serve immediately alongside the arugula.

Per Serving
calories: 283 | fat: 21.4g | protein: 23g | carbs: 1.9g | net carbs:1.28g | fiber: 0.7g

Salmon Lettuce Wraps

1 Leaner | 3 Greens | 1 Healthy Fat | 1 Condiments
Prep time: 10 minutes | Cook time: 0 minutes | Serves 2

¼ cup part-skim mozzarella cheese, cubed
¼ cup tomato, chopped
2 tablespoons fresh dill, chopped
1 teaspoon fresh lemon juice
Salt, as required
4 lettuce leaves
⅓ pound (9.45) cooked salmon, chopped

1. In a small bowl, combine mozzarella, tomato, dill, lemon juice, and salt until well combined.
2. Arrange the lettuce leaves onto serving plates.
3. Divide the salmon and tomato mixture over each lettuce leaf and serve immediately.

Per Serving
calories: 124 | fat: 5.5g | protein: 16.6g | carbs: 3.1g | net carbs: 2.3g | fiber: 0.8g

Shrimp Stew

1 Leaner | 3 Greens | 1 Healthy Fat | 4 Condiments
Prep time: 10 minutes | Cook time: 20 minutes | Serves 6

¼ cup olive oil
¼ cup yellow onion, chopped
¼ cup green bell pepper, seeded and chopped
1 garlic clove, minced
1½ pounds (680 g) raw shrimp, peeled and deveined
1 (14-ounce/ 397 g) can diced tomatoes with chilies
1 cup unsweetened coconut milk
2 tablespoons Sriracha
2 tablespoons fresh lime juice
Salt and ground black pepper, as required
¼ cup fresh cilantro, chopped

1. Heat oil in a pan over medium heat and sauté the onion for about 4 to 5 minutes.
2. Add the bell pepper and garlic and sauté for about 4 to 5 minutes.
3. Add the shrimp and tomatoes and cook for about 3 to 4 minutes.
4. Stir in the coconut milk and Sriracha and cook for about 4 to 5 minutes.
5. Stir in the lime juice, salt, and black pepper, and remove from the heat.
6. Garnish with cilantro and serve hot.

Per Serving
calories: 236 | fat: 11.1g | protein: 26.6g | carbs: 6.7g | net carbs: 5.5g | fiber: 1.2g

Lemony Salmon

1 Leaner | 1 Greens | 1 Healthy Fat | 3 Condiments
Prep time: 10 minutes | Cook time: 7 minutes | Serves 4

2 garlic cloves, minced
1 tablespoon fresh lemon zest, grated
2 tablespoons olive oil
2 tablespoons fresh lemon juice
Salt and ground black pepper, as required
4 (6-ounce/ 170 g) boneless, skinless salmon fillets
6 cups fresh spinach

1. Preheat the grill to medium-high heat.
2. Grease the grill grate.
3. In a bowl, place all ingredients except for salmon and spinach and mix well.
4. Add the salmon fillets and coat with garlic mixture generously.
5. Grill the salmon fillets for about 6 to 7 minutes per side.
6. Serve immediately alongside the spinach.

Per Serving
calories: 300 | fat: 17.8g | protein: 34.5g | carbs: 2.6g | net carbs: 1.5g | fiber: 1.1g

Salmon with Asparagus

1 Leaner | 1 Greens | 1 Healthy Fat | 2 Condiments
Prep time: 5 minutes | Cook time: 20 minutes | Serves 6

6 (4-ounce/ 113 g) salmon fillets
2 tablespoons extra-virgin olive oil
3 tablespoons fresh parsley, minced
¼ teaspoon ginger powder
Salt and freshly ground black pepper, as required
1½ pounds fresh asparagus

1. Preheat your oven to 400°F (204°C).
2. Grease a large baking dish.
3. In a bowl, place all ingredients and mix well.
4. Arrange the salmon fillets into the prepared baking dish in a single layer.
5. Bake for approximately 15-20 minutes or until desired doneness of salmon.
6. Meanwhile, in a pan of boiling water, add asparagus and cook for about 4-5 minutes.
7. Drain the asparagus well.
8. Divide the asparagus onto serving plates evenly.
9. Top each plate with 1 salmon fillet and serve.

Per Serving
calories: 214 | fat: 11.8g | protein: 24.6g | carbs: 4.6 g | net carbs: 2.1g | fiber: 2.5g

Chapter 5 Fueling Hacks

Iced Vanilla Shake

1 Fueling | 1 Condiment
Prep time: 5 minutes | Cook time: 0 minutes | Serves 1

½ packet Optavia Vanilla Shake Fueling
½ packet Optavia Gingerbread Fueling
½ cup unsweetened almond milk
½ cup water
8 ice cubes

1. In a small blender, place all ingredients and pulse until smooth.
2. Transfer the shake into a serving glass and serve immediately.

Per Serving
calories: 62 | fat: 1g | protein: 1g | carbs: 12g | net carbs: 11g | fiber: 1g

Cappuccino Shake

1 Fueling |1 Condiment
Prep time: 5 minutes | Cook time: 0 minutes | Serves 1

1 packet Medifast cappuccino mix
1 tablespoon sugar-free chocolate syrup
½ cup water
½ cup ice, crushed

1. In a small blender, place all ingredients and pulse until smooth and creamy.
2. Transfer the shake into a serving glass and serve immediately.

Per Serving
calories: 150 | fat: 8g | protein: 3g | carbs: 17g | net carbs: 13g | fiber: 4g

Vanilla-Almond Frappe

1 Fueling | 2 Condiments
Prep time: 5 minutes | Cook time: 0 minutes | Serves 1

1 sachet Optavia Essential Vanilla Shake
8 ounces (227 g) unsweetened almond milk
½ cup ice
1 tablespoon whipped topping

1. In a blender, add the Vanilla Shake sachet, almond milk and ice and pulse until smooth.
2. Transfer the mixture into a glass and top with whipped topping.
3. Serve immediately.

Per Serving
calories: 146 | fat: 8g | protein: 4g | carbs: 32g | net carbs: 30g | fiber: 2g

Pumpkin Coffee Frappe

1 Fueling | 3½ Condiments
Prep time: 5 minutes | Cook time: 0 minutes | Serves 1

1 sachet Optavia Essential Spiced Gingerbread
4 ounces (113 g) strong brewed coffee
4 ounces (113 g) unsweetened almond milk
⅛ teaspoon pumpkin pie spice
½ cup ice
1 tablespoon whipped topping

1. In a blender, add the Spiced Gingerbread sachet, coffee, almond milk, pumpkin pie spice and ice and pulse until smooth.
2. Transfer the mixture into a glass and top with whipped topping.
3. Serve immediately.

Per Serving
calories: 195 | fat: 9g | protein: 6g | carbs: 21g | net carbs: 18g | fiber: 3g

Hot Chocolate with Cinnamon

1 Fueling| 2½ Condiments
Prep time: 10 minutes | Cook time: 2 minutes | Serves 1

1 sachet Optavia Essential Velvety Hot Chocolate
½ teaspoon ground cinnamon
Pinch of cayenne pepper
6 ounces (170 g) unsweetened almond milk
1 tablespoon whipped cream

1. In a serving mug, place all the ingredients except for whipped cream and beat until well blended.
2. Microwave on high for about 2 minutes.
3. Top with whipped cream and serve.

Per Serving
calories: 142 | fat: 8g | protein: 6g | carbs: 10g | net carbs: 9g | fiber: 1g

Classic Eggnog

1 Fueling | 2 Condiments
Prep time: 10 minutes | Cook time: 0 minutes | Serves 1

1 sachet Optavia Essential Vanilla Shake
8 ounces (227 g) unsweetened almond milk
1 organic egg (yolk and white separated)
¼ teaspoon rum extract
Pinch of ground nutmeg

1. In a blender, add the Vanilla Shake sachet, almond milk and egg yolk and pulse until smooth.
2. In the bowl of a stand mixer, place egg white and beat on medium speed until stiff peaks form.
3. Place the whipped egg whites into a serving glass and top with shake mixture.
4. Stir the mixture and sprinkle with nutmeg.
5. Serve immediately.

Per Serving
calories: 246 | fat: 14g | protein: 16g | carbs: 12g | net carbs: 12g | fiber: 0g

Oatmeal Sticks

2 Fueling | 1 Condiment
Prep time: 10 minutes | Cook time: 4 minutes | Serves 3

2 sachets Optavia Essential Cinnamon Crunchy Oat Cereal
6 tablespoons egg liquid substitute
2 tablespoons low-fat cream cheese, softened
Olive oil cooking spray

1. In a food processor, add the Oat Cereal sachets and pulse until fine breadcrumbs like consistency is achieved.
2. Add the egg liquid substitute and cream cheese and pulse until a dough forms.
3. Divide the dough into 6 equal-sized pieces and shape each into a breadstick.
4. Grease a wok lightly with cooking spray and heat over medium-high heat.
5. Add the French toast sticks and cook for about 2 minutes per side or until golden brown.
6. Serve warm.

Per Serving
calories: 106 | fat: 4g | protein: 11g | carbs: 6g | net carbs: 6g | fiber: 0g

Chocolate Fudge Balls

2 Fueling | 1 Condiment
Prep time: 10 minutes | Cook time: 0 minutes | Serves 2

1 sachet Medifast chocolate pudding
1 sachet Medifast chocolate shake
4 tablespoons peanut butter powder
¼ cup unsweetened almond milk
2 tablespoons water

1. In a small bowl, add all ingredients and stir until well blended.
2. Make 8 small equal-sized balls from the mixture.
3. Arrange the balls onto a parchment paper-lined baking sheet and refrigerate until set before serving.

Per Serving
calories: 108 | fat: 2g | protein: 6g | carbs: 10g | net carbs: 9g | fiber: 1g

Chocolate Brownie Cookies

2 Fueling
Prep time: 10 minutes | Cook time: 2 minutes | Serves 2

1 sachet Optavia Essential Decadent Double Brownie
1 sachet Peanut Butter Chocolate Crunch Bar
3 tablespoons water

1. In a bowl, add the Brownie sachet and water and mix well. Set aside.
2. In a microwave-safe bowl, place the Crunch Bar and microwave on High for about 20 seconds or until it is slightly melted.
3. Add the crunch bar into the brownie mixture and mix until well blended.
4. Divide the mixture into 2 greased ramekins and microwave on High for about 2 minutes.
5. Remove from microwave and set aside to cool for about 5 minutes before serving.

Per Serving
calories: 264 | fat: 7g | protein: 3g | carbs: 50g | net carbs: 37g | fiber: 13g

Vanilla Oatmeal Cookies

2 Fueling | 1 Condiment
Prep time: 10 minutes | Cook time: 15 minutes | Serves 2

1 Optavia Oatmeal Raisin Crunch Bar
1 packet Optavia Oatmeal
⅛ teaspoon ground cinnamon
1 packet stevia powder
⅛ teaspoon baking powder
½ teaspoon vanilla extract
⅓ cup water

1. Preheat your oven to 350°F (180°C).
2. Line a cookie sheet with parchment paper.
3. In a microwave-safe bowl, place the Crunch Bar and microwave on High for about 15 seconds or until it is slightly melted.
4. In the bowl of the bar, add the remaining ingredients and mix until well blended.
5. Set the mixture aside for about 5 minutes.
6. With a spoon, place 4 cookies onto the prepared cookie sheet in a single layer and with your fingers, press each ball slightly.
7. Bake for approximately 12-15 minutes.
8. Remove from the oven and place the cookie sheet onto a wire rack to cool for about 5 minutes.
9. Now, invert the cookies onto the wire rack to cool before serving.

Per Serving
calories: 109 | fat: 2g | protein: 11g | carbs: 14g | net carbs: 10g | fiber: 4g

Cinnamon Chocolate Haystacks

2 Fueling | 1 Condiment
Prep time: 10 minutes | Cook time: 0 minutes | Serves 2

1 sachet Optavia Brownie Mix
3 tablespoons water
1 tablespoon peanut butter powder
1 packet stevia powder
1 packet Medifast Cinnamon Pretzel Sticks, crushed

1. In a small bowl, add the brownie mix and water and mix until paste forms.
2. Add the peanut butter powder and stevia and mix until well blended.
3. Add the crushed pretzels and mix until well blended.
4. With a spoon, place 6 haystacks onto a piece of foil and freeze for about 1 hour or until set.

Per Serving
calories: 63 | fat: 3g | protein: 1g | carbs: 5g | net carbs: 5g | fiber: 0g

Vanilla Chocolate Crepes

1 Fueling | 3 Condiments
Prep time: 10 minutes | Cook time: 4 minutes | Serves 1

1 packet Medifast Chocolate Chip Pancakes
¼ cup water
2 tablespoons part-skim ricotta cheese
½ packet stevia powder
⅛ teaspoon vanilla extract
1 teaspoon sugar-free chocolate syrup

1. In a bowl, add the pancake packet and water and mix well.
2. Heat a lightly greased non-stick wok over medium heat.
3. Place the mixture into the wok and spread in a thin circle.
4. Cook for about 1-2 minutes per side or until golden brown.
5. Remove from the heat and place the crepe onto a plate.
6. In a small bowl, add the ricotta cheese, stevia and vanilla extract and mix until well blended.
7. Place the mixture inside the crepe.
8. Drizzle with chocolate syrup and serve.

Per Serving
calories: 363 | fat: 16g | protein: 11g | carbs: 44g | net carbs: 41g | fiber: 3g

Cheddar Potato Pancakes

1 Fueling | 2½ Condiments
Prep time: 10 minutes | Cook time: 12 minutes | Serves 2

1 Optavia Garlic Mashed Potatoes
¼ cup low-fat Cheddar cheese, shredded
¼ teaspoon baking powder
½ cup water
2 tablespoons low-fat sour cream

1. In a bowl, add all the ingredients except for sour cream and mix until well blended.
2. Set the bowl of the mixture aside for about 5 minutes.
3. Heat a lightly greased cast-iron wok over medium heat.
4. Place half of the mixture and with the back of a spoon, spread the mixture into a circle.
5. Cook for about 2-3 minutes per side or until golden brown.
6. Repeat with the remaining mixture.
7. Serve warm with the topping of sour cream.

Per Serving
calories: 224 | fat: 6g | protein: 9g | carbs: 33g | net carbs: 29g | fiber: 4g

Biscuit Pizza with Cheddar

1 Fueling | 2 Condiments
Prep time: 10 minutes | Cook time: 14 minutes | Serves 1

1 sachet Optavia Buttermilk Cheddar and Herb Biscuits
2 tablespoons water
1 tablespoon sugar-free tomato sauce
1 tablespoon low-fat Cheddar cheese, shredded

1. Preheat your oven to 350°F (180°C).
2. In a small bowl, add the biscuit and water and mix well.
3. Place the biscuit mixture onto a parchment paper-lined baking sheet and with a spoon, spread into a thin circle.
4. Bake for approximately 10 minutes.
5. Remove the baking sheet of pizza from the oven and spread the tomato sauce over the biscuit circle.
6. Sprinkle with Cheddar cheese.
7. Bake for approximately 2-4 minutes or until cheese is melted.
8. Remove the baking sheet of pizza from the oven and set aside for about 3-5 minutes.
9. Serve warm.

Per Serving
calories: 1,202 | fat: 107g | protein: 17g | carbs: 49g | net carbs: 7g | fiber: 18g

Cheddar Pizza Bread

1 Fueling | 2 Condiments
Prep time: 10 minutes | Cook time: 10 minutes | Serves 1

1 packet Optavia Cream of Tomato Soup
¼ teaspoon baking powder
Salt and ground black pepper, as required
2 tablespoons water
2 tablespoons low-fat Cheddar cheese, shredded

1. Preheat your oven to 425°F (220°C).
2. Grease a small baking sheet.
3. In a bowl, add the soup, baking powder, salt, black pepper and water and mix until well blended.
4. Place the mixture onto the prepared baking sheet and shape into a circle.
5. Bake for approximately 5 minutes.
6. Remove from the oven and with a spatula, flip the bread.
7. Top with the cheese and bake for approximately 5 minutes more.
8. Serve warm.

Per Serving
calories: 80| fat: 3g | protein: 5g | carbs: 7g | net carbs: 6g | fiber: 1g

Cheddar Avocado Toast

1 Fueling | 1 Healthy Fat
Prep time: 5 minutes | Cook time: 15 minutes | Serves 1

1 sachet Optavia Select Buttermilk Cheddar Herb Biscuit
1½ ounces (43 g) avocado, mashed

1. Bake the Buttermilk Cheddar Herb Biscuit according to the package directions.
2. Allow to cool before serving with mashed avocado on top.

Per Serving
calories: 233 | fat: 11g | protein: 4g | carbs: 28g | net carbs: 24g | fiber: 4g

Chocolate Chip Cookie with Yogurt

1 Fueling | ½ Leaner
Prep time: 5 minutes | Cook time: 0 minutes | Serves 1

1 sachet Optavia Essential Chewy Chocolate Chip Cookie
1 (5.3-ounce / 150-g) container low-fat plain Greek yogurt

1. Combine the Chewy Chocolate Chip Cookie with the Greek yogurt in a bowl.
2. Chill until ready to serve.

Per Serving
calories: 174 | fat: 5g | protein: 9g | carbs: 21g | net carbs: 21g | fiber: 0g

Pecans Oatmeal Bake with Cinnamon

1 Fueling | 1 Healthy Fat | 1 Condiment
Prep time: 10 minutes | Cook time: 20 to 25 minutes |
   Serves 4

4 sachets Optavia Indonesian Cinnamon and Honey Hot Cereal
½ teaspoon baking powder
1 cup unsweetened almond milk
3 tablespoons egg whites
1½ ounces (43 g) chopped pecans
¼ teaspoon cinnamon
Cooking spray

Special Equipment:
4 (4.2-ounce / 125-ml) mini mason jars

1. Preheat the oven to 350°F (180°C).
2. Combine the Indonesian Cinnamon and Honey Hot Cereal and baking powder in a bowl. Stir in the almond milk and egg white. Fold in the pecans.
3. Spritz 4 mason jars with cooking spray. Divide the mixture evenly between the jars, leaving 2 inches at the top. Sprinkle with cinnamon.
4. Bake in the preheated oven for 20 to 25 minutes on a baking sheet or until golden.
5. Allow to cool. Close the lid, refrigerate, and serve chilled.

Per Serving
calories: 470 | fat: 38g | protein: 16g | carbs: 19g | net carbs: 15g | fiber: 4g

Mozzarella Tomato Pizza Bites with Basil

1 Fueling | ¼ Lean | ½ Green | ½ Healthy Fat | 2 Condiments
Prep time: 10 minutes | Cook time: 12 minutes | Serves 4

4 sachets Optavia Buttermilk Cheddar Herb Biscuit
½ cup unsweetened almond milk
2 teaspoons olive oil
1 cup basil leaves, julienned
4 ounces (113 g) fresh Mozzarella log, cut into 12 small pieces
3 Roma tomatoes, thinly sliced
2 tablespoons balsamic vinegar
Cooking spray

1. Preheat the oven to 450°F (235°C).
2. In a bowl, mix Buttermilk Cheddar Herb Biscuit, almond milk, and olive oil until well combined.
3. Divide the biscuit mixture among 12 slots of a greased muffin tin.
4. Layer a slice of Mozzarella, then a slice of tomato, and then a few pieces of basil into each slot.
5. Bake in the preheated oven for 12 minutes or until biscuit mixture is well browned and cheese is bubbly.
6. Drizzle with balsamic vinegar on top before serving.

Per Serving
calories: 249 | fat: 8g | protein: 12g | carbs: 90g | net carbs: 88g | fiber: 2g

Yogurt Berry Bagels

1 Fueling | ½ Healthy Fat | 1½ Condiments
Prep time: 10 minutes | Cook time: 15 minutes | Serves 2

2 sachets Optavia Essential Yogurt Berry Blast Smoothie
2 tablespoons liquid egg substitute
⅓ cup unsweetened almond milk
½ teaspoon baking powder
Cooking spray
1 ounce (28 g) light cream cheese

1. Preheat the oven to 350°F (180°C).
2. In a bowl, mix the Yogurt Berry Blast Smoothie with egg substitute, almond milk, and baking powder.
3. Divide mixture among 4 greased slots of a donut pan.
4. Bake in the preheated oven for 15 minutes or until set.
5. Spread the cream cheese on top and allow to cool before serving.

Per Serving
calories: 110 | fat: 5g | protein: 3g | carbs: 12g | net carbs: 11g | fiber: 1g

Macadamia Smoothie Bowl with Chia Seeds

1 Fueling | 2 Healthy Fats | 2½ Condiments
Prep time: 10 minutes | Cook time: 0 minutes | Serves 1

1 sachet Optavia Essential Tropical Fruit Smoothie
½ cup unsweetened coconut milk
½ cup ice
1 tablespoon shredded, unsweetened coconut
½ ounce (14 g) macadamias, chopped
½ teaspoon lime zest
½ tablespoon chia seeds

1. Add the Tropical Fruit Smoothie, coconut milk, and ice to a blender. Pulse until smooth.
2. Pour the smoothie into a bowl. Spread the remaining ingredients on top and serve.

Per Serving
calories: 545 | fat: 49g | protein: 6g | carbs: 26g | net carbs: 19g | fiber: 7g

Spinach-Stuffed Mushrooms with Basil

1 Fueling | ½ Healthy Fat | 1 Condiment | 1 Optional Snack
Prep time: 15 minutes | Cook time: 25 minutes | Serves 4

4 sachets Optavia Spinach Pesto Mac and Cheese
2 cups raw spinach, torn into small pieces
¼ cup fresh basil, torn into small pieces
8 ounces (227 g) water
2 (10- to 12-ounce / 283- to 340-g) packages baby bella mushrooms, rinsed and stems removed
2 sachets Rosemary Sea Salt Crackers, finely crushed
2 tablespoons grated Pecorino Romano cheese
2 teaspoons olive oil
Cooking spray

1. Preheat the oven to 350°F (180°C).
2. In a microwave-safe bowl, mix the Spinach Pesto Mac and Cheese, spinach, basil, and water until well combined.
3. Microwave on high for 1½ minutes. Stir and let stand for 1 minute. Microwave on high for an additional minute. Stir and let sit.
4. Meanwhile, in a small bowl, combine the Rosemary Sea Salt Crackers, cheese, and olive oil.
5. Arrange the baby bella mushroom caps, cavity-side up, onto a greased and foil-lined baking sheet.
6. Fill each cavity with Mac and Cheese mixture. Top with Cracker mixture and press to secure.
7. Bake in the preheated oven for 22 minutes or until lightly browned.
8. Serve immediately

Per Serving
calories: 58| fat: 4g | protein: 1g | carbs: 4g | net carbs: 3g | fiber: 1g

Pumpkin Almond Gingerbread Latte

1 Fueling | 2½ Condiments
Prep time: 5 minutes | Cook time: 1 minutes | Serves 1

2 tablespoons pumpkin purée
½ cup unsweetened almond milk
1 sachet Optavia Essential Spiced Gingerbread
½ cup strong brewed coffee

1. Combine the pumpkin purée and milk in a microwave-safe mug. Microwave for 1 minute and stir.
2. Mix in the coffee and Spiced Gingerbread. Serve immediately.

Per Serving
calories: 73 | fat: 4g | protein: 6g | carbs: 2g | net carbs: 1g | fiber: 1g

Iced Ginger Ale Coconut Colada

½ Fueling | 3 Condiments
Prep time: 10 minutes | Cook time: 0 minutes | Serves 1

1 sachet Optavia Essential Creamy Vanilla Shake
6 ounces (170 g) unsweetened, original coconut milk
¼ teaspoon rum extract
6 ounces (170 g) diet ginger ale
½ cup ice
2 tablespoons shredded, unsweetened coconut, plus 2 teaspoons for topping

1. Combine all the ingredients in a blender. Pulse until creamy.
2. Divide the mixture among two pina colada glasses. Spread remaining 2 teaspoons of shredded coconut on top.
3. Serve immediately.

Per Serving
calories: 611 | fat: 50g | protein: 6g | carbs: 40g | net carbs: 33g | fiber: 7g

Chocolate Brownie and Peanut Butter Whoopie

1 Fueling | ½ Healthy Fat | 1 Condiment | 1 Optional Snack
Prep time: 10 minutes | Cook time: 18 minutes | Serves 2

2 sachets Optavia Decadent Double Chocolate Brownie
6 tablespoons unsweetened almond milk, divided
3 tablespoons liquid egg substitute
¼ teaspoon baking powder
1 teaspoon vegetable oil
¼ cup powdered peanut butter
Cooking spray

1. Preheat the oven to 350°F (180°C).
2. In a bowl, combine the Decadent Double Chocolate Brownie, ¼ cup almond milk, egg substitute, baking powder, and vegetable oil. Stir to mix well.
3. Divide the Chocolate Brownie batter among 4 slots of a greased muffin tin.
4. Bake in the preheated oven for 18 minutes or until a toothpick inserted in the center comes out clean.
5. Meanwhile, combine the powdered peanut butter and remaining almond milk in a small bowl.
6. When baking is complete, allow to cool, then slice each muffin in half horizontally.
7. Spread 1 tablespoon of peanut butter mixture on the bottom half of each muffin, then top with the remaining muffin halves.
8. Serve immediately.

Per Serving
calories: 151 | fat: 9g | protein: 5g | carbs: 10g | net carbs: 9g | fiber: 1g

Vanilla Sweet Potato Muffins with Pecans

1 Fueling | 1 Healthy Fat | 1 Condiment
Prep time: 15 minutes | Cook time: 20 minutes | Serves 4

2 sachets Optavia Select Honey Sweet Potatoes
2 sachets Optavia Essential Spiced Gingerbread
¼ cup unsweetened almond milk
6 tablespoons liquid egg substitute
½ teaspoon pumpkin pie spice
½ teaspoon baking powder
½ teaspoon vanilla extract
1 cup water
1½ ounces (43 g) chopped pecans
Cooking Spray

1. Preheat the oven to 350°F (180°C).
2. Cook the Honey Sweet Potatoes according to the package directions. Allow to cool before using.
3. Combine the cooked Honey Sweet Potatoes with remaining ingredients, except for the pecans in a large bowl.
4. Divide the mixture among 8 slots of a greased muffin pan. Sprinkle with pecans on top.
5. Bake in the preheated oven for 20 minutes or until a toothpick inserted in the center comes out clean.
6. Serve immediately.

Per Serving
calories: 95 | fat: 8g | protein: 3g | carbs: 3g | net carbs: 2g | fiber: 1g

Blueberry Almond Scones with Flaxseeds

1 Fueling | 2 Healthy Fats | 2 Condiments
Prep time: 15 minutes | Cook time: 15 minutes | Serves 4

4 sachets Optavia Blueberry Almond Hot Cereal
¼ cup ground flaxseeds
2 packets stevia
½ teaspoon baking powder
3 tablespoons unsalted butter, frozen and cut into ½-inch pieces
3 tablespoons liquid egg white
3 tablespoons plain, low-fat Greek yogurt
¼ teaspoon cinnamon

1. Preheat the oven to 400°F (205°C).
2. Add the Blueberry Almond Hot Cereal, ground flaxseeds, stevia, and baking powder to a food processor. Pulse until smooth.
3. Add the frozen butter and pulse until mixture resembles a coarse meal.
4. Add the egg white and Greek yogurt, and pulse until the dough is sanity.
5. Form the dough into a 6-inch circle, then transfer the dough onto a parchment-lined baking sheet. Sprinkle with cinnamon.
6. Bake in the preheated oven for 15 minutes or until lightly browned.
7. After baking, allow to cool before cutting into eight wedges, then serve.

Per Serving
calories: 244 | fat: 24g | protein: 7g | carbs: 8g | net carbs: 4g | fiber: 4g

Cinnamon French Toast Sticks

1 Fueling | 3 Condiments
Prep time: 5 minutes | Cook time: 8 minutes | Serves 2

2 sachets Optavia Essential Cinnamon Crunchy O's Cereal
2 tablespoons low-fat cream cheese, softened
6 tablespoons liquid egg substitute
Cooking spray

1. Put the Cinnamon Crunchy O's in a blender. Pulse until it has a breadcrumb-like consistency.
2. Pour in the cream cheese and liquid egg substitute, and pulse until a sanity dough forms.
3. Divide and shape the dough into 6 French toast stick pieces.
4. Spritz a skillet with cooking spray. Heat over medium high heat and cook the French toast sticks for 8 minutes on all sides or until lightly browned.
5. Serve immediately.

Per Serving
calories: 52 | fat: 5g | protein: 2g | carbs: 2g | net carbs: 7g | fiber: 0g

Vanilla Zombie Frappe

1 Fueling | 3 Condiments
Prep time: 15 minutes | Cook time: 0 minutes | Serves 1

1 sachet Optavia Essential Creamy Vanilla Shake
1 cup unsweetened almond milk
1 tablespoon caramel syrup
½ cup ice
McCormick Color From Nature Food Colors- blue, yellow, and red
2 tablespoons plain, low-fat Greek yogurt
1 tablespoon unsweetened vanilla milk
2 tablespoons pressurized whipped topping

1. Put the Creamy Vanilla Shake, almond milk, caramel syrup, and ice in a blender. Pulse until smooth.
2. Add equal portions of blue and yellow food coloring until the shade of green is achieved.
3. In a bowl, mix the Greek yogurt and equal portions of blue and red food coloring until the shade of purple is achieved.
4. In a separate bowl, mix the vanilla milk with equal portions of blue and red food coloring until the shade of purple is achieved.
5. Drizzle purple Greek yogurt mixture down the sides of a cup. Fill cup with green shake mixture. Top with whipped topping and sprinkle with purple milk mixture.
6. Serve immediately.

Per Serving
calories: 201 | fat: 9g | protein: 5g | carbs: 23g | net carbs: 21g | fiber: 2g

Chocolate, Vanilla and Strawberry Popsicles

1 Fueling | ¼ Leaner | ½ Condiment
Prep time: 15 minutes | Cook time: 0 minutes | Serves 6

1 sachet Optavia Essential Creamy Chocolate Shake
1 cup unsweetened almond milk, divided
2 cups plain, low-fat Greek yogurt, divided
1 packet stevia
1 sachet Optavia Essential Creamy Vanilla Shake
1 sachet Optavia Essential Wild Strawberry Shake

1. Add the Creamy Chocolate Shake, ⅓ cup of almond milk, ⅔ cup of Greek yogurt, and ⅓ packet stevia to a blender. Pulse until smooth.
2. Divide the mixture among 6 large popsicle molds, and place in the freezer for 15 minutes.
3. Repeat with the Creamy Vanilla Shake and the Wild Strawberry Shake. Freeze for at least 4 hours or overnight until set.
4. Serve the popsicles chilled.

Per Serving
calories: 75 | fat: 3g | protein: 5g | carbs: 5g | net carbs: 5g | fiber: 0g

Iced Pumpkin Frappe

1 Fueling | 2 Condiments
Prep time: 5 minutes | Cook time: 0 minutes | Serves 1

1 sachet Optavia Essential Spiced Gingerbread
4 ounces (113 g) strong brewed coffee, chilled
4 ounces (113 g) unsweetened almond milk
⅛ teaspoon pumpkin pie spice
½ cup ice
2 tablespoons pressurized whipped topping

1. Combine all the ingredients, except for the whipped topping, in a blender. Pulse until smooth.
2. Pour the mixture in a serving bowl. Top with whipped topping and serve.

Per Serving
calories: 222 | fat: 11g | protein: 6g | carbs: 22g | net carbs: 20g | fiber: 2g

Cranberry Cheesecakes with Orange

1 Fueling | ¼ Leaner | 3 Condiments
Prep time: 10 minutes | Cook time: 0 minutes | Serves 4

4 Optavia Honey Chili Cranberry Nut Bars, broken in half
1½ cups plain, low-fat Greek yogurt
2 tablespoons sugar-free, fat-free cheesecake-flavored pudding mix
1 teaspoon orange zest

1. Line a muffin tin with eight cupcake liners.
2. Arrange the Honey Chili Cranberry Nut Bar halves, crunch-side down, on a microwave-safe plate. Microwave for 30 seconds or until softened.
3. Arrange each half of the nut bar into a cupcake liner, and press. Repeat to fill all cupcake liners.
4. In a large bowl, mix Greek yogurt and pudding mix until well combined.
5. Divide the yogurt mixture among cupcake liner and spread with orange zest.
6. Freeze in the freezer for 45 minutes or until firm. Serve chilled.

Per Serving
calories: 72 | fat: 3g | protein: 3g | carbs: 8g | net carbs: 6g | fiber: 2g

Chocolate Whoopie

1 Fueling | 1 Healthy Fat | 1½ Condiments
Prep time: 15 minutes | Cook time: 15 minutes | Serves 4

2 sachets Optavia Essential Golden Chip Pancakes
2 sachets Optavia Essential Chewy Chocolate Chip Cookie
½ tablespoon unsweetened cocoa powder
½ teaspoon baking powder
6 tablespoons liquid egg substitute
½ cup unsweetened almond milk
1 teaspoon apple cider vinegar
Cooking spray
½ cup low-fat cream cheese
2 packets stevia

1. Preheat the oven to 350°F (180°C).
2. Mix the Golden Pancakes, Chewy Chocolate Chip Cookies, cocoa powder, and baking powder in a bowl.
3. Whisk in the egg substitute, almond milk, and apple cider vinegar, and mix until it forms a batter.
4. Divide the batter among 8 slots of a greased muffin tin. Bake in the preheated oven for 15 minutes or until a toothpick inserted in the center comes out clean.
5. Meanwhile, combine the cream cheese and stevia.
6. When baking is complete, allow to cool, then slice each muffin in half horizontally.
7. Spread one tablespoon of cream cheese mixture onto the bottom half of each muffin, and top with the remaining muffin halves.
8. Serve immediately.

Per Serving
calories: 344 | fat: 16g | protein: 12g | carbs: 38g | net carbs: 36g | fiber: 2g

Vanilla and Rum Eggnog

1 Fueling | ⅓ Lean | 1½ Condiments
Prep time: 5 minutes | Cook time: 0 minutes | Serves 1

1 sachet Optavia Essential Creamy Vanilla Shake
8 ounces (227 g) unsweetened almond milk
1 egg, white and yolk separated
¼ teaspoon rum extract
Pinch nutmeg

1. Combine the Creamy Vanilla Shake, almond milk, and egg yolk in a blender and pulse until smooth.
2. Whip the egg white until stiff peaks form in a bowl. Pour the whipped egg white in a glass.
3. Pour the Vanilla Shake mixture over the egg white. Sprinkle with nutmeg and serve.

Per Serving
calories: 688 | fat: 68g | protein: 25g | carbs: 24g | net carbs: 7g | fiber: 14g

Chocolate Peppermint Mocha

1 Fueling | 1½ Condiments
Prep time: 5 minutes | Cook time: 0 minutes | Serves 1

1 sachet Optavia Essential Velvety Hot Chocolate
6 ounces (170 g) brewed coffee
¼ teaspoon peppermint extract
¼ cup unsweetened almond milk, warmed
2 tablespoons pressurized whipped topping
Pinch cinnamon

1. Combine the Velvety Hot Chocolate, coffee, peppermint extract, and milk in a mug and stir to mix well.
2. Spread with whipped topping and sprinkle with cinnamon. Serve immediately.

Per Serving
calories: 53 | fat: 2g | protein: 1g | carbs: 8g | net carbs: 8g | fiber: 0g

Cheese Smashed Potatoes with Spinach

1 Fueling | ½ Lean | 1 Healthy Fat | 1 Green | 1 Condiment
Prep time: 5 minutes | Cook time: 0 minutes | Serves 1

1 sachet Optavia Essential Roasted Garlic Creamy Smashed Potatoes
1 cup baby spinach
1 teaspoon water
½ cup reduced-fat shredded Mozzarella cheese
1 tablespoon grated Parmesan cheese

1. Cook the Roasted Garlic Creamy Smashed Potatoes according to package directions.
2. Steam the spinach with water in a microwave-safe bowl in the microwave for 1 minute or until wilted.
3. Combine the Roasted Garlic Creamy Smashed Potatoes, spinach, and cheeses in a large serving bowl.
4. Serve warm.

Per Serving
calories: 199 | fat: 6g | protein: 10g | carbs: 26g | net carbs: 23g | fiber: 3g

Yogurt Berry Bark

½ Fueling | ½ Leaner | 1 Condiment
Prep time: 5 minutes | Cook time: 0 minutes | Serves 2

12 ounces (340 g) plain low-fat Greek yogurt
2 packets stevia
1 sachet Optavia Essential Red Berry Crunchy O's Cereal

1. Combine the Greek yogurt and stevia in a bowl.
2. Line a baking dish with foil. Pour the Greek yogurt in the baking dish.
3. Sprinkle the Red Berry Crunchy O's Cereal on top of the yogurt.
4. Put the baking dish in the freezer and freeze for 4 hours or overnight, or until firm.
5. Break the bark before serving.

Per Serving
calories: 107 | fat: 8g | protein: 8g | carbs: 11g | net carbs: 11g | fiber: 0g

Cheddar Jalapeño Poppers

½ Fueling | ¼ Lean | 1 Green | 1 Healthy Fat | 2½ Condiments
Prep time: 15 minutes | Cook time: 15 minutes | Serves 2

¼ cup plain low-fat Greek yogurt
½ cup reduced-fat, shredded Cheddar jack cheese
2 ounces (57 g) light cream cheese, softened
¼ teaspoon chili powder
¼ teaspoon garlic powder
⅛ teaspoon salt
6 jalapeños, halved lengthwise, seeds and membranes removed
Cooking spray
1 sachet Optavia Essential Jalapeño Cheddar Poppers, finely crushed to breadcrumb-like consistency

1. Preheat the oven to 350°F (180°C).
2. Whisk together the Greek yogurt, Cheddar jack cheese, cream cheese, chili powder, garlic powder, and salt in a bowl.
3. Spoon the cheese mixture into the jalapeño cavity.
4. Arrange the stuffed jalapeños on a greased, foil-lined baking sheet. Sprinkle with crushed Jalapeño Cheddar Poppers.
5. Bake in the preheated oven for 15 minutes. Serve immediately.

Per Serving
calories: 557 | fat: 59g | protein: 3g | carbs: 3g | net carbs: 3g | fiber: 0g

Minty Vanilla Chocolate Parfaits

1 Fueling | ¼ Leaner | 1 Condiment
Prep time: 10 minutes | Cook time: 0 minutes | Serves 2

1 Sachet Optavia Essential Decadent Double Chocolate Brownie
1 Sachet Optavia Essential Creamy Vanilla Shake
¾ cup plain, low-fat Greek yogurt
¼ cup unsweetened almond milk
⅛ teaspoon peppermint extract
Green food coloring
¼ cup pressurized whipped topping

1. Cook the Decadent Double Chocolate Brownie according to package directions. Allow to cool, then crumble into small pieces.
2. Combine the Creamy Vanilla Shake, Greek yogurt, almond milk, peppermint extract, and green food coloring in a bowl. Stir to mix well.
3. Arrange the brownie crumbles in two mason jars. Pour the yogurt mixture and whipped topping over.
4. Serve immediately.

Per Serving
calories: 92 | fat: 4g | protein: 3g | carbs: 9g | net carbs: 8g | fiber: 0g

Boo-Nila Shake

1 Fueling | 2 Condiments
Prep time: 5 minutes | Cook time: 0 minutes | Serves 1

1 sachet Optavia Essential Creamy Vanilla Shake
8 ounces (227 g) unsweetened almond milk
½ cup ice
2 tablespoons pressurized whipped topping

1. Combine the Creamy Vanilla Shake, almond milk, and ice in a food processor. Pulse until smooth.
2. Pour the mixture in a mason jar and spread with whipped topping over.
3. Serve immediately.

Per Serving
calories: 151 | fat: 8g | protcin: 4g | carbs: 13g | net carbs: 7g | fiber: 8g

Cheddar Buffalo Cauliflower

1 Fueling | 3 Greens | ½ Healthy Fat | 3 Condiments
Prep time: 15 minutes | Cook time: 28 minutes | Serves 2

2 sachets Optavia Select Buttermilk Cheddar Herb Biscuit
½ cup water
3 cups cauliflower florets
Cooking spray
¼ cup hot buffalo sauce
½ tablespoon butter, melted
¼ cup low-fat plain Greek yogurt
1 teaspoon dry ranch dressing mix

1. Preheat the oven to 425°F (220°C).
2. In a bowl, mix the Buttermilk Cheddar Herb Biscuits and water. Add cauliflower florets and toss to coat well.
3. Arrange the cauliflower florets on a greased, foil-lined baking sheet. Bake in the preheated oven for 20 minutes.
4. In a separate bowl, mix the hot sauce and butter. Transfer the baked cauliflower into the bowl of hot sauce mixture and toss to coat.
5. Put the cauliflower back onto the baking sheet and bake an additional 8 minutes or until golden brown and crispy.
6. In a small bowl, mix the Greek yogurt and the ranch dressing mix. Stir to combine well.
7. Serve the golden cauliflower with the yogurt ranch dip.

Per Serving
calories: 322 | fat: 10g | protein: 8g | carbs: 49g | net carbs: 39g | fiber: 10g

Egg & Vanilla Shake

1 Fueling | 1½ Condiment
Prep time: 5 minutes | Cook time: 5 minutes | Serves 2

2 sachets (each sachet 1.13oz/368.5 g) optavia essential creamy vanilla shake
16 ounces (453 g) vanilla almond milk, unsweetened
2 egg pasteurized; yolk separated
½ teaspoon rum extract
¼ teaspoon nutmeg

1. Preheat the oven to 425°F (220°C).
2. In a bowl, mix the Buttermilk Cheddar Herb Biscuits and water. Add cauliflower florets and toss to coat well.
3. Arrange the cauliflower florets on a greased, foil-lined baking sheet. Bake in the preheated oven for 20 minutes.
4. In a separate bowl, mix the hot sauce and butter. Transfer the baked cauliflower into the bowl of hot sauce mixture and toss to coat.
5. Put the cauliflower back onto the baking sheet and bake an additional 8 minutes or until golden brown and crispy.
6. In a small bowl, mix the Greek yogurt and the ranch dressing mix. Stir to combine well.
7. Serve the golden cauliflower with the yogurt ranch dip.

Per Serving
calories: 288 | fat: 16g | protein: 17g | carbs: 41g | net carbs: 41g | fiber: 0g

Chocolate Shake

1 Fueling | 1 Condiment
Prep time: 5 minutes | Cook time: 0 minutes | Serves 1

1 packet Medifast cappuccino mix
1 tablespoon sugar-free chocolate syrup
½ cup water
½ cup ice, crushed

1. In a small blender, place all ingredients and pulse until smooth and creamy.
2. Transfer the shake into a serving glass and serve immediately.

Per Serving
calories: 150 | fat: 8g | protein: 2g | carbs: 17g | net carbs: 14g | fiber: 3g

Vanilla Frappe

1 Fueling | 2 Condiments
Prep time: 5 minutes | Cook time: 0 minutes | Serves 1

1 sachet Optavia Essential Vanilla Shake
8 ounces unsweetened almond milk
½ cup ice
1 tablespoon whipped topping

1. In a blender, add the Vanilla Shake sachet, almond milk and ice and pulse until smooth.
2. Transfer the mixture into a glass and top with whipped topping.
3. Serve immediately.

Per Serving
calories: 266 | fat: 13g | protein: 9g | carbs: 26g | net carbs: 23g | fiber: 3g

Chocolate Waffles

1 Fueling | 2 Condiments
Prep time: 5 minutes | Cook time: 4 minutes | Serves 2

1 packet Medifast Chocolate Chip Pancakes
¼ teaspoon pumpkin pie spice
1 tablespoon 100% canned pumpkin
¼ cup water
2 teaspoons sugar-free pancake syrup

1. Preheat a mini waffle iron and then grease it.
2. In a bowl, add all the ingredients except for pancake syrup and mix until well blended.
3. Place ½ of the mixture into the preheated waffle iron and cook for about 3 to 4 minutes or until golden brown.
4. Repeat with the remaining mixture.
5. Transfer the waffles onto serving plates.
6. Serve warm with the topping of pancake syrup.

Per Serving
calories: 211 | fat: 11g | protein: 6g | carbs: 21g | net carbs: 19g | fiber: 2g

Berry Mojito

1 Fueling | 2 Condiment
Prep time: 5 minutes | Cook time: 0 minutes | Serves 2

2 tablespoons fresh lime juice
6 fresh mint leaves
1 packet Mixed Berry Flavor Infuser
16 ounces (453 g) seltzer water
Ice cubes, as required

1. In the bottom of 2 cocktail glasses, divide the lime juice and mint leaves.
2. With the bottom end of a spoon, gently muddle the mint leaves.
3. Now, divide the Berry Infuser and seltzer water into each glass and stir to combine.
4. Place ice cubes in each glass and serve.

Per Serving
calories: 99| fat: 0g | protein: 1g | carbs: 23g | net carbs: 22g | fiber: 1g

Appendix 1 Measurement Conversion Chart

MEASUREMENT CONVERSION CHART

VOLUME EQUIVALENTS(DRY)

US STANDARD	METRIC (APPROXIMATE)
1/8 teaspoon	0.5 mL
1/4 teaspoon	1 mL
1/2 teaspoon	2 mL
3/4 teaspoon	4 mL
1 teaspoon	5 mL
1 tablespoon	15 mL
1/4 cup	59 mL
1/2 cup	118 mL
3/4 cup	177 mL
1 cup	235 mL
2 cups	475 mL
3 cups	700 mL
4 cups	1 L

VOLUME EQUIVALENTS(LIQUID)

US STANDARD	US STANDARD (OUNCES)	METRIC (APPROXIMATE)
2 tablespoons	1 fl.oz.	30 mL
1/4 cup	2 fl.oz.	60 mL
1/2 cup	4 fl.oz.	120 mL
1 cup	8 fl.oz.	240 mL
1 1/2 cup	12 fl.oz.	355 mL
2 cups or 1 pint	16 fl.oz.	475 mL
4 cups or 1 quart	32 fl.oz.	1 L
1 gallon	128 fl.oz.	4 L

TEMPERATURES EQUIVALENTS

FAHRENHEIT(F)	CELSIUS(C) (APPROXIMATE)
225 °F	107 °C
250 °F	120 °C
275 °F	135 °C
300 °F	150 °C
325 °F	160 °C
350 °F	180 °C
375 °F	190 °C
400 °F	205 °C
425 °F	220 °C
450 °F	235 °C
475 °F	245 °C
500 °F	260 °C

WEIGHT EQUIVALENTS

US STANDARD	METRIC (APPROXIMATE)
1 ounce	28 g
2 ounces	57 g
5 ounces	142 g
10 ounces	284 g
15 ounces	425 g
16 ounces	455 g
(1 pound)	
1.5 pounds	680 g
2 pounds	907 g

Appendix 2 Index

Made in the USA
Las Vegas, NV
16 October 2024

96941578R00070